POSTCARD HISTORY SERIES

The William Penn Highway

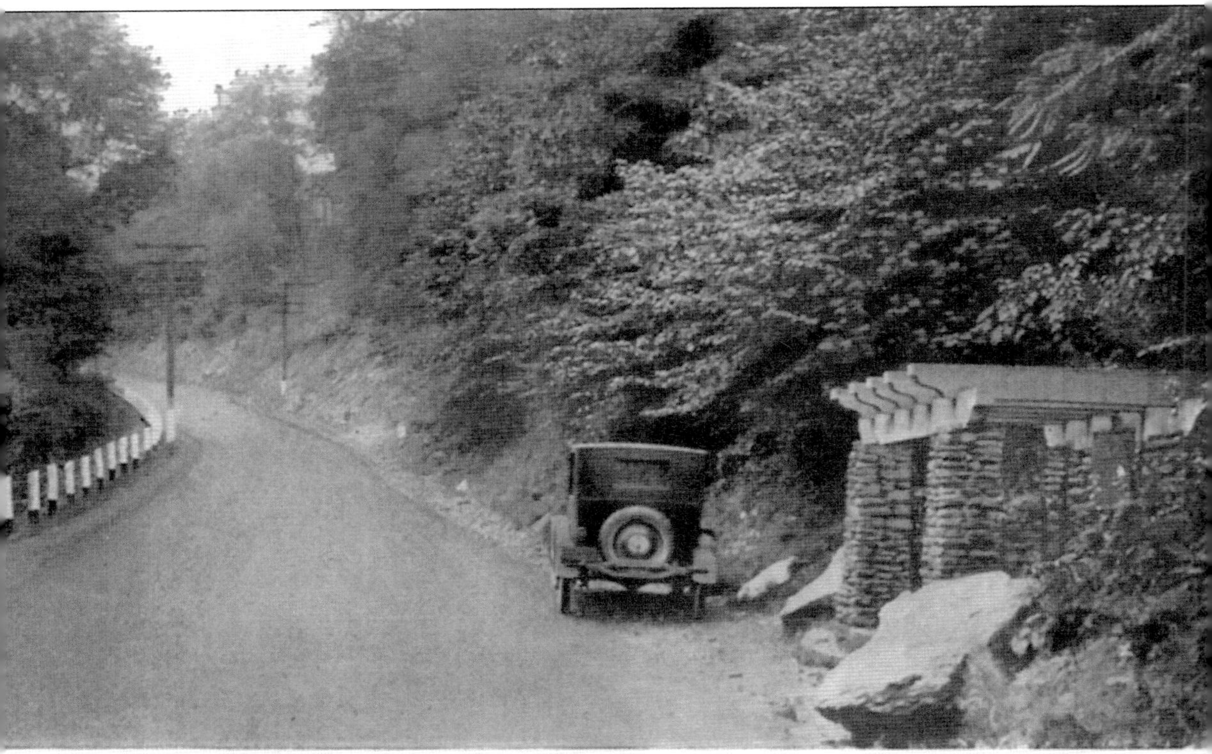

PRINCE GALLITZIN SPRING, BETWEEN CRESSON AND ALTOONA, PA. ON WM. PENN HIGHWAY.

This small spring, located midway along the Cresson Grade, was a favorite stopping point for many early settlers making the journey up the mountain. One of these was its namesake, Prince Gallitzin, the Russian aristocrat who became a Catholic priest and founded the town of Loretto several miles to the west. Shown here in the 1920s, the spring was located directly along the original Northern Turnpike and William Penn Highway. (Author's collection.)

On the Cover: The Pennsylvania Turnpike was extended westward to cross Route 22 in Monroeville in the late 1940s, and within several years a large group of motels appeared along the older highway to take advantage of travelers approaching Pittsburgh. One of these lodgings was the William Penn Motel, shown with its oversized neon sign on this card from the 1960s. (Author's collection.)

On the Back Cover: Kelley's Korner was an early gas station along the William Penn Highway in Huntingdon. It offered a lunchroom, bar, and "sanitary rest room." The owners are posing in front of their establishment in 1935. (Author's collection.)

POSTCARD HISTORY SERIES

The William Penn Highway

Robert A. Musson, MD

ARCADIA
PUBLISHING

ISBN 978-1-4671-3477-4

Published by Arcadia Publishing
Charleston, South Carolina

Printed in the United States of America

Library of Congress Control Number: 2015948906

For all general information contact Arcadia Publishing at:
Telephone 843-853-2070
Fax 843-853-0044
E-mail sales@arcadiapublishing.com
For customer service and orders:
Toll-Free 1-888-313-2665

Visit us on the Internet at www.arcadiapublishing.com

This book is dedicated to my family. My late parents, Irv and Fritz Musson, allowed me to hijack many of our family vacations by taking the older, scenic, and time-consuming highways instead of the interstates. Today, my wife, Jennifer, and my daughters, Ana, Alex, and Athena, get to follow these older roads with me, and we have enjoyed many of their attractions along the way.

Contents

Acknowledgments

Finding interstate highways to be fairly boring, even as a child, I have always been one to prefer driving on the nation's older highways. In more recent years, I have begun to accumulate photographs, postcards, and other information about the history of these roads as well as the scenery and attractions along them.

When researching the nation's highway system, postcards are a natural source of images, since a large percentage of small businesses in the first half of the 20th century, particularly motels and restaurants, produced promotional postcards for patrons to send to friends and family. It was inexpensive advertising, and many of them have long outlasted the businesses they originally advertised. Therein lies their tremendous historical value, as they show images of many companies, buildings, and people that do not appear in traditional history books.

I would particularly like to thank the staff of the Cambria County Historical Society in Ebensburg for allowing me to research their archives for information about the highway in central Pennsylvania. One of the most helpful publications was the Cambria Freeman promotional pamphlet, titled *Ebensburg and the William Penn Highway*, published in 1916 by Deck Lane and Orville Jones. It was published to help promote the newly completed highway and has a great deal of information about the road and the region as well as numerous rare photographs of scenery along the road.

I would also like to thank Doug Bosley, ranger for the National Park Service, and the staff of the Allegheny Portage Railroad National Historic Site for providing a tremendous amount of information about the site. I would also like to thank the owners of Lincoln Caverns in Huntingdon and Roadside America in Shartlesville. Both of these attractions are operated by descendants of their founders and have made a tremendous amount of history of their establishments available to the public.

Finally, I would like to thank Abby Henry and Lily Watkins, my contacts at Arcadia Publishing, for their enthusiasm and input during the production of this book.

Unless otherwise noted, all postcard images and photographs are from the author's collection.

Introduction

The William Penn Highway and its predecessors played a vital role in the development of many communities in Pennsylvania, providing a route for settlers, travelers, and goods from the East Coast to move into the new territories in the West. A primary reason for this is that it was one of only three major east-west highways through the sometimes treacherous mountains in the central part of the state (the others being the Lincoln and Roosevelt Highways) in the pre-interstate era. The highway's origins began during the Native American era, as it followed the courses of some of the earliest footpaths through the wilderness.

Around 1788, as pioneer settlers from the East were increasingly moving westward, the state appropriated funds for the improvement of the trails. In the process, the trails were cleared of rocks and stumps in order to allow the easier passage of horse-drawn wagons and stagecoaches, although a lack of bridges meant that streams and rivers still had to be forded. After several years of construction, the privately funded Huntingdon, Cambria, and Indiana Turnpike opened in 1820 to connect Huntingdon and Blairsville; a series of tolls along its course paid for the costs of construction. This road was a significant improvement over the earlier paths, as it included bridges over rivers and creeks, and some segments received gravel pavement of the narrow roadbed. This later became a part of a larger road, known as the Northern Turnpike, which connected Philadelphia and Pittsburgh.

In 1834, the Pennsylvania Canal opened, traveling parallel to the road through the Juniata River valley between Harrisburg and Hollidaysburg. This allowed larger shipments of goods from the East to find their way to Pittsburgh and the rest of western Pennsylvania. However, the canal ran into a major obstacle with the Allegheny Mountain range west of Hollidaysburg.

A solution was found in the creation of what was known as the Allegheny Portage Railroad, in which passengers and cargo on the canal were transferred to railroad cars at Hollidaysburg before beginning a gradual ascent of 1,400 feet via a series of inclined planes, being pulled from one level to the next by means of a motor-pulled cable. Upon reaching the summit, the cars would descend to Johnstown via a similar series of inclined planes. Once in Johnstown, the passengers and cargo would return to canalboats, which would continue on their voyage to downtown Pittsburgh. Covering a total of 36 miles, the railroad-incline was an engineering marvel of its day and was vital for the port of Philadelphia to be able to send goods westward, thus remaining competitive with other coastal ports (New York City had already overtaken Philadelphia as the East Coast's busiest port due to the completion of the Erie Canal across New York State, and Baltimore was set to benefit from the Chesapeake and Ohio Canal, although that was never completed).

The Allegheny Portage Railroad, which ran parallel to the Northern Turnpike on its course through Blair Gap up the mountain (also known as the Cresson Grade), was rendered obsolete by the 1850s upon the completion of the Pennsylvania Railroad, which was able to ascend the Allegheny Front more quickly via Horseshoe Curve, several miles to the north. While the canal remained in operation for some years after this, its importance as a major transportation route quickly faded. The rails of the inclined planes were later removed, leaving very little today at the site, although the area at the summit of the mountain has been designated as a national historic park, with a replica of an engine house and a section of track near Cresson.

Despite the appearance of the Pennsylvania Railroad through the region, carrying both passengers and cargo, the Northern Turnpike remained operational for many years, carrying primarily local horse-drawn vehicles as well as stagecoaches on longer trips. Tolls had largely been eliminated by the late 1800s, and as a result there were few improvements made in the road until well after the turn of the 20th century. The appearance of motorized automobiles by this time, however, had created the need for a significantly improved road system.

That improved system came about in 1916, when 650 people gathered in Harrisburg to establish the William Penn Highway Association. Most of these were business owners along the proposed route who stood to benefit from the increase in traffic. Once in operation, the privately funded organization brought the road to a new level of quality and safety. Bridges were improved, roadbeds were widened and paved with gravel, and many guardrails were built along dangerous segments of the highway. The route extended primarily from Philadelphia to Pittsburgh but also had branch alignments that traveled southward to Baltimore and northeastward to New York City. Although its name was overshadowed by the Lincoln Highway, completed three years earlier, the William Penn Highway nevertheless carried a significant amount of traffic by virtue of its course through Harrisburg.

Five years after the establishment of the highway, the government passed the Federal Aid Highway Act, which provided federal money for the upgrading and maintenance of major roads, with the eventual goal being the creation of a national system of numbered routes to replace privately funded highways. Although coordinated by the federal government, the roads were to be maintained by the individual states in which the roads traveled.

In 1926, this goal became a reality, as the new federal highway system was established, with numbered highways crossing the country from coast to coast. In the case of the William Penn Highway, it became Federal Route 22, although the new highway was extended eastward to Elizabeth, New Jersey, and westward to Cambridge, Ohio. Within several years, the eastern endpoint had been shifted northward to Newark, and the western endpoint was shifted farther west to Cincinnati.

Over the following 80-plus years, Route 22 has remained an important transportation artery throughout the state, particularly in the Pittsburgh area, the mountains and Juniata River valley in the central part of the state, and the Lehigh Valley region. The highway has been improved in most areas, with most of its course in Pennsylvania now following limited-access four-lane highways. The full length of the road from Cincinnati to Newark in 1940 was 665 miles, while today its more direct alignments have given it a total length of 651 miles, 337 miles of which are in Pennsylvania. This book focuses primarily on images of scenery, motels, restaurants, and so forth from the original alignments through the state, although there are some images from the modern road as well.

The name "William Penn Highway" is largely used interchangeably with "Route 22" in this book, although the two are not exactly the same. The William Penn Highway Association remained in operation into the 1950s, still promoting commerce along the highway, but after that era, it gradually faded away. Although Route 22 is the highway's standard name today, many of its original segments through the state have retained various forms of the name William Penn Highway, as well as Olde 22 and Old Route 22. Hopefully, this book will evoke nostalgic interest for some readers; for others, it might stir some curiosity about the old road and encourage travel along its scenic course.

One

Coming from the West

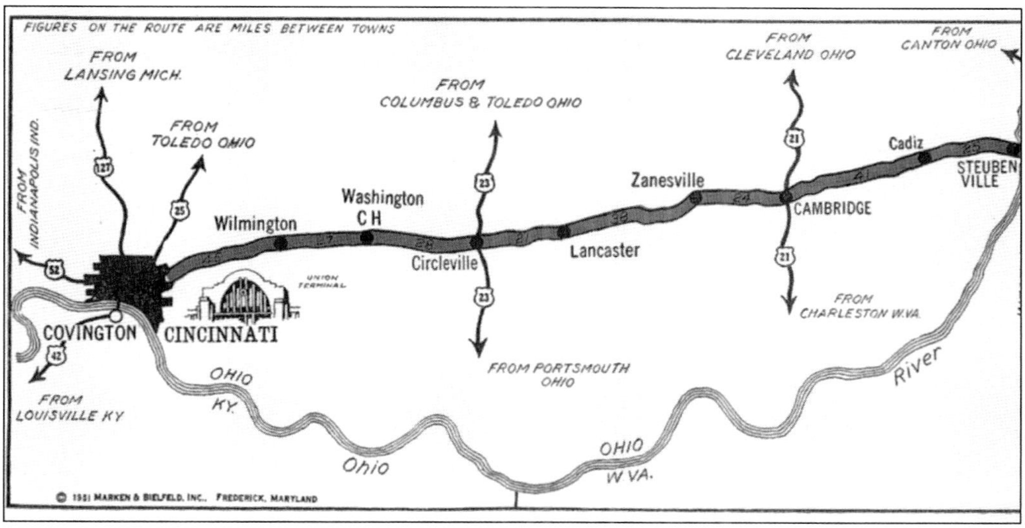

This map is from a 1951 brochure encouraging travel on the William Penn Highway, showing the segment of Route 22 from Cincinnati to the Ohio River. Produced by the Route 22 Association, consisting mostly of businesses along the highway, it lists many sites of interest along the way and features rarely seen references to the William Penn Highway outside of Pennsylvania.

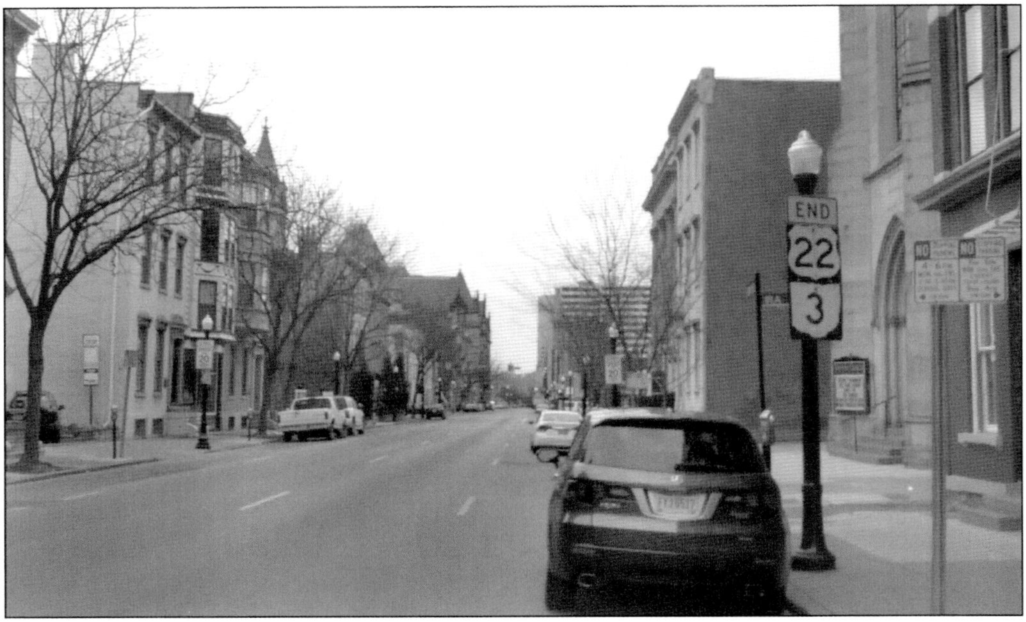

Route 22 continues westward through the flat rural territory that makes up much of southern Ohio. Upon reaching Cincinnati, it descends into the Ohio River valley and continues just north of the downtown area. Its well-marked western endpoint is at the intersection of Seventh Street and Central Avenue, several blocks from the river.

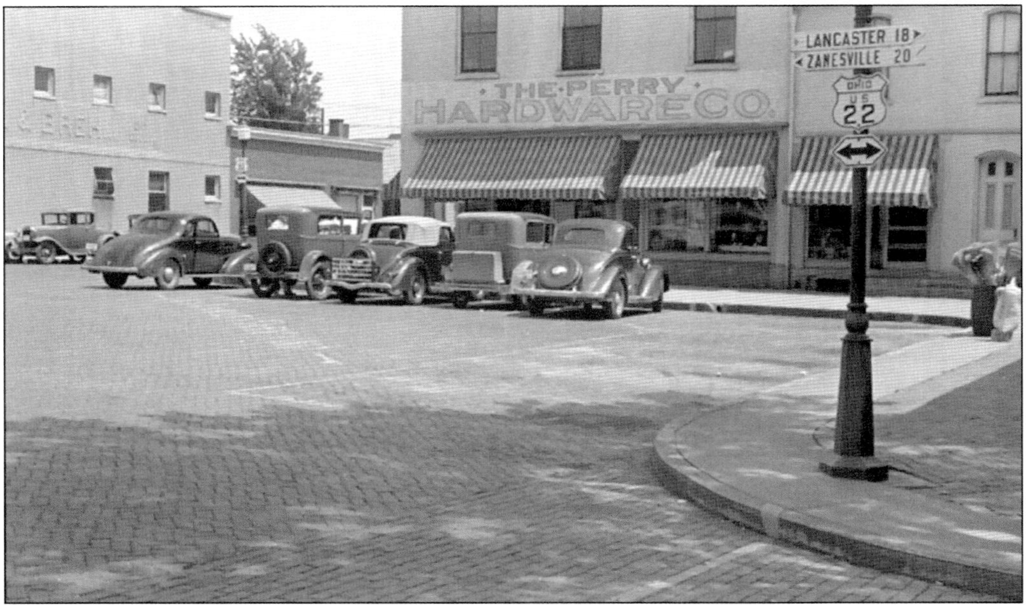

Portions of Route 22 in southern Ohio follow the pioneer trail known as Zane's Trace, traversing many rolling hills and rural territory. The road's course is dotted with small towns such as Somerset, shown here in 1938 with a prominent view of a shield sign. Somerset's main claim to fame is being the hometown of Civil War general Philip Sheridan. (Courtesy of the Library of Congress, Farm Security Administration Collection.)

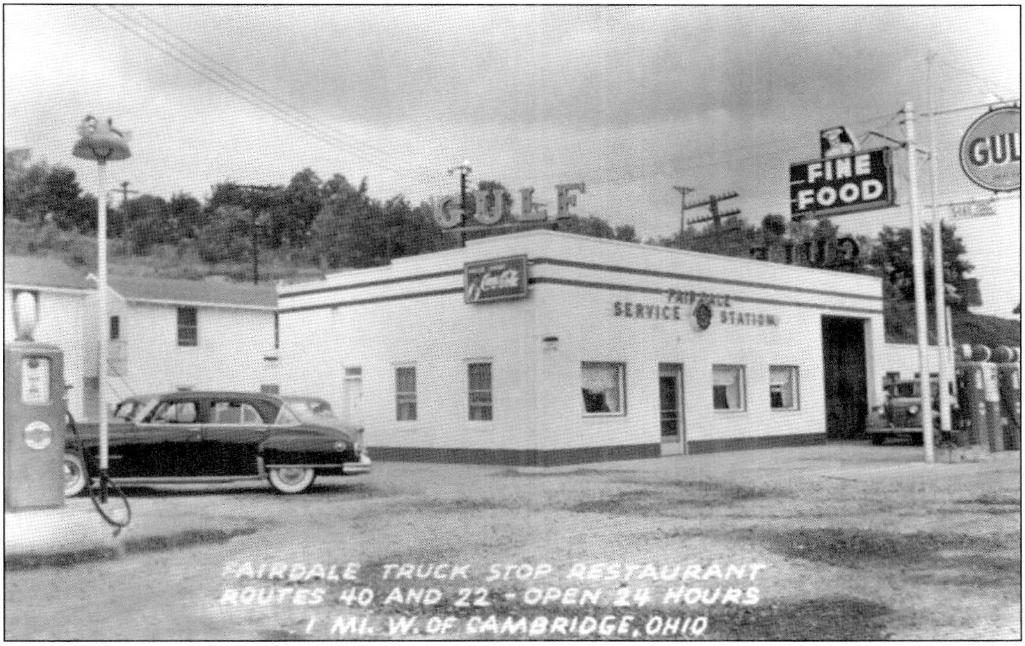

Fairdale is a small locality just west of Cambridge. Shown here around 1950 is the Fairdale Service Station, which sold Gulf gasoline and Coca-Cola and offered fine food. Between Zanesville and Cambridge, the road carries both US Routes 22 and 40 (the latter following the early trail known as the National Road.)

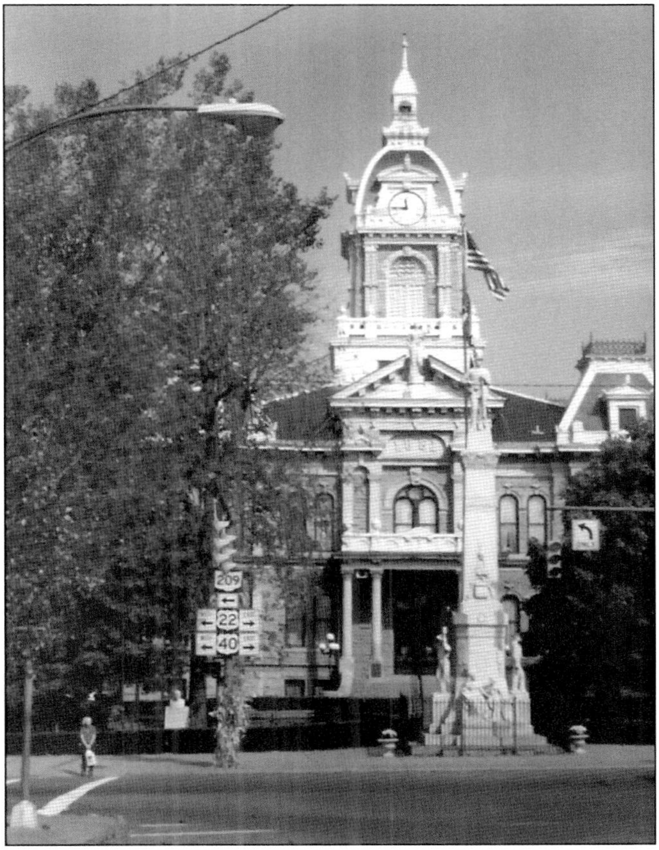

The Guernsey County seat, the city of Cambridge was founded in 1806 and has a population of more than 10,000. The county courthouse stands along Wheeling Avenue, which carries Routes 22 and 40. Built between 1881 and 1883 in the Second Empire architectural style, the building is listed in the National Register of Historic Places.

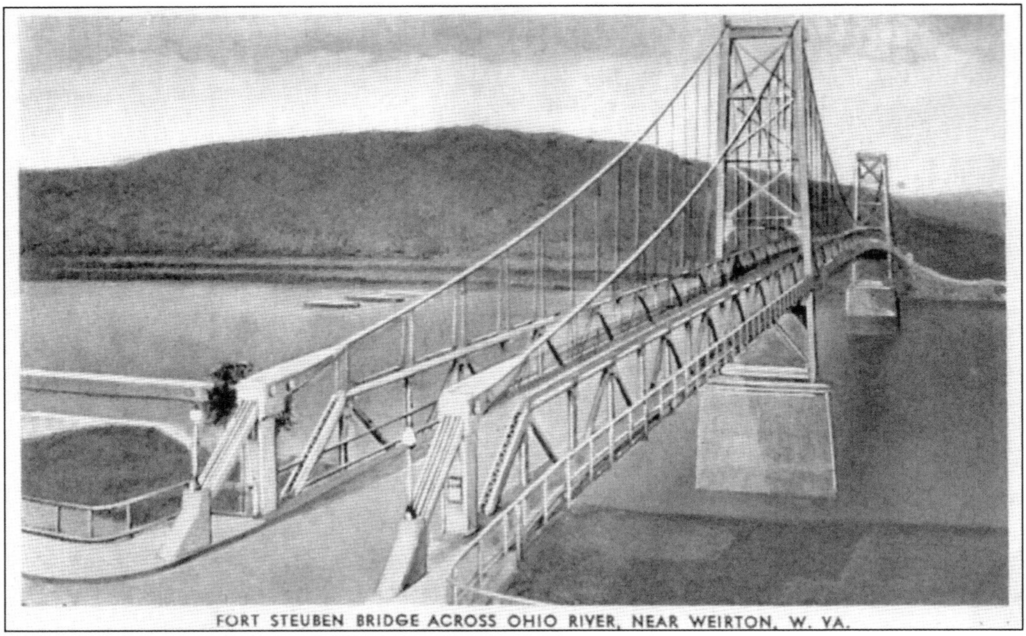

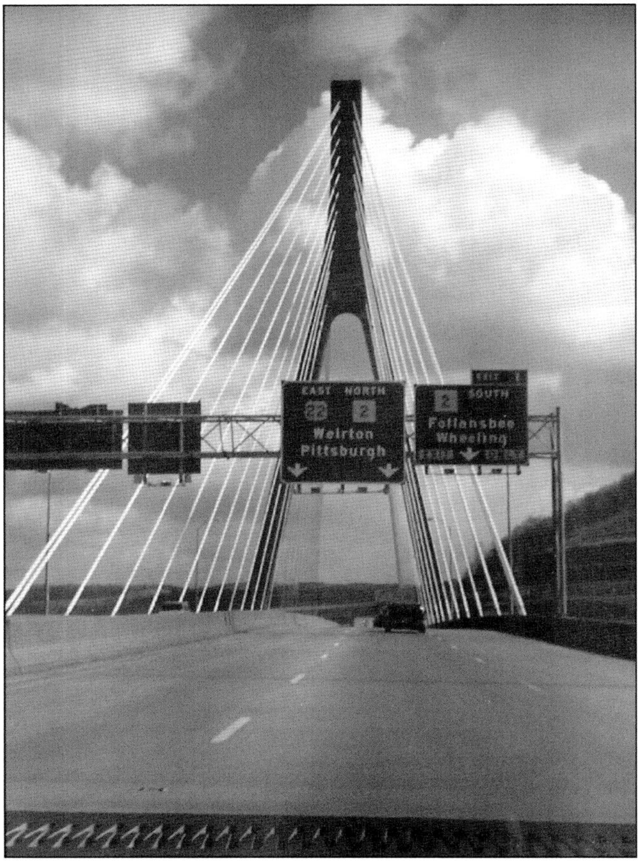

The Fort Steuben Bridge was built in 1928 to carry Route 22 traffic over the Ohio River. The steel suspension bridge was nearly 1,600 feet in length and required a 25¢ toll for crossing until 1947. After being closed to traffic in 2009 due to structural deterioration, the bridge sat unused for three years before being demolished in a spectacular series of controlled explosions in February 2012.

The Veteran's Memorial Bridge is a single-tower stayed-cable structure that replaced the Fort Steuben Bridge in 1990. Carrying Route 22 across the Ohio River between Steubenville and Weirton, it cost $70 million and took a decade to build. Carrying 30,000 automobiles every day, it was the last link in allowing direct highway access between the Ohio River valley and Pittsburgh.

Two

From the Ohio River to Pittsburgh

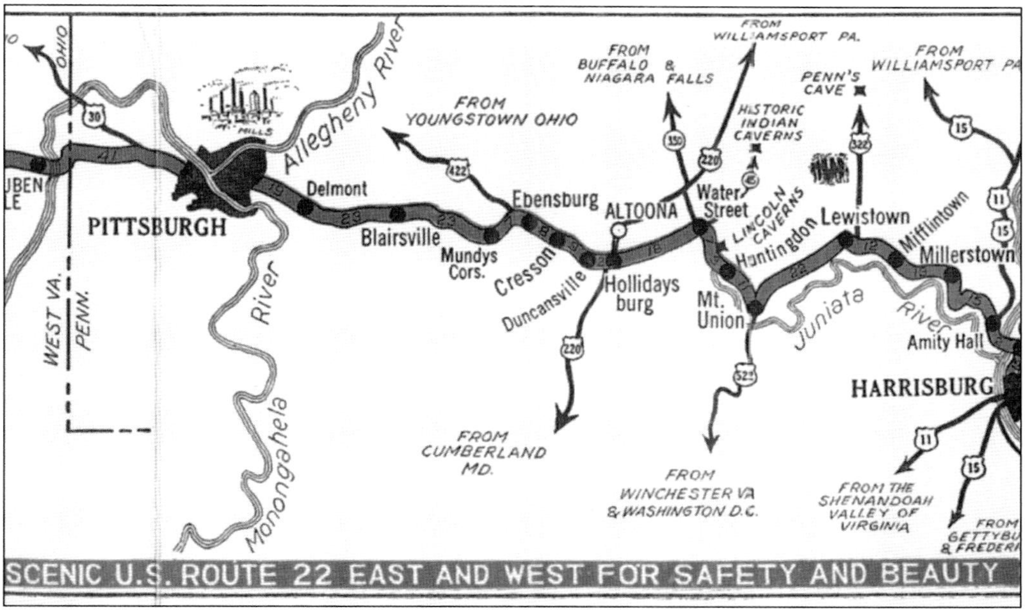

This map from 1951 shows the William Penn Highway through western Pennsylvania. Although the route continues to follow the same basic path today, nearly all segments of the route have since been realigned onto modern four-lane highways. By the end of the decade, the William Penn Highway name was rarely if ever being used, as the interstate system began to slowly replace the older highways.

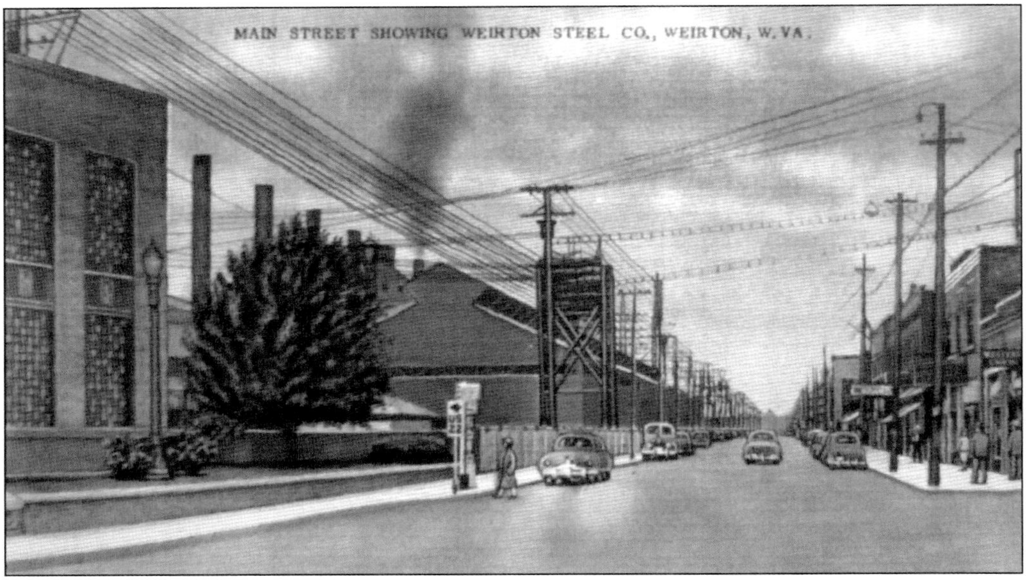

The original course of Route 22 passed the massive mills of the Weirton Steel Company in Weirton, West Virginia, as seen here in the 1940s. Founded in 1909, Weirton was one of the world's largest producers of steel and tin-plated products for the military and the automobile industry for many years. Though downsized significantly in later years, it remains in operation today.

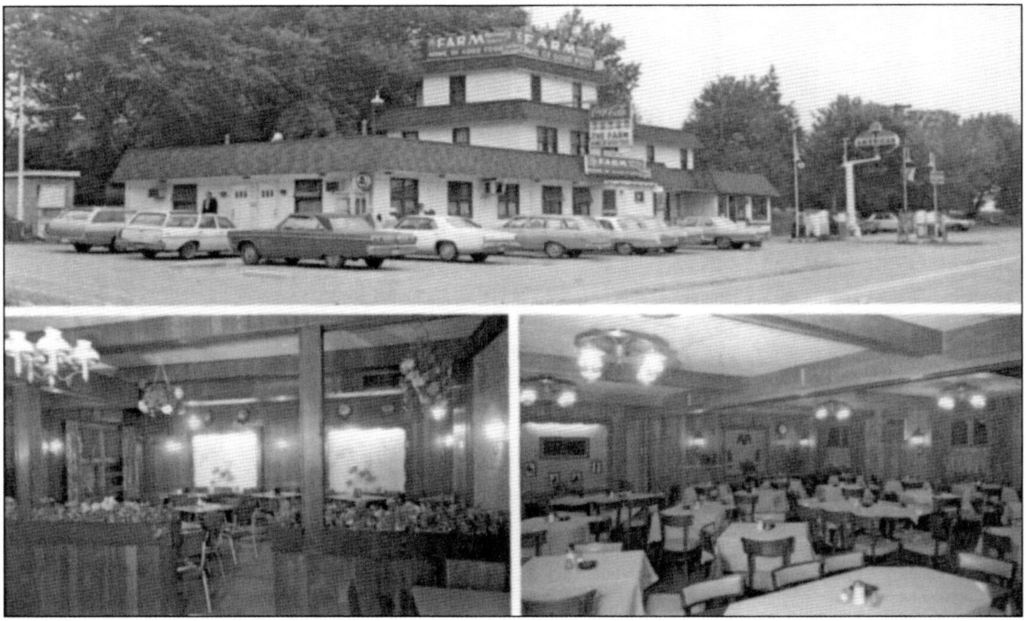

Much of Route 22 between the West Virginia panhandle and the western suburbs of Pittsburgh is isolated and rural. The locality of Florence stands at the original route's intersection with Pennsylvania Route 18 and was once the site of the three-story Farm restaurant and ice-cream bar, shown here around 1970. It was a popular stop for drivers making the hour-long trip from the Ohio River valley to Pittsburgh.

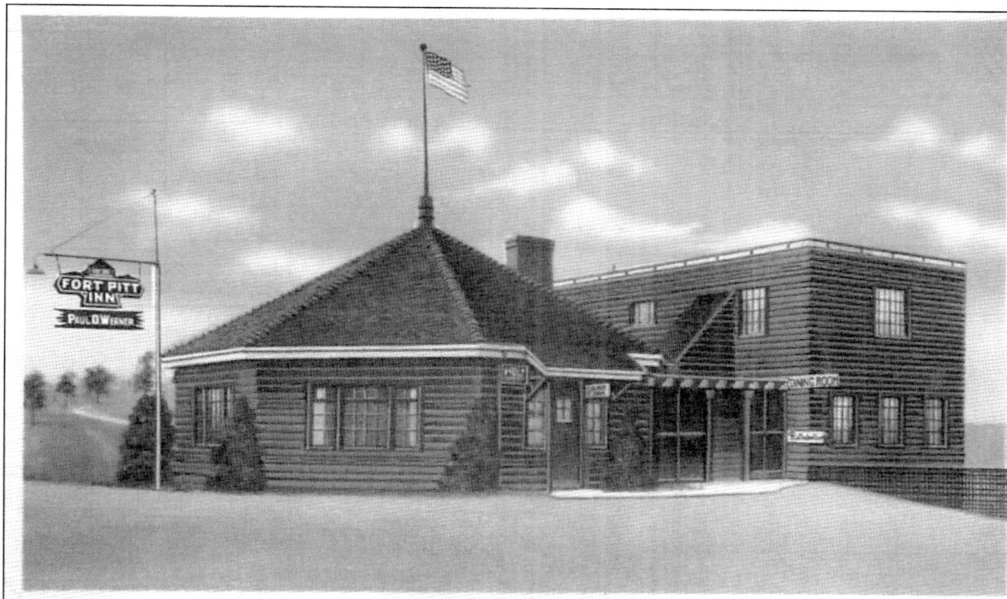

FORT PITT INN 4A-H856

Built 13 miles west of downtown Pittsburgh in the 1930s, the Fort Pitt Inn Restaurant was designed to resemble the blockhouse of its namesake in downtown Pittsburgh. Shown above, the building's unusual shape is a reminder of the road's early days, when businesses were often housed in unique structures to attract more attention and hopefully more business. Below, the interior of the tavern was built to resemble a Revolutionary War–era rathskeller (a tavern or restaurant housed in a cellar), with stone walls, pewter mugs, and a grandfather clock. The building remains in use today as a bar at 7780 Steubenville Pike, the original alignment of Route 22 through the area.

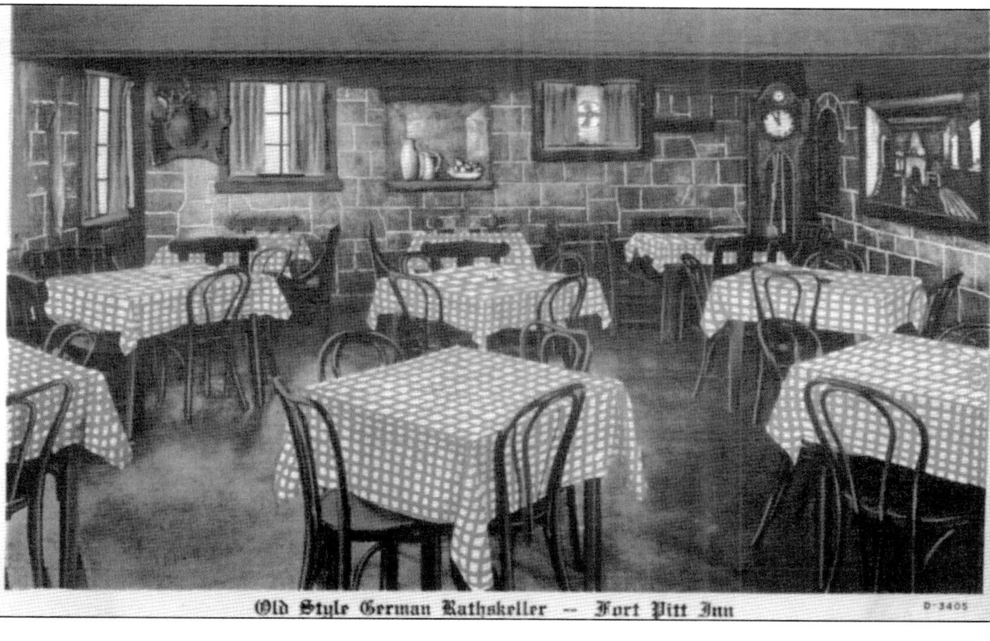

Old Style German Rathskeller -- Fort Pitt Inn D-3405

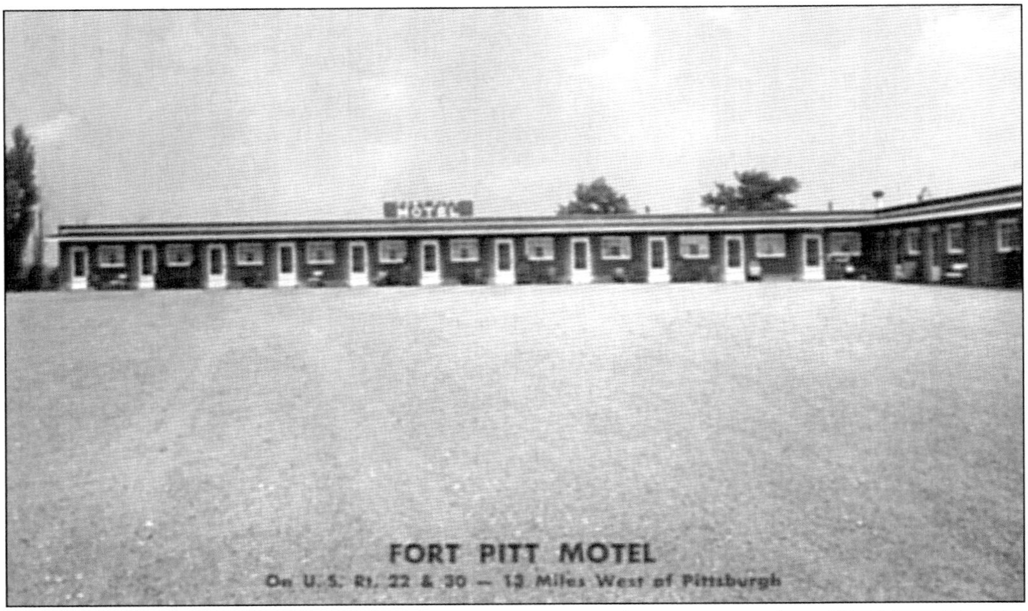

Two doors east of the Fort Pitt Inn is the Fort Pitt Motel, at 7750 Steubenville Pike, 13 miles west of Pittsburgh. Shown here in the 1950s, it was typical of the early roadside motels and is one of few survivors from that era. Surrounded today by trees, it remains in business with its 20 rooms and specializes in romantic getaways.

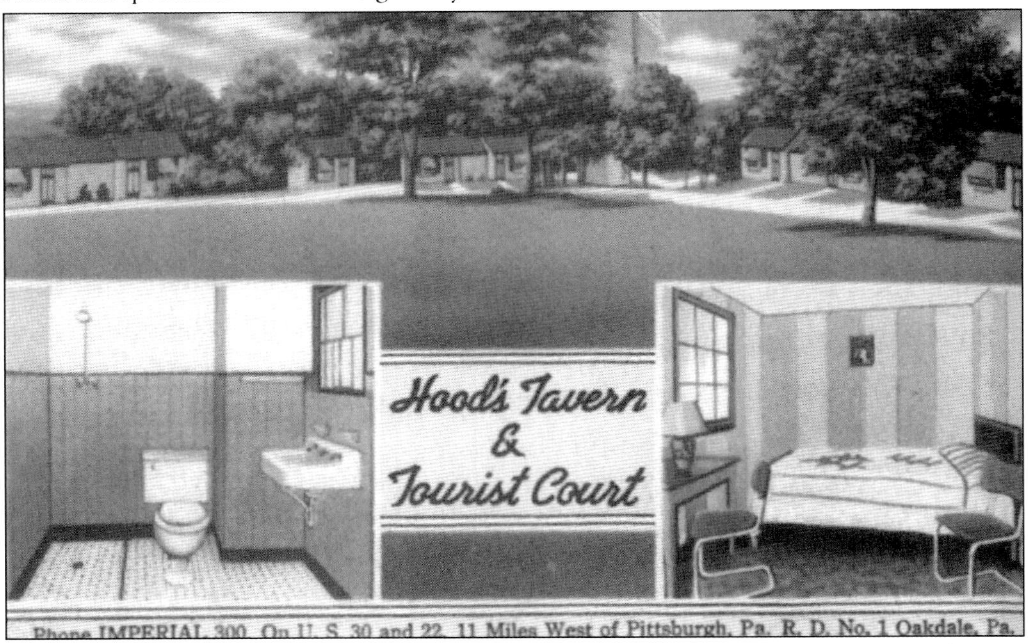

Hood's Tavern & Tourist Court, shown here in the 1940s, stood along Steubenville Pike near the village of Imperial, 11 miles west of Pittsburgh. Accommodations were sparse by today's standards, yet they were welcomed by thousands of tourists over the years. After Routes 22 and 30 were realigned onto the modern highway nearby, patronage dropped off steeply for all of the businesses on the old road.

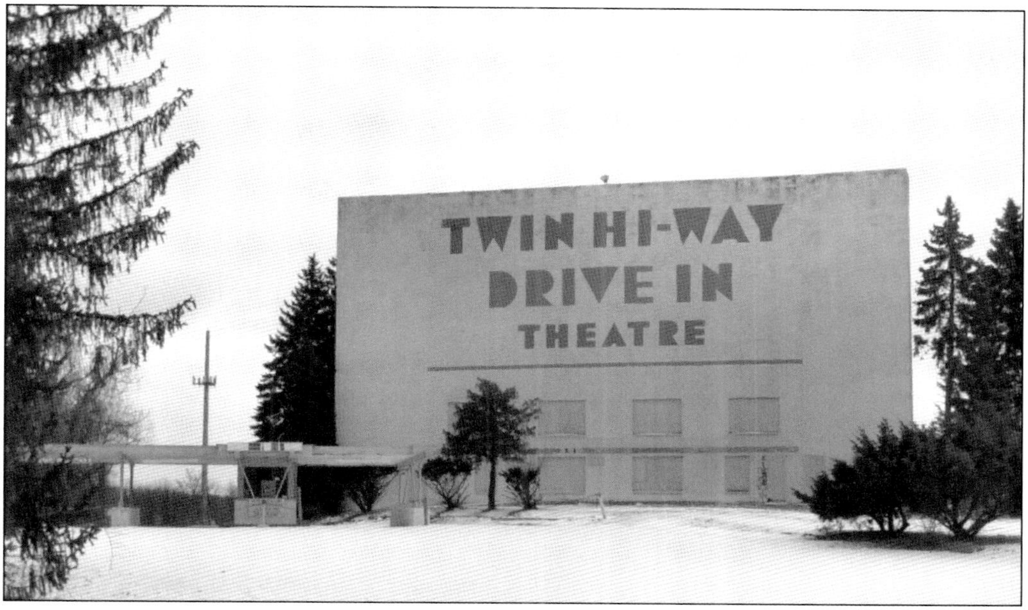

One of the Pittsburgh area's first outdoor theaters, the Twin Hi-Way Drive In opened in 1950 on Steubenville Pike, several miles west of the city. Its name came from its location along both Routes 22 and 30, and the theater remained in operation until the 1990s. It has reopened in recent years and remains an area favorite in the summer.

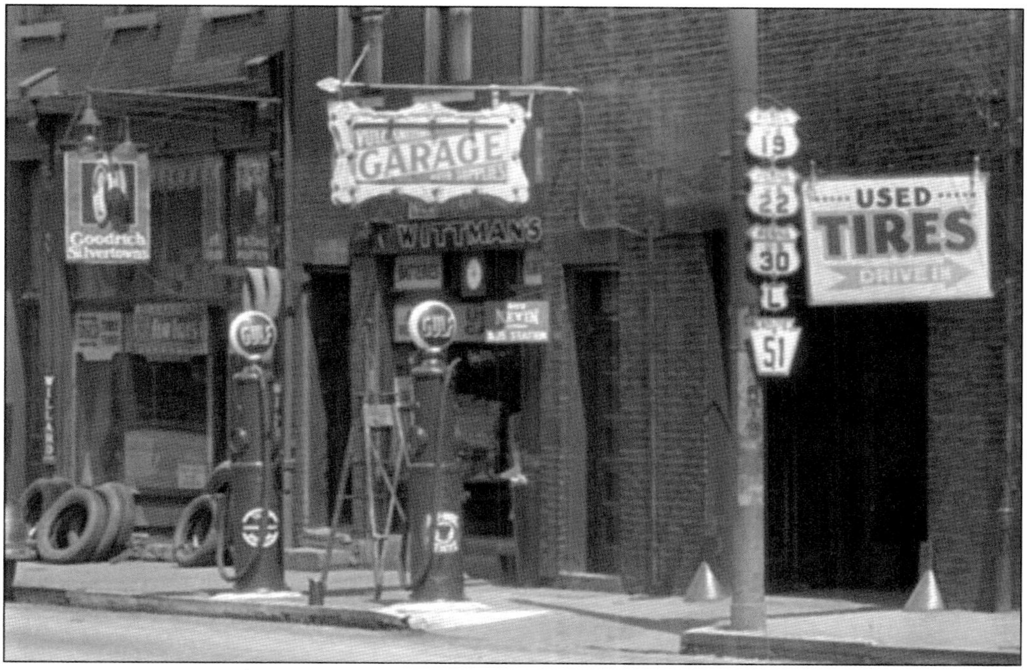

Prior to construction of the Penn-Lincoln Parkway through Pittsburgh, Route 22 traveled through the valley of Saw Mill Run in the city's West End district in conjunction with US Routes 19 and 30, as well as state Route 51. This real-photo postcard shows a combination tire store and gas station along the road, selling Gulf gasoline and Goodrich tires.

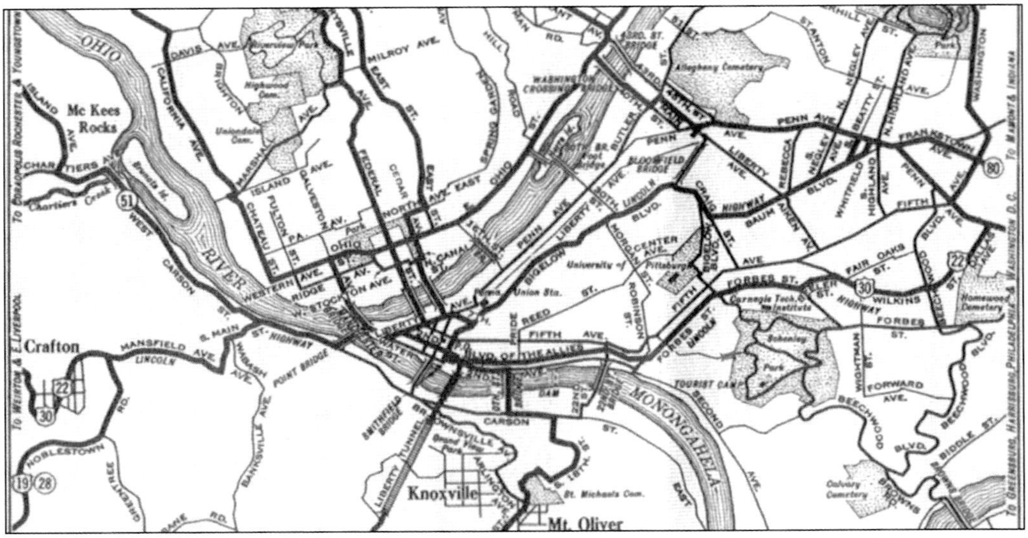

This is a map of downtown Pittsburgh in 1937, showing the course of Routes 22 and 30 on a series of city streets. The map would soon begin to undergo dramatic changes with the construction of the Penn-Lincoln Parkway, followed by the rebuilding of the Point District and then the opening of the Fort Pitt Tunnel and Bridge by 1960.

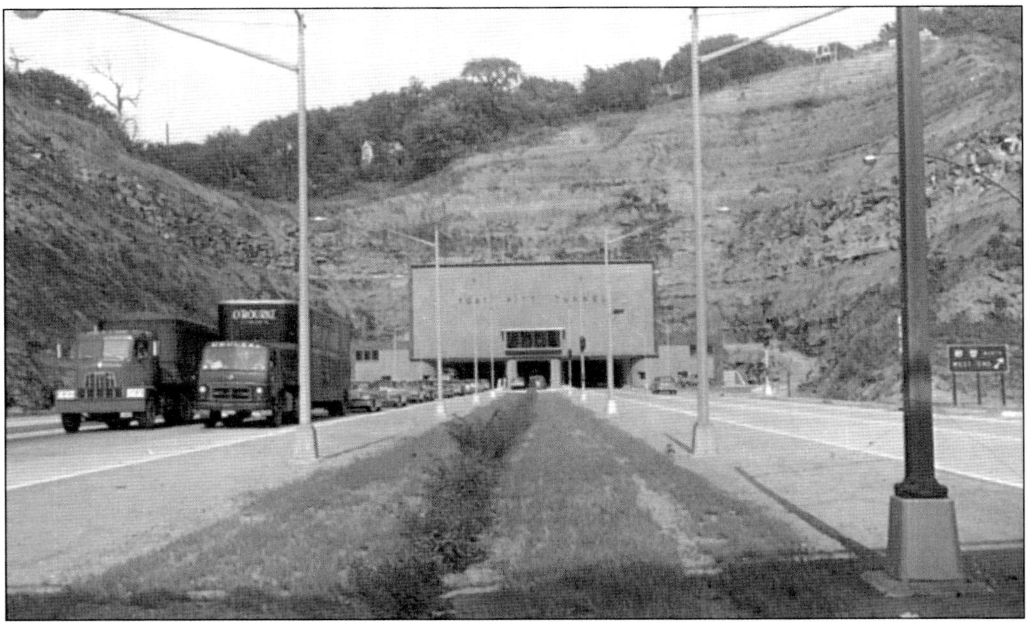

The Fort Pitt Tunnel, seen at its western end in the early 1960s, opened in 1960 under Pittsburgh's Mount Washington to complete the Penn-Lincoln Parkway and allow traffic from the city's east side to reach the airport directly. Originally carrying Routes 22 and 30, it now carries Interstate 376 as well. Its two parallel traffic tubes carry more than 100,000 cars every day.

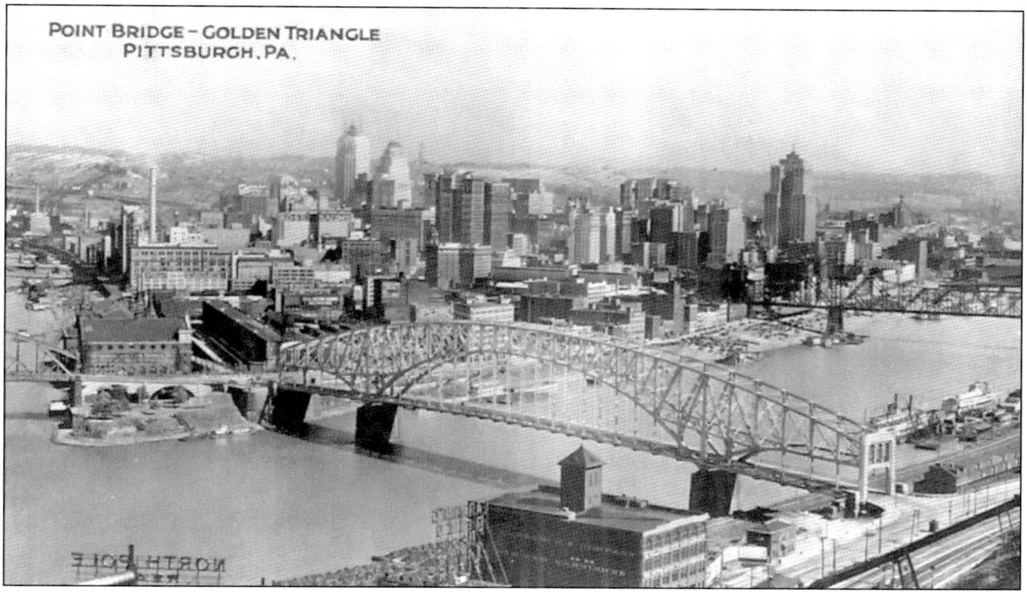

The Point Bridge (the second bridge by that name at the same site) was opened in 1927 to carry traffic across the Monongahela River, just to the east of its confluence with the Allegheny River. The bridge carried Route 22 for more than 30 years before it was replaced in 1959 by the current Fort Pitt Bridge. The Point Bridge remained standing for another decade before being demolished in 1970.

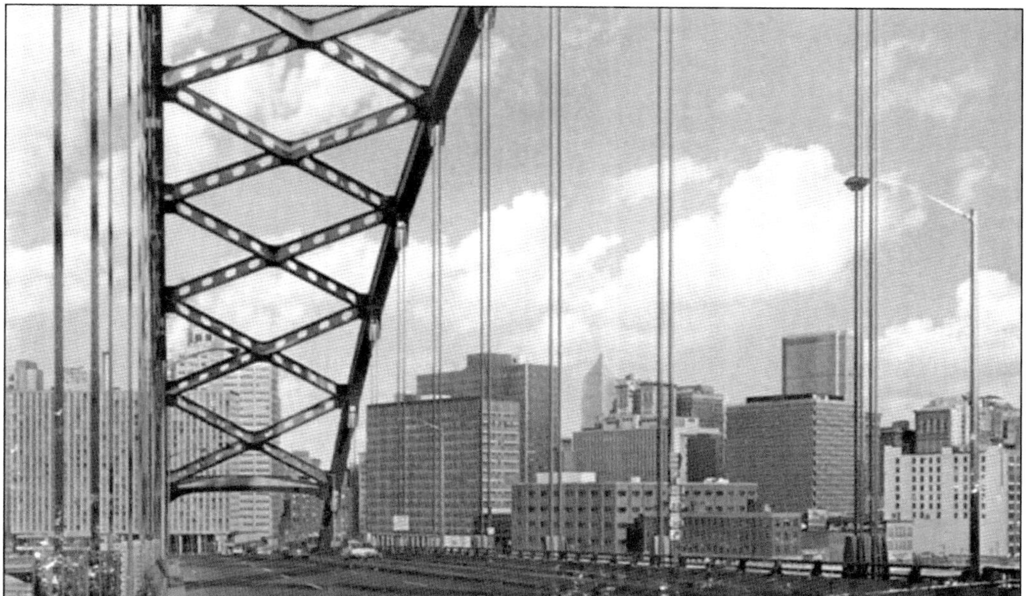

The Fort Pitt Bridge, shown here shortly after its opening in 1959, is roughly 1,200 feet long and carries more than 150,000 cars across the Monongahela River every day, making it one of the state's busiest segments of road. This view shows the new gleaming towers of the city's Gateway Project in the background, and shield-shaped signs for Routes 22 and 30 can be seen at bottom center.

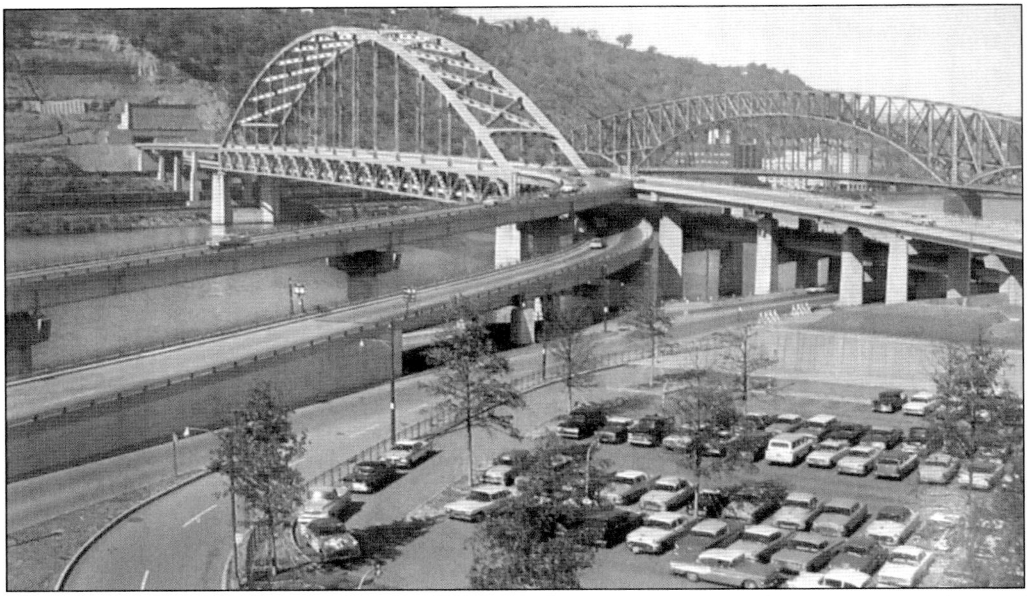

This view shows Pittsburgh's Penn-Lincoln Parkway leading onto the Fort Pitt Bridge and toward the Fort Pitt Tunnel in the mid-1960s. A similar view today would likely show the traffic congestion that is typical of both the highway and bridge. In the background is the massive Point Bridge, which was open from 1927 to 1959. It then remained standing until being razed in 1970.

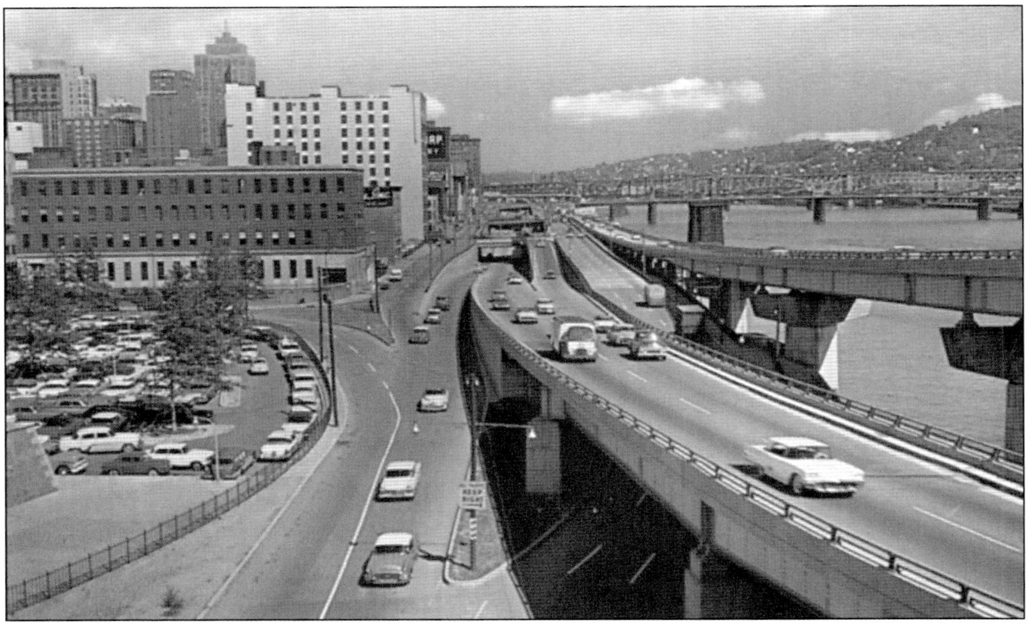

The Penn-Lincoln Parkway was built to allow traffic from both the William Penn and Lincoln Highways to bypass Pittsburgh's city streets. Most of the construction through downtown took place in the early 1950s, and was then completed after the opening of the Fort Pitt Bridge and Tunnel. This segment, seen in a view looking eastward along the Monongahela River, is shown in the early 1960s.

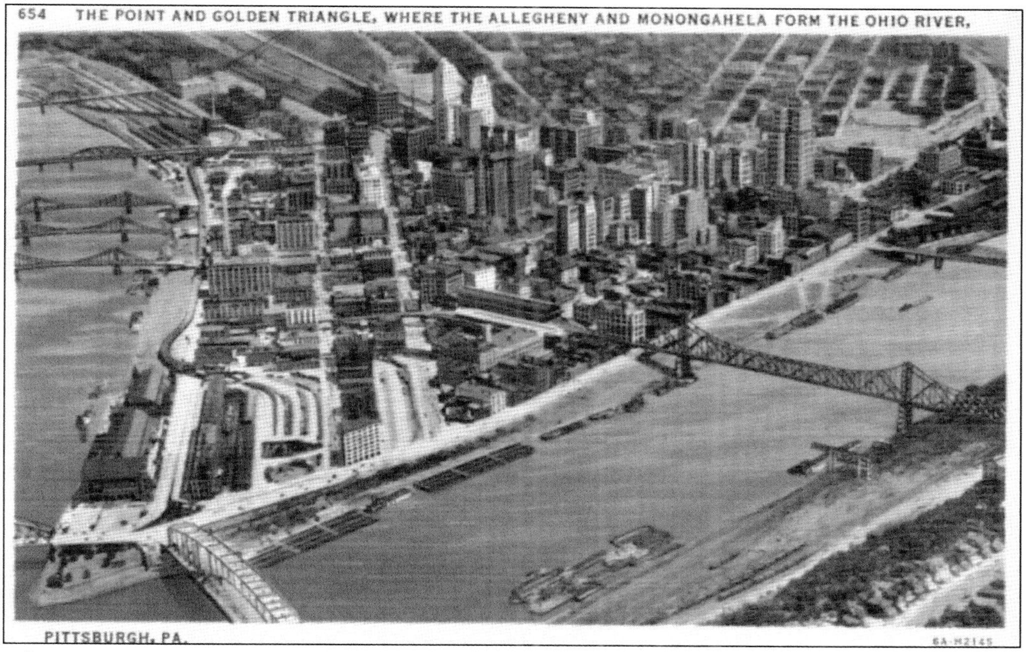

After crossing the Monongahela River, the original course of Route 22 passed through Pittsburgh's Point district, also known as the Golden Triangle (shown above in the 1930s). After leaving the bridge, the route turned onto Water Street, Liberty Avenue, and Boulevard of the Allies to continue eastward. The 1950s saw a dramatic renaissance in the district, with the razing of nearly every structure in favor of Point State Park and new buildings, collectively known as the Gateway Project (shown below as it appears today). In the process, Route 22 was realigned onto the new Fort Pitt Bridge, allowing it to bypass the traffic of the city streets.

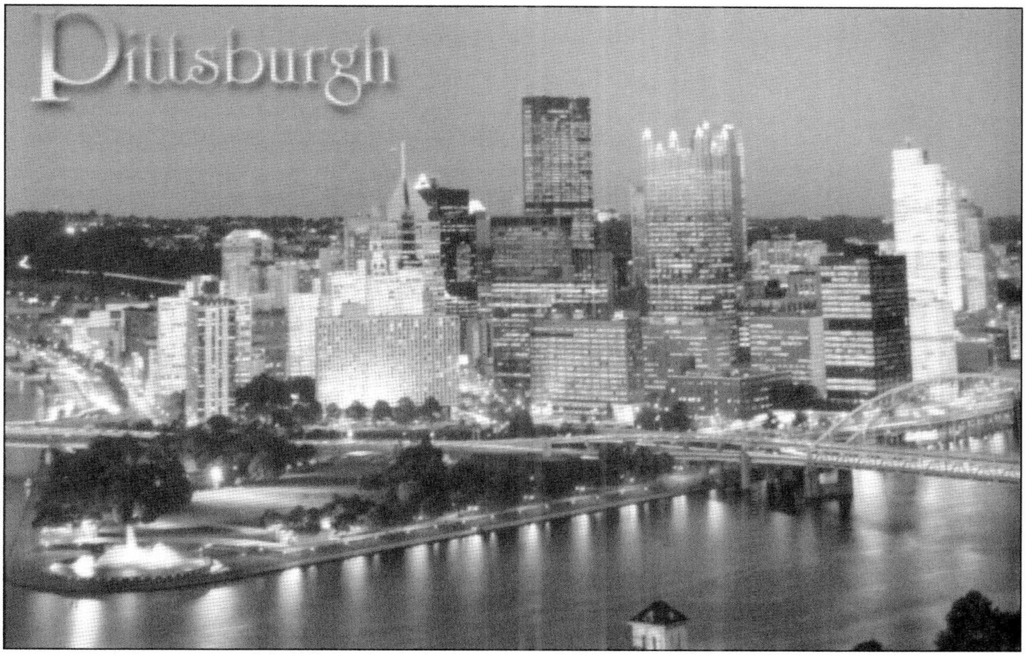

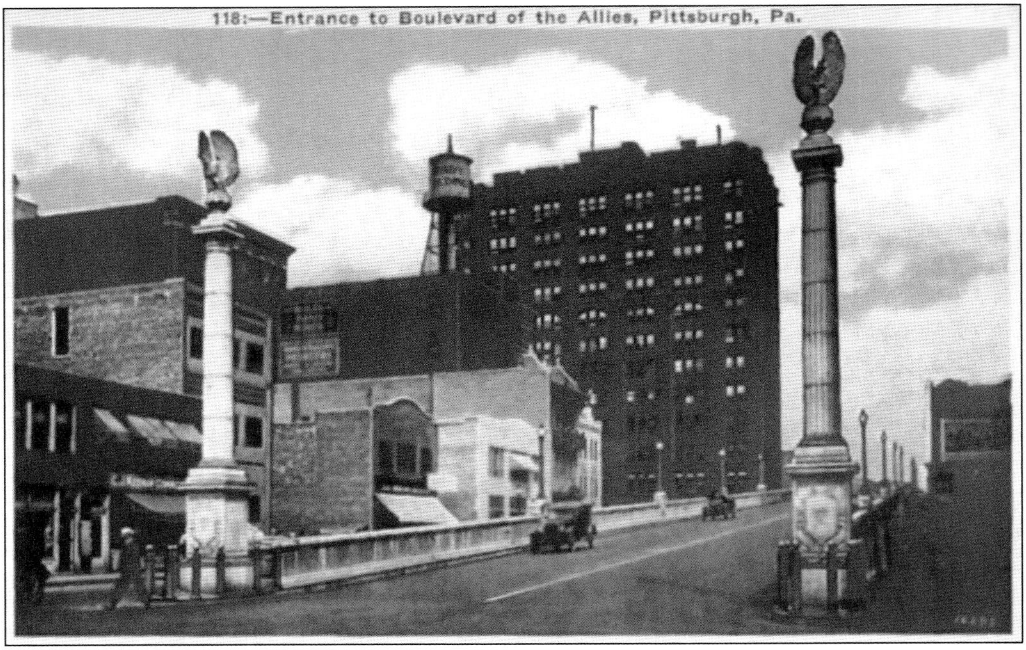

In 1921, most of Second Avenue in Pittsburgh was renamed as Boulevard of the Allies, in honor of the Allies in World War I. In the process, it was extended eastward to Forbes Avenue in Oakland, a distance of roughly three miles. As a result, it passes just south of the campus of Duquesne University and along the top of the high bluff overlooking the Monongahela River. With a cost of $1.6 million per mile, it was considered to be the most expensive road in the world at the time. Until the opening of the Penn-Lincoln Parkway, the Boulevard carried Routes 22 and 30 eastward. Today, much of the road is designated as State Route 885. Above is a view of the downtown entrance to the road in the 1930s; below is a view of the road farther east.

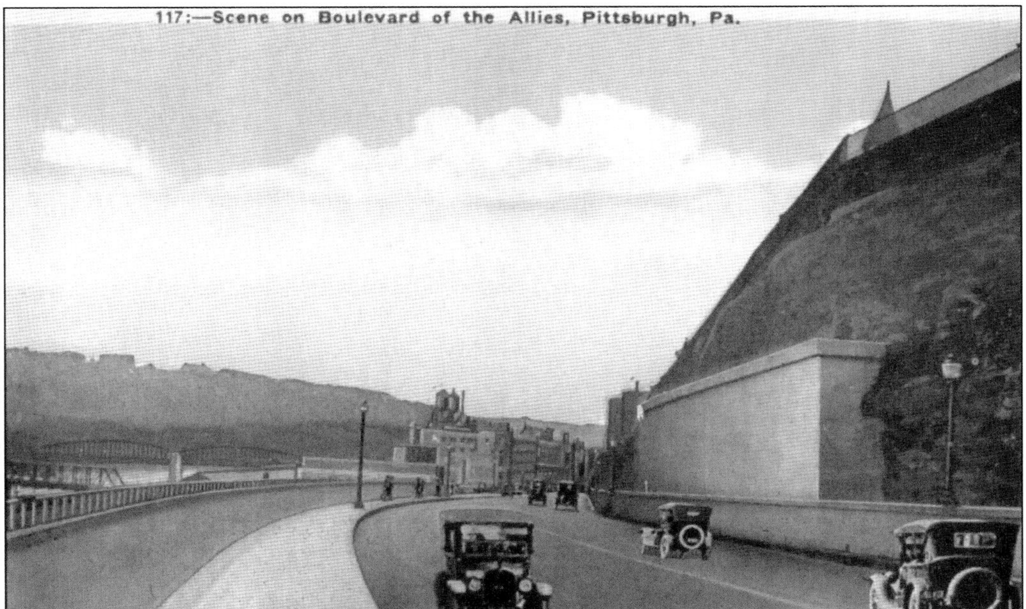

The landmark Cathedral of Learning is the most prominent site on the University of Pittsburgh campus. Located on Forbes Avenue (the original course of Route 22) in the city's Oakland district, the building was completed in 1931. Seen here in the 1950s, the Gothic Revival structure is 42 stories and 535 feet in height, and it houses classrooms, administrative office, and study areas.

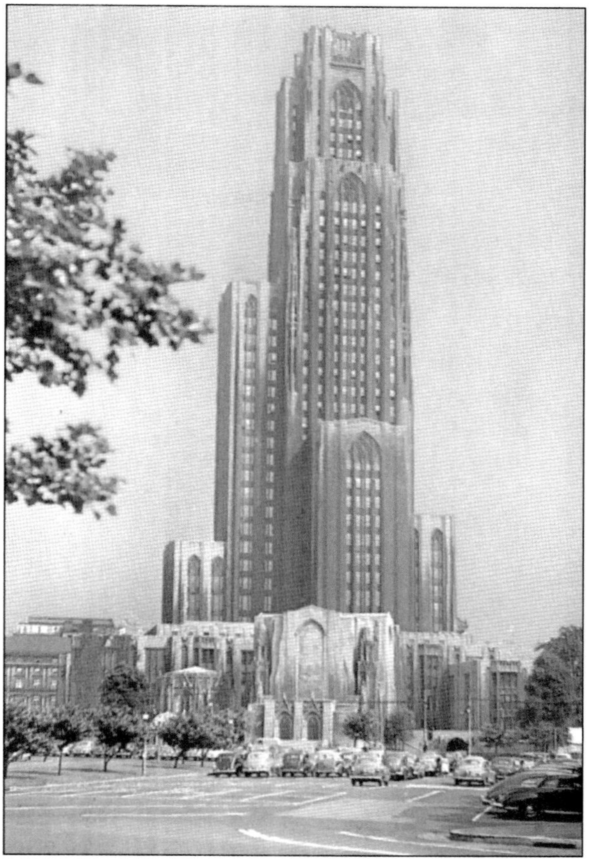

This postcard shows an aerial illustration of the University of Pittsburgh campus in the city's Oakland district, about 1950. The original course of Route 22, following Forbes Avenue through the campus, can be seen in the center foreground. As it traveled through the campus, the route passed the university's huge medical complex, Forbes Field (home of the Pittsburgh Pirates baseball team at the time), and the Cathedral of Learning.

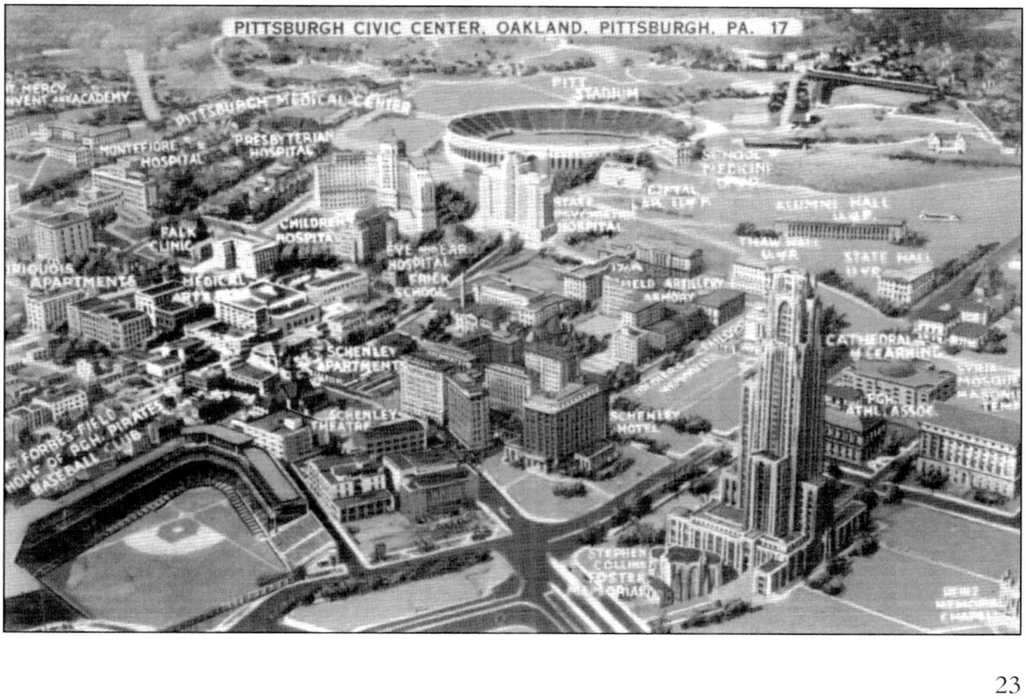

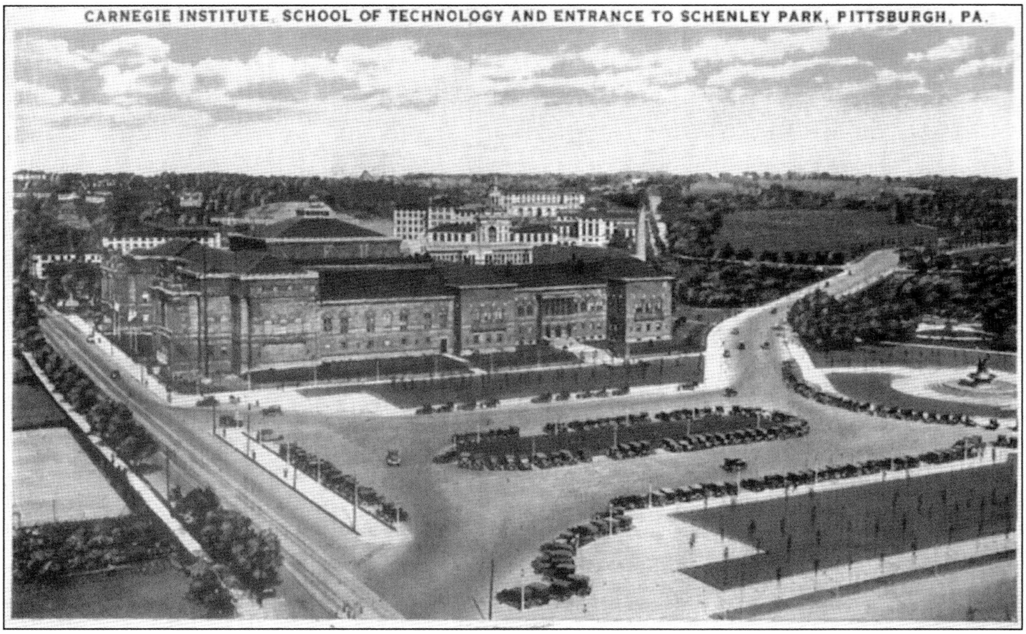

Continuing eastward after passing the University of Pittsburgh campus, Forbes Avenue (former Route 22, shown here at left) passed the huge building housing the Carnegie Museum of Natural History. Built in 1895, the structure also houses the Carnegie Library of Pittsburgh and the Carnegie Museum of Art. Just east of this, the road passes the Carnegie Institute (today known as Carnegie Mellon University), seen in the background.

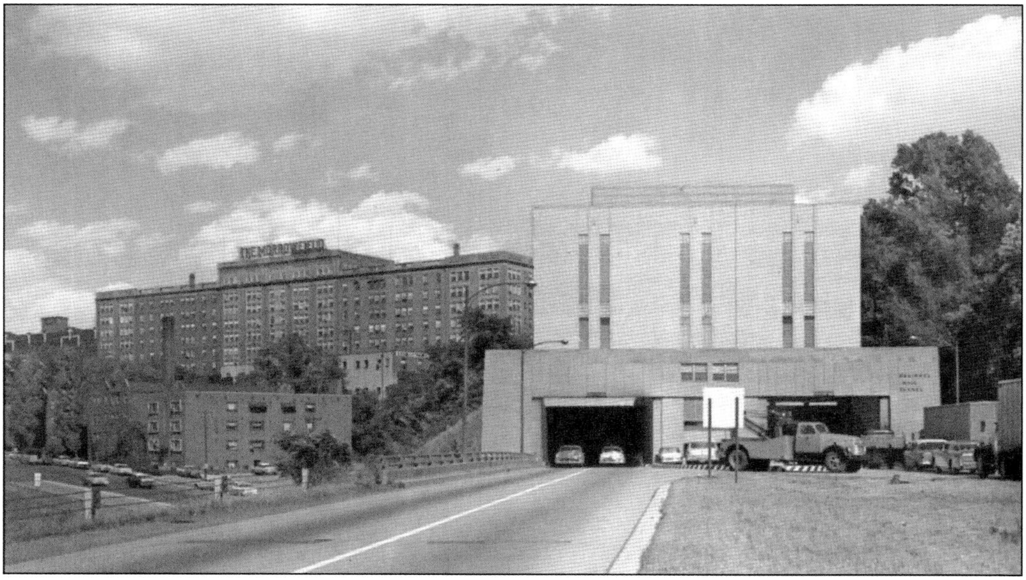

Five miles east of Pittsburgh's Point is the Squirrel Hill Tunnel, constructed in 1953 as part of the Penn-Lincoln Parkway, which carries Routes 22 and 30. Built over eight years, the tunnel consists of two parallel tubes, which travel 4,200 feet under the residential hillside neighborhood of Squirrel Hill. The tunnel remains a major part of the local road system today, with roughly 106,000 vehicles traveling through it every day.

Three

Pittsburgh to Blairsville

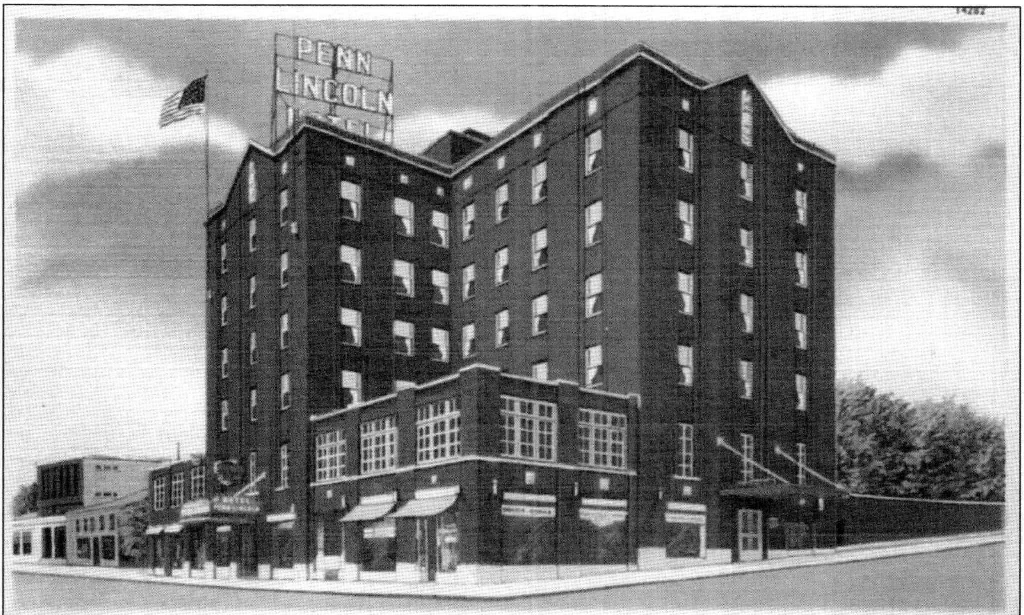

The Penn Lincoln Hotel, so named by its location along both the Lincoln and William Penn Highways, stood at the corner of Penn and Center Streets in the Pittsburgh suburb of Wilkinsburg. Opened in 1927, it stood six stories in height and featured 150 rooms, but by 1968 it had been converted into apartments. After closing for good in 1995, it fell into disrepair and was demolished in 2014.

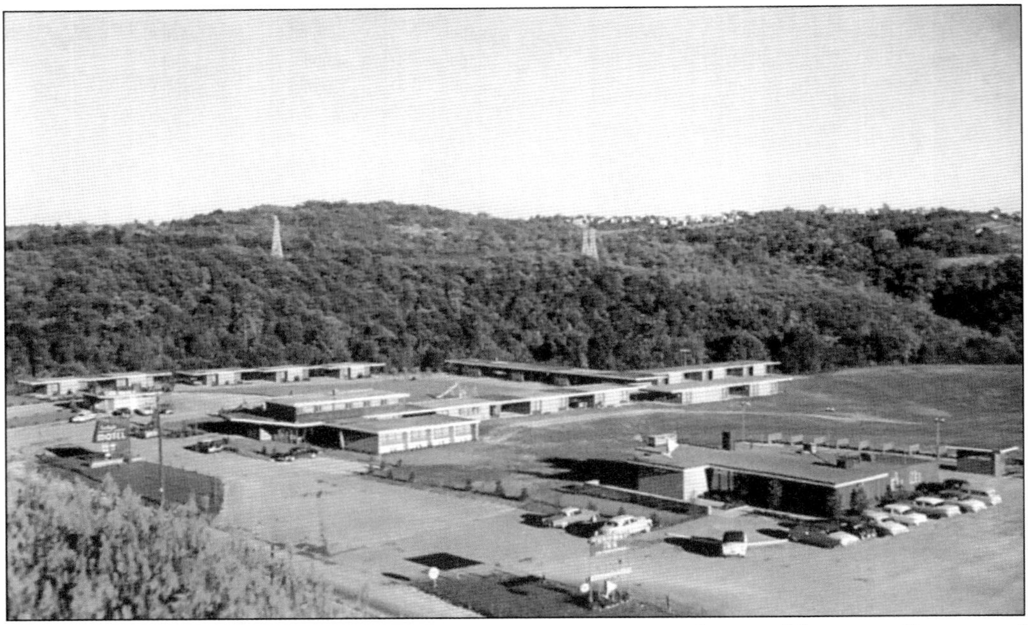

Conley's Motel opened in 1950s along Route 22 in Monroeville, roughly two miles west of the turnpike entrance. One of several motels in the Conley's chain near freeways in greater Pittsburgh, it operated in conjunction with the Thruway Inn restaurant, also seen here. The motels remained in business into the 1990s before closing.

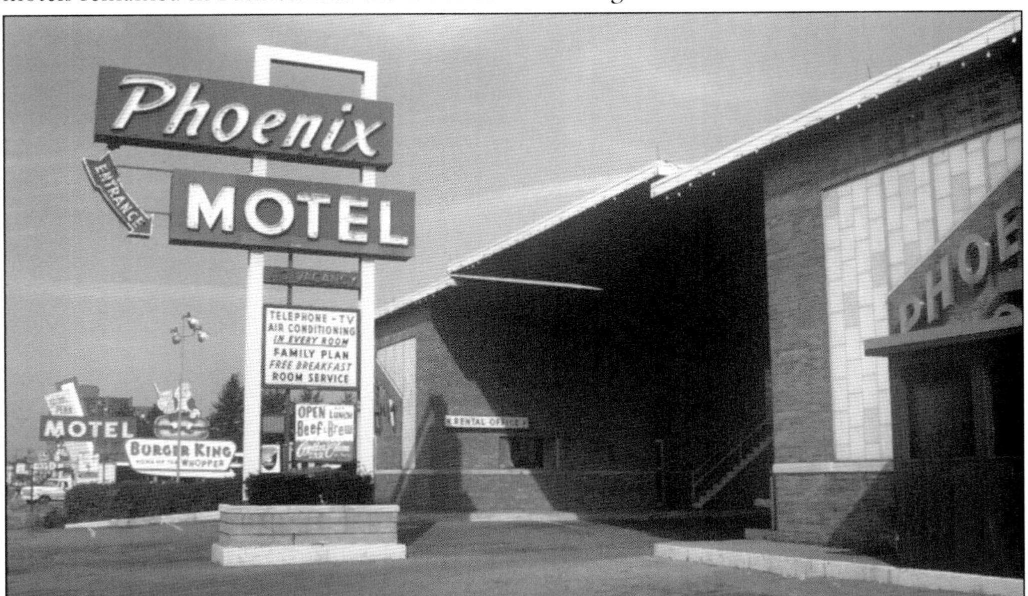

Much of Monroeville's growth can be traced to commerce related to the turnpike, although in recent years, nearly all of the early motels have been razed in favor of modern businesses. One of the few survivors is the former Phoenix Motel, shown here in the early 1970s with a sign that glowed with bright red neon at night. It remains standing today, doing business as the Sunrise Inn.

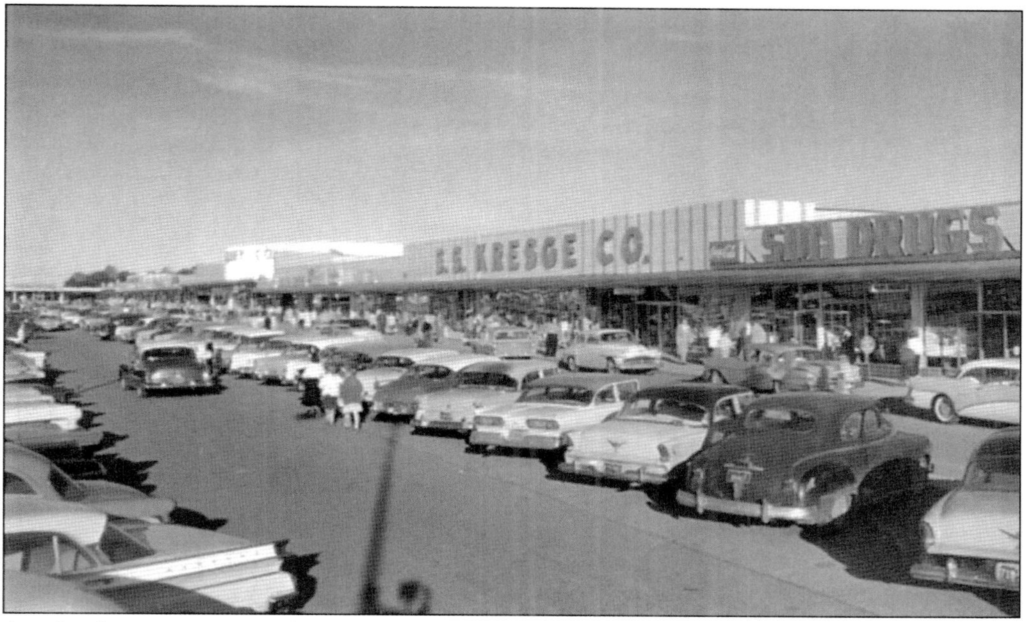

Another business venture that benefitted from its proximity to the Pennsylvania Turnpike was the Miracle Mile Shopping Center, shown here in 1959. Built in the 1950s, it stands less than half a mile west of the turnpike entrance on Business Route 22, which is officially known here as William Penn Highway. One of the region's oldest shopping centers, the Miracle Mile remains a busy retail site today.

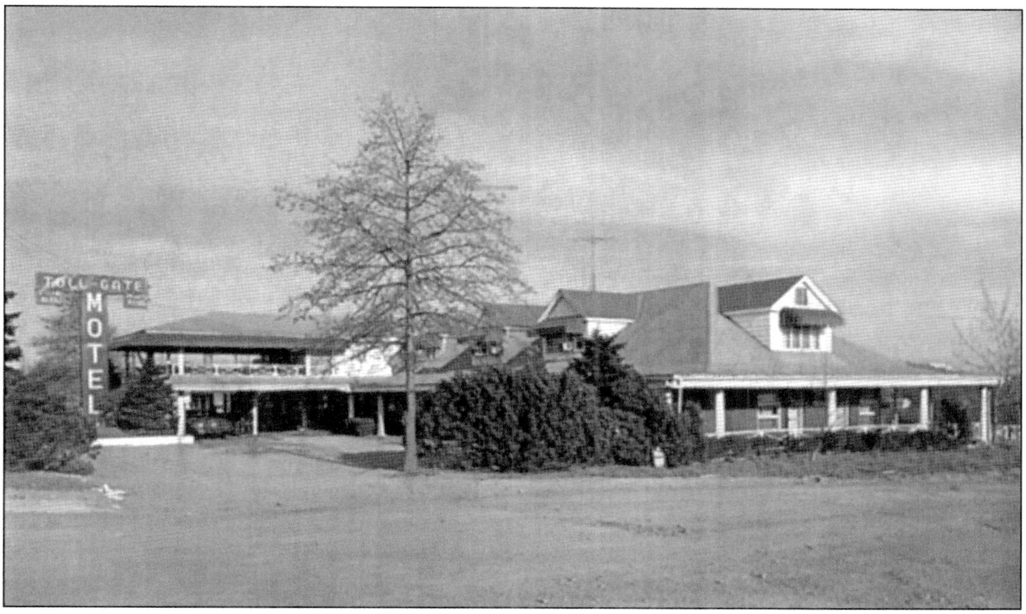

If proximity to the Pennsylvania Turnpike led to more business, then the Toll Gate Motel would certainly have been a successful establishment. Shown here in 1961, the motel was situated just 100 feet from the turnpike exit onto Route 22 in Monroeville. It offered 40 rooms with private baths and air-conditioning.

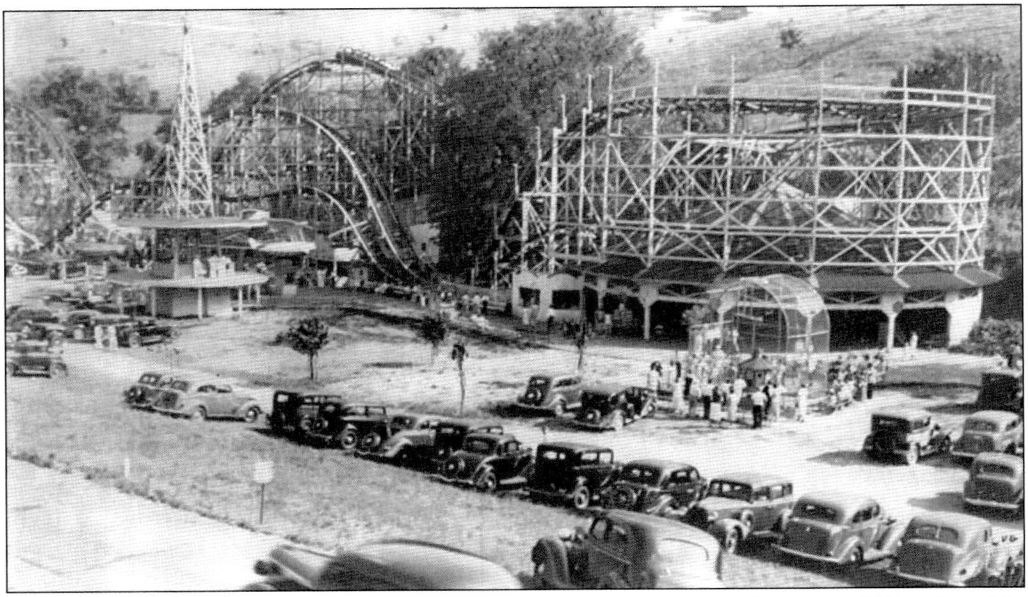

Burke Glen Park stood near the intersection of the William Penn Highway and Elliott Road in Monroeville, roughly one mile east of the Pennsylvania Turnpike. Established in 1926 by the Burke family, it featured the Speed Hound roller coaster, a large swimming pool, miniature golf, and smaller rides. As the road was gradually widened over the years, the park grew increasingly smaller until it closed in 1974.

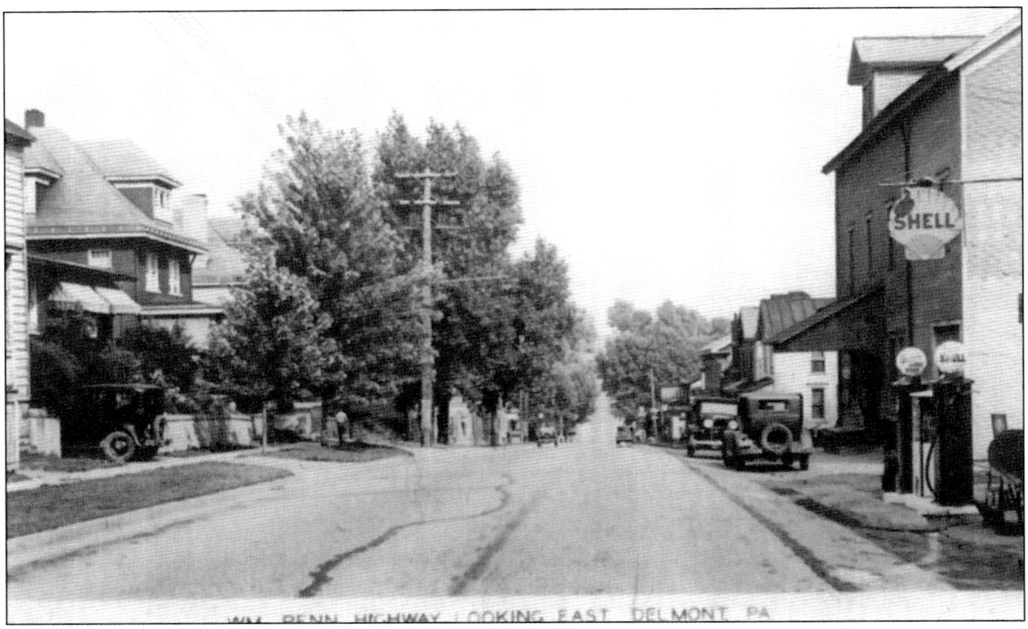

This is a view of the William Penn Highway as it passed eastward through the quiet town of Delmont in Westmoreland County in about 1930. On the right is a Shell gasoline station, its pumps adorned with lighted shell-shaped glass globes. Known today as Pittsburgh Avenue, this original segment of the highway was bypassed by the modern highway just to the south in the 1940s.

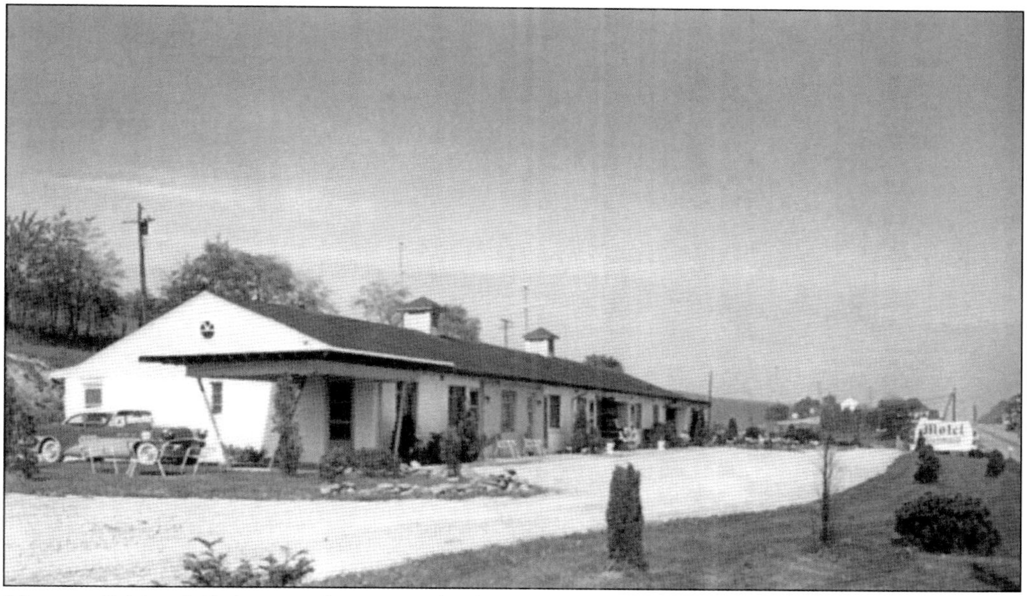

The small Motel Delmont, shown in the late 1950s, stood along modern Route 22 in the borough of Delmont. At the time, this was still a quiet area in Westmoreland County, outside the growth of suburban Pittsburgh. Today, its population continues to grow, as the Route 22 corridor becomes more commercial all the time.

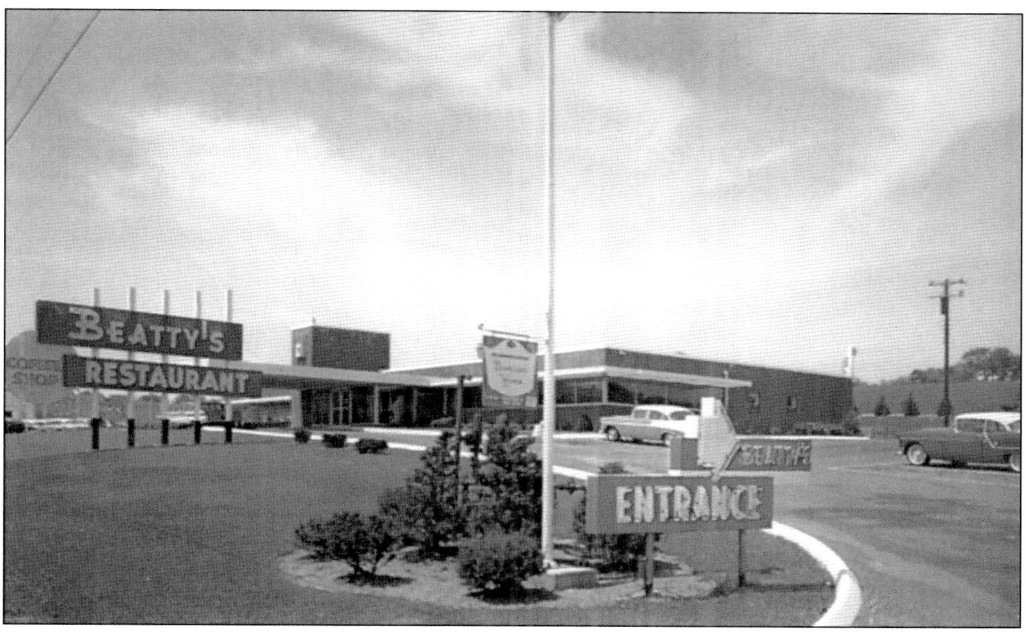

Beatty's Restaurant was built soon after the opening of the Route 22 bypass of Delmont in the late 1940s. Known today as the Lamplighter, it remains in business at 6566 William Penn Highway, providing upscale dining and entertainment. The restaurant is particularly known for its desserts, made in the on-site bakery.

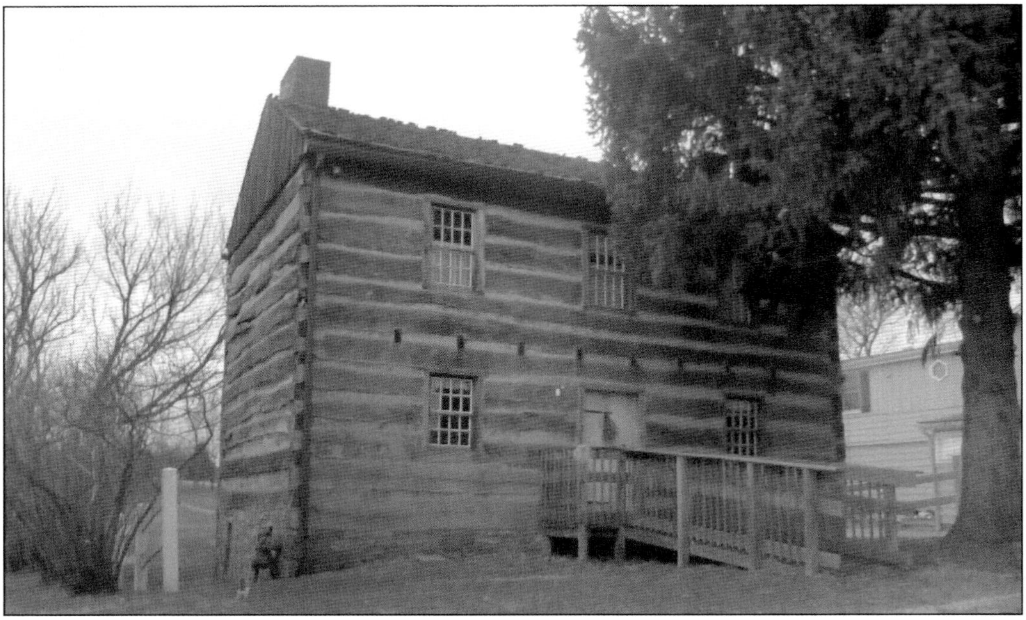

The borough of Delmont was founded in the 1780s and was originally known as Salem Crossroads. The Northern Turnpike (and later the original William Penn Highway) followed what is today known as Pittsburgh Street, and the town became a busy travel stop, with as many as five stagecoach lines coming through the village. This log house just east of the town's center dates from the turnpike's early days.

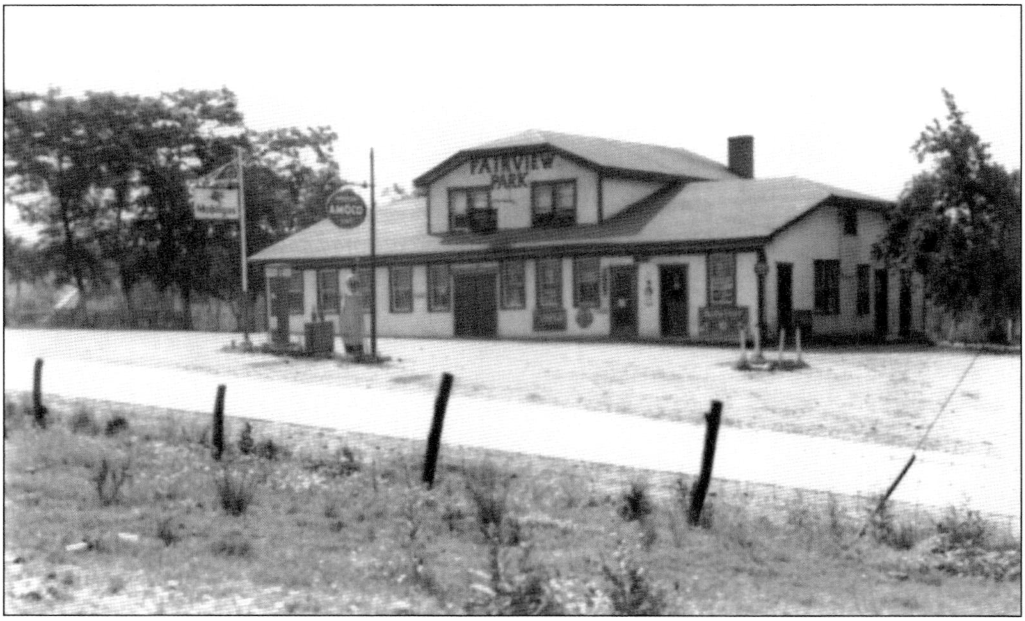

Fairview Park was a combination gas station and restaurant that stood along Route 22 near Delmont. See here in the 1930s, it sold both Amoco and Mobilgas. A sign for Budweiser beer, served in the lunchroom, can also be seen on the building's front wall. This stretch of the highway was very rural at the time, although today it has a great deal of commerce and traffic.

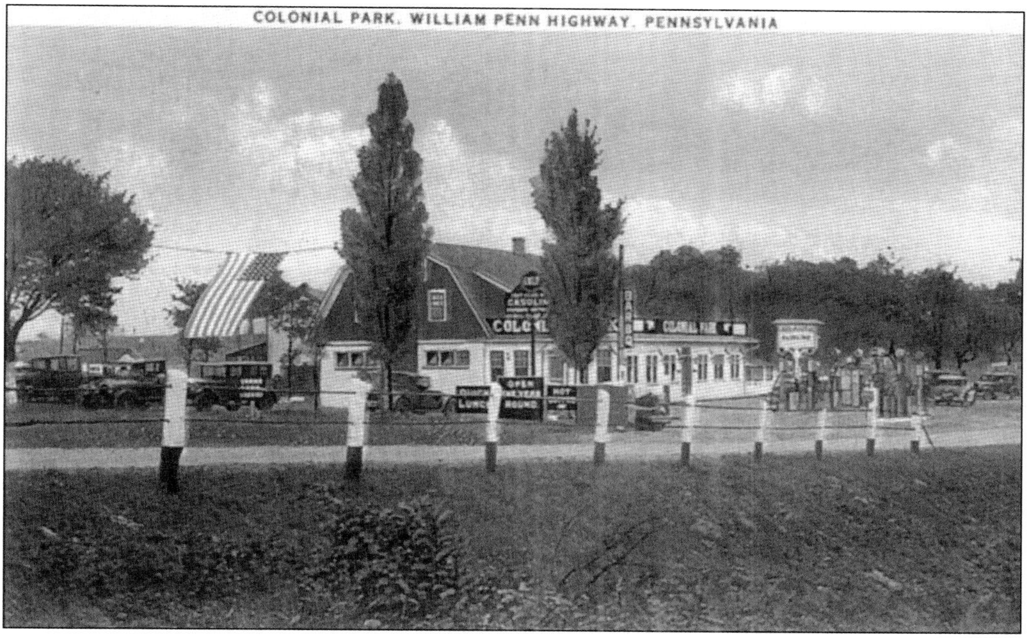

The Colonial Park was located just outside of Delmont and was one of several road stops along the rural stretch of Route 22 between Murrysville and Blairsville. Seen above in the 1930s, it was essentially a large country residence, with the addition of a small restaurant and gas station in the front. In this era, before gas stations were committed to one single brand, it was not uncommon to see two or even more brands available at a single station; this one sold both Gulf and Atlantic gasoline. The original course of the William Penn Highway and Route 22 through this region was gradually bypassed by the current highway, beginning in the 1940s. The building remains standing today as shown below, housing a small business. Its address is Croft Road, which is a segment of the original highway.

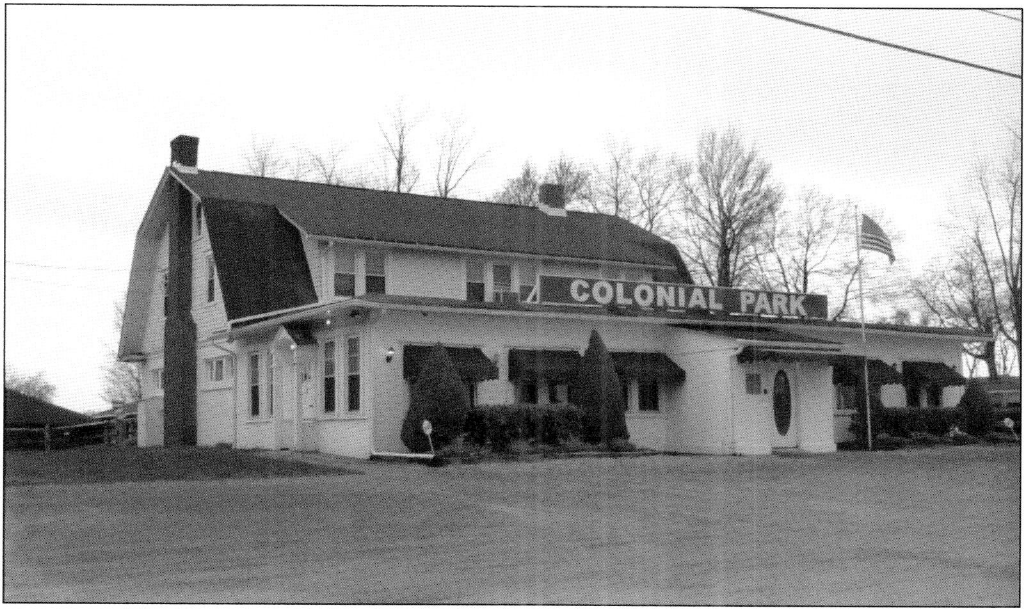

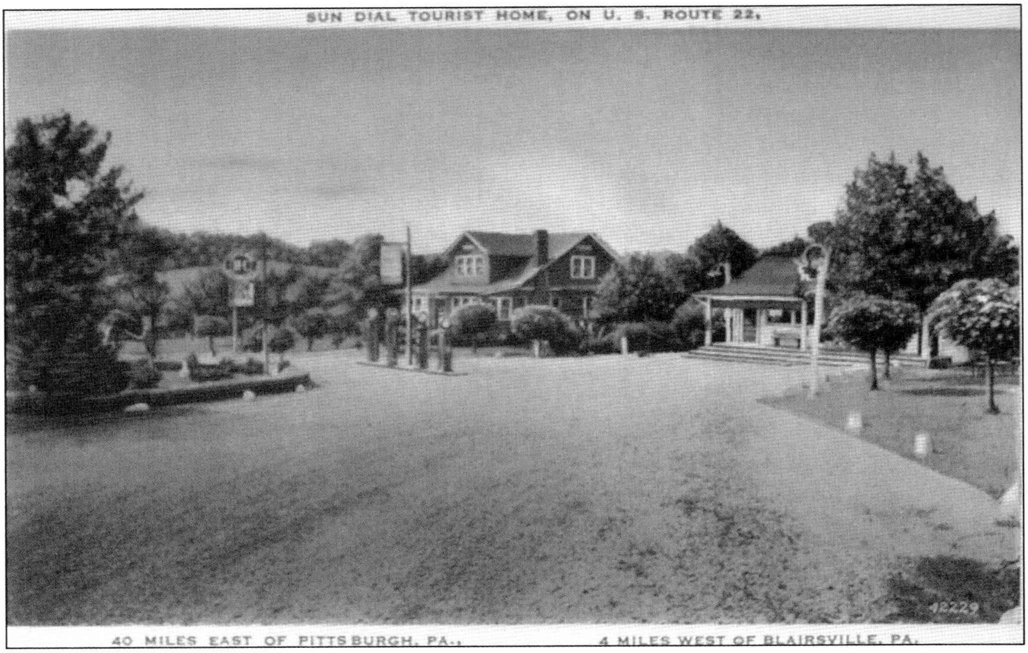

The Sun Dial Tourist Home, shown above in the 1940s, was a popular stop with travelers along the William Penn Highway for many years. Located at the intersection with Livermore Road, four miles west of Blairsville and 40 miles east of Pittsburgh, the small establishment sold Sinclair gasoline and offered a small restaurant and tourist cabins. Although no longer a business, the home and several of the cabins remain standing today, as seen below. The original alignment of the highway in front of the house is now known as Truman Road, having been bypassed by the modern highway nearby in the 1940s.

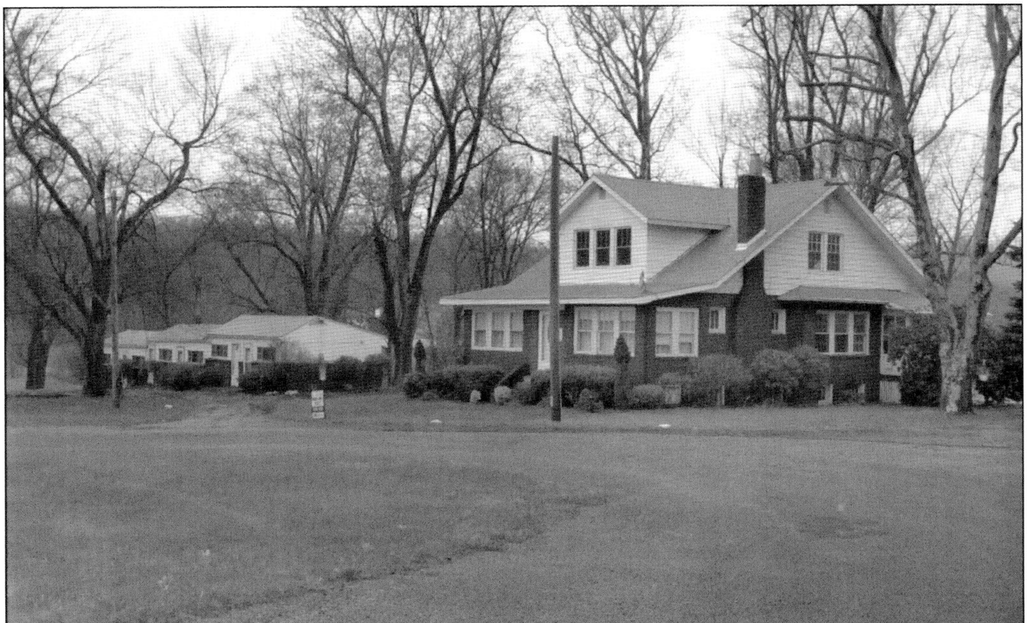

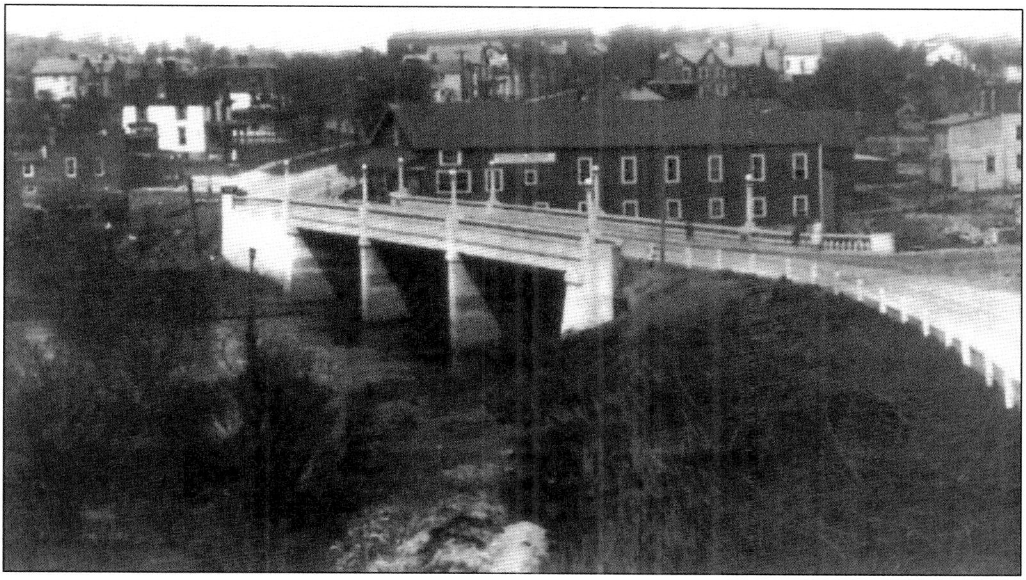

Shown here in the 1930s is the William Penn Highway Bridge over Loyalhanna Creek, just east of the borough of New Alexandria. When the modern highway was constructed just to the north of this in the 1940s, the bridge was abandoned and eventually razed. The eastern side of the original road is now abandoned and ends abruptly at the creek.

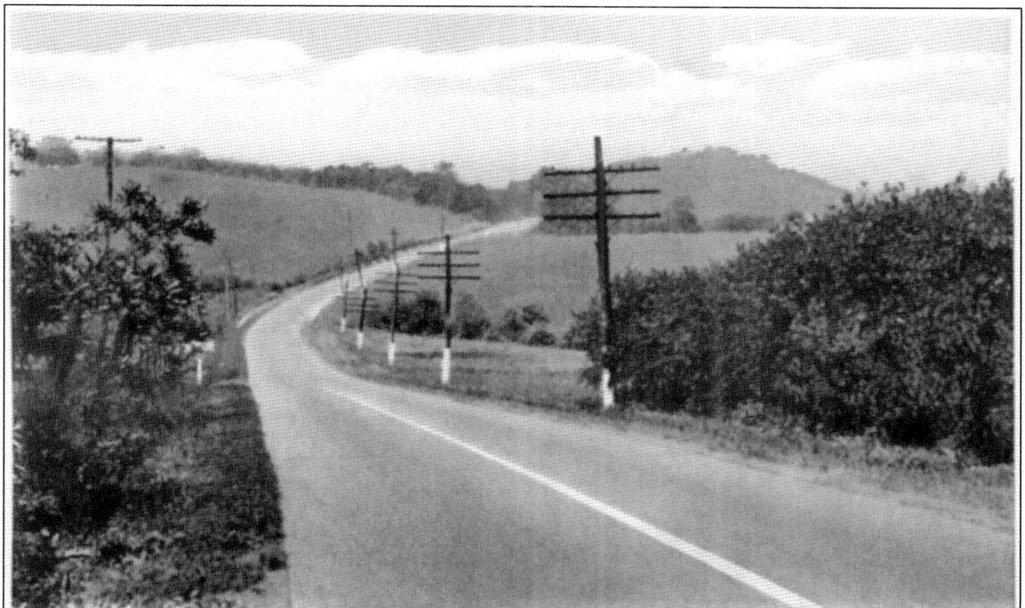

WM. PENN HIGHWAY BETWEEN PITTSBURGH AND BLAIRSVILLE, PA.

This view of the rolling hills between Pittsburgh and Blairsville in the 1920s has a typically rural appearance. The area was largely undeveloped at the time, aside from the occasional filling station, small restaurant, or overnight cabins. By the 1950s, however, the Greater Pittsburgh area had begun to slowly spread eastward into the countryside, and much of the Route 22 corridor in that area is well developed today.

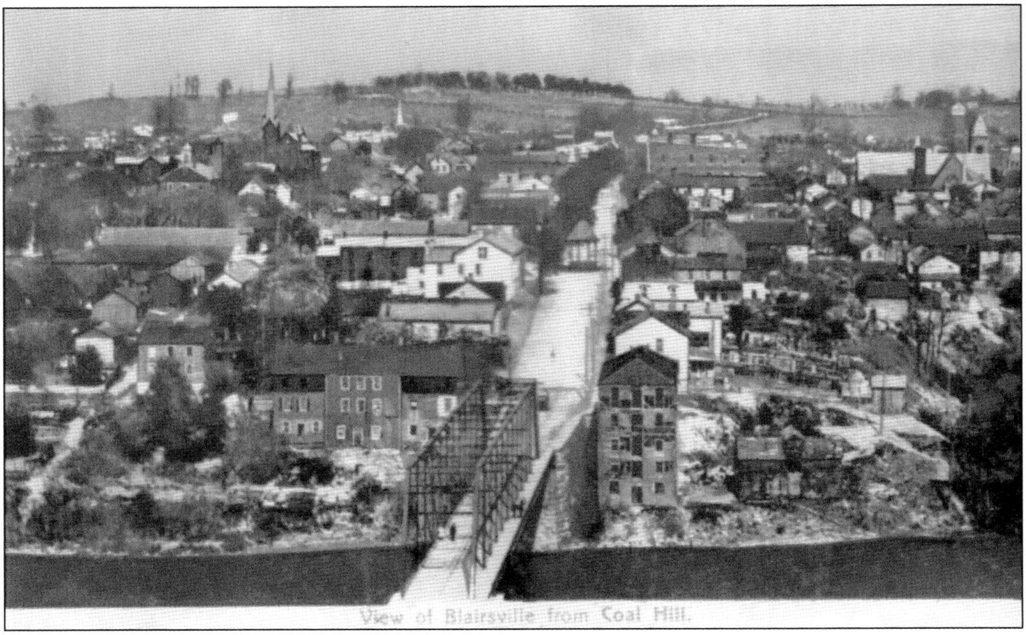

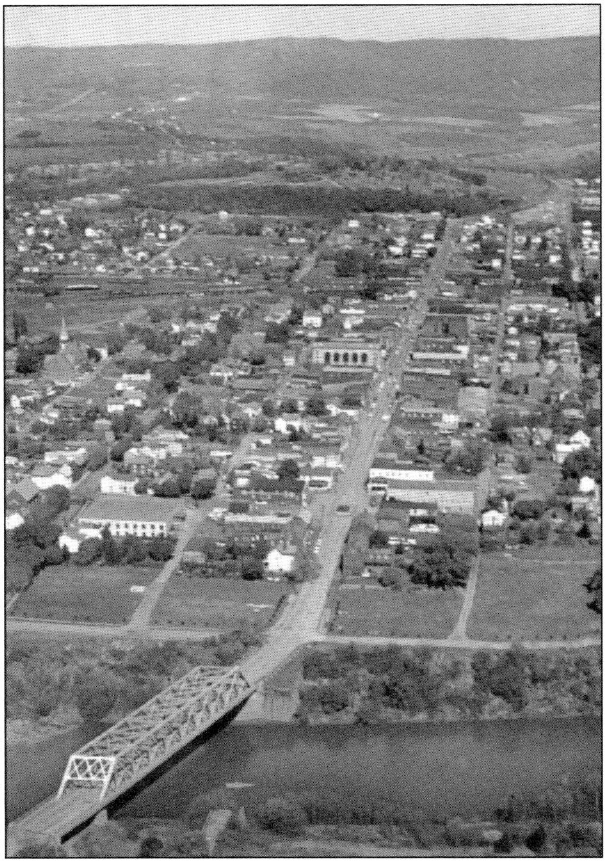

Above is an early eastward view of Blairsville from Coal Hill, about 1920. The William Penn Highway crosses the bridge over the river and enters town as West Market Street. The narrow bridge shown here was replaced in the 1930s by the much wider current structure, seen at left in an aerial view from a similar vantage point in the 1960s. The city was bypassed entirely by the modern Route 22 highway north of town in the early 1950s. The thousand-foot rise of Chestnut Ridge, the westernmost of the Allegheny Mountains, can be seen towering in the background.

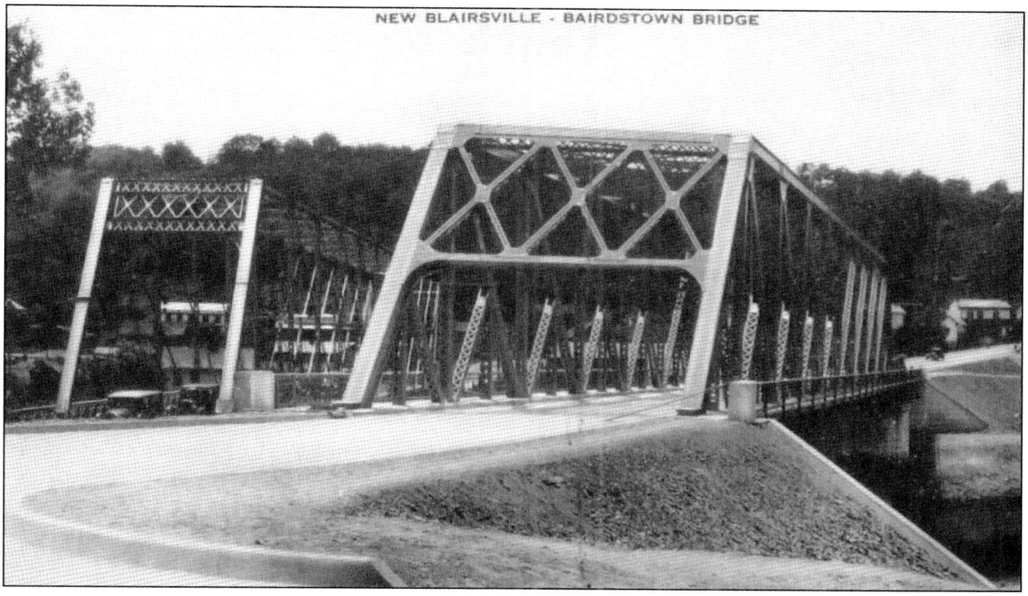

After it was designated as a federal route, a gradual improvement of the William Penn Highway and upgrading of bridges and road quality took place over the following decade. Seen in the postcard above, the bridge at right opened in 1935 to cross the Conemaugh River near Blairsville, replacing the older bridge at left. The new bridge, which remains in use today, only carried Route 22 for about 15 years before being bypassed by the modern highway nearby. This bridge and the current span can both be seen below around 1970 in an aerial view of the borough looking southeastward. Chestnut Ridge, the westernmost front of the Allegheny Range, is again in the distance.

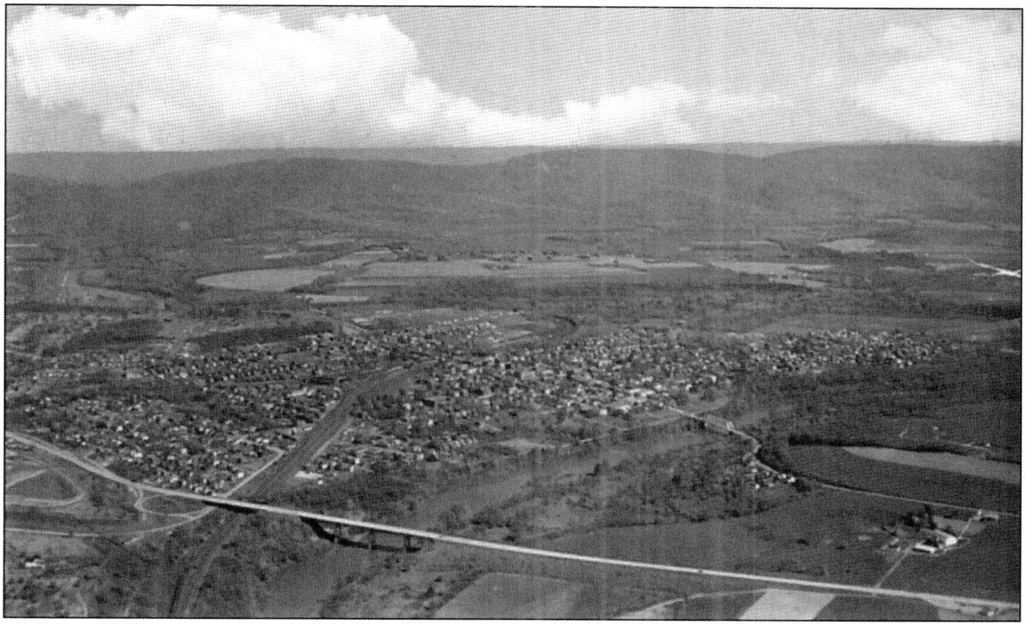

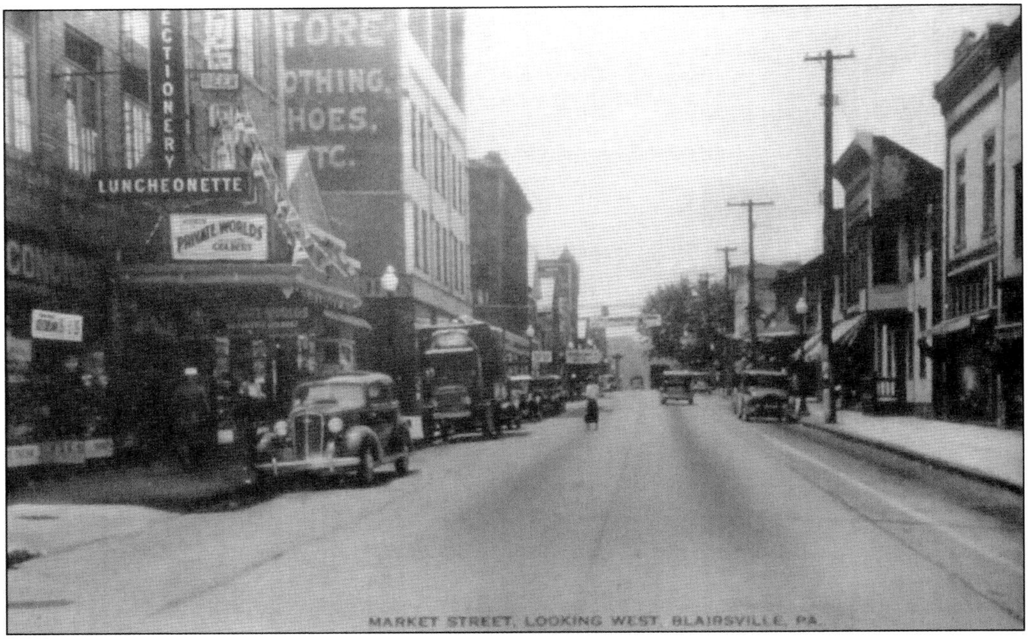

Settled in 1818 along the Conemaugh River, Blairsville has a current population of more than 3,400. Shown here in a 1940s view looking eastward along Market Street (Route 22), its downtown was a bustling business district. Once the bypass of downtown was completed in the early 1950s, however, the appearance gradually changed as the area's primary business district shifted to the corridor of the modern highway.

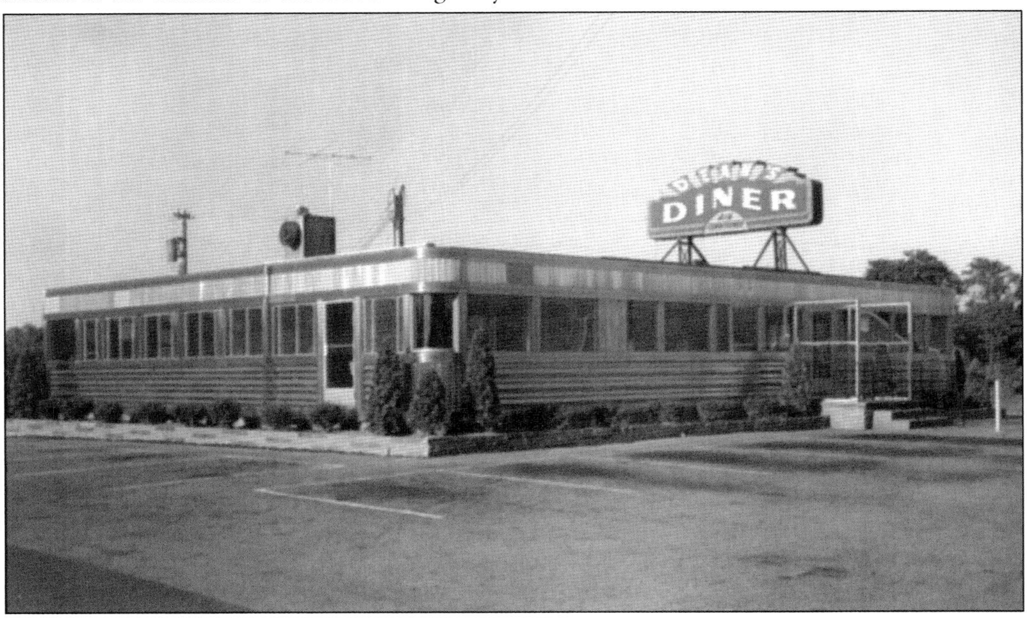

Emerson Dean opened this diner in Blairsville in 1953, shortly after the Route 22 bypass of the city was opened. Made by the Fodero Dining Car Company of New Jersey, it was built in the classic Art Deco style with a stainless-steel exterior and quickly became a popular stop for travelers. It remained under family ownership for more than 50 years and is still in operation today.

Four

Across the Mountains

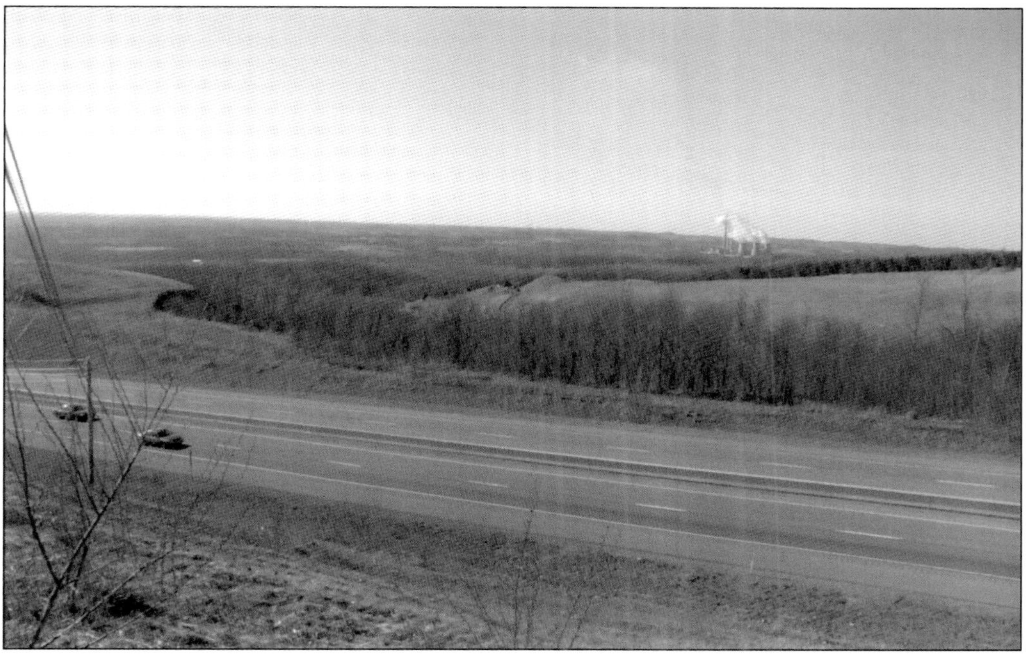

The western front of the Allegheny Ridge of the Appalachian Mountains is also known as Chestnut Ridge. Encountering the ridge immediately east of Blairsville, Route 22 climbs more than 1,000 feet over several miles, providing a dramatic view of the countryside to the west. Of note is the Homer City Generating Station, five miles north, which has the nation's tallest smokestack at 1,217 feet in height.

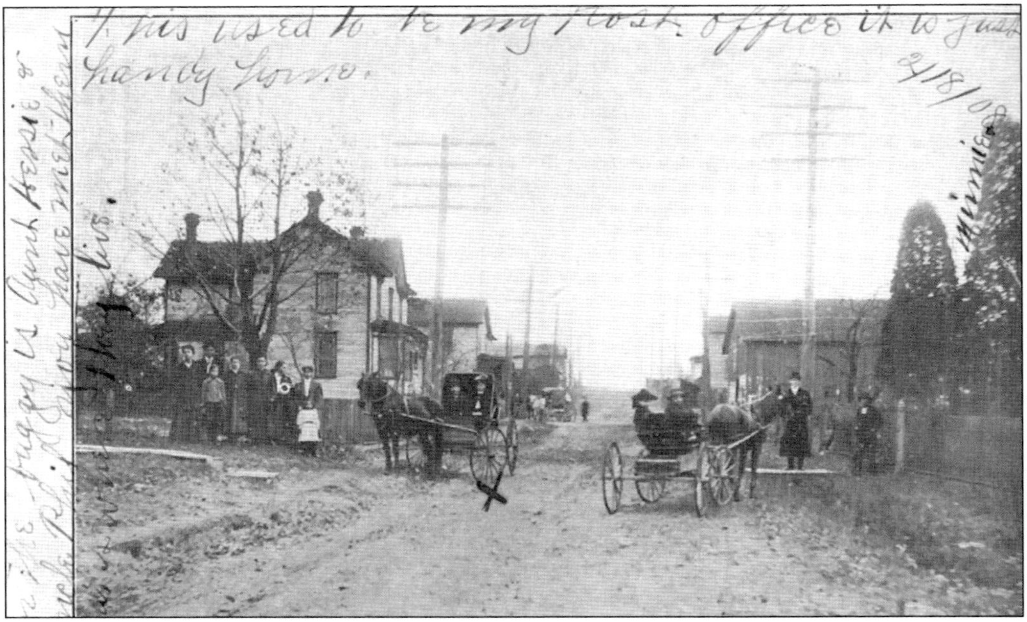

One of the earliest postcards in this collection, this one shows a view of Clyde, a small village in Indiana County, in 1908. At that time, the road was still known as the Philadelphia-Pittsburg Turnpike. The road was paved in the 1920s and remained in use until 2010, when Route 22 was finally realigned onto the modern highway that passes just to the south of the village.

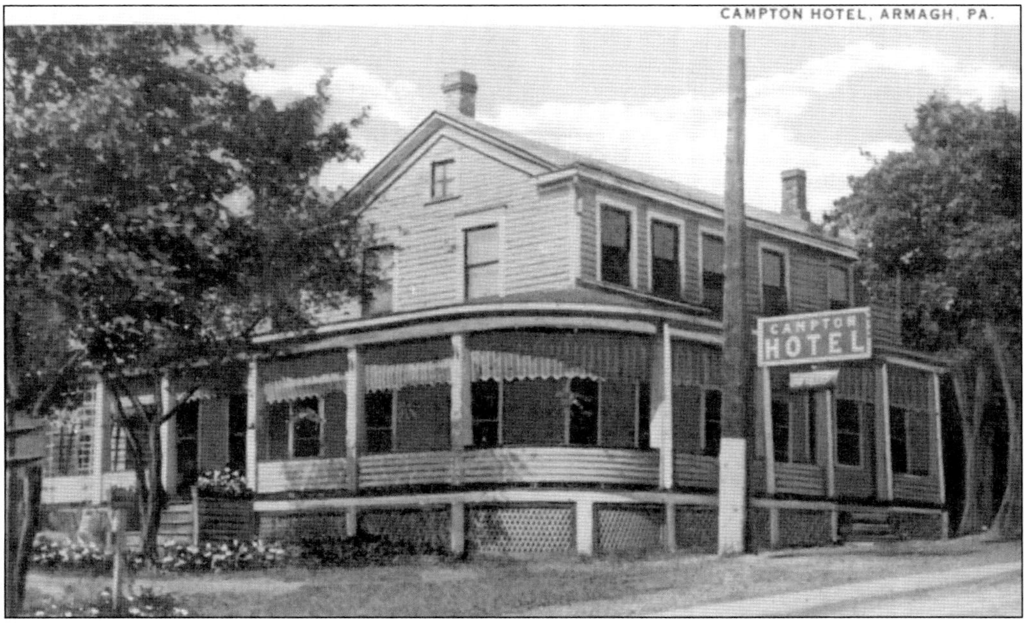

Midway between Blairsville and Ebensburg in the Laurel Highlands, the small borough of Armagh was settled by Irish immigrants in 1792, and it served as a stop along the Northern Turnpike in the 19th century. This card shows the Campton Hotel, housed in a large residence, in the 1930s. The original course of the turnpike and Route 22, known today as Philadelphia Street, was later bypassed by the modern highway.

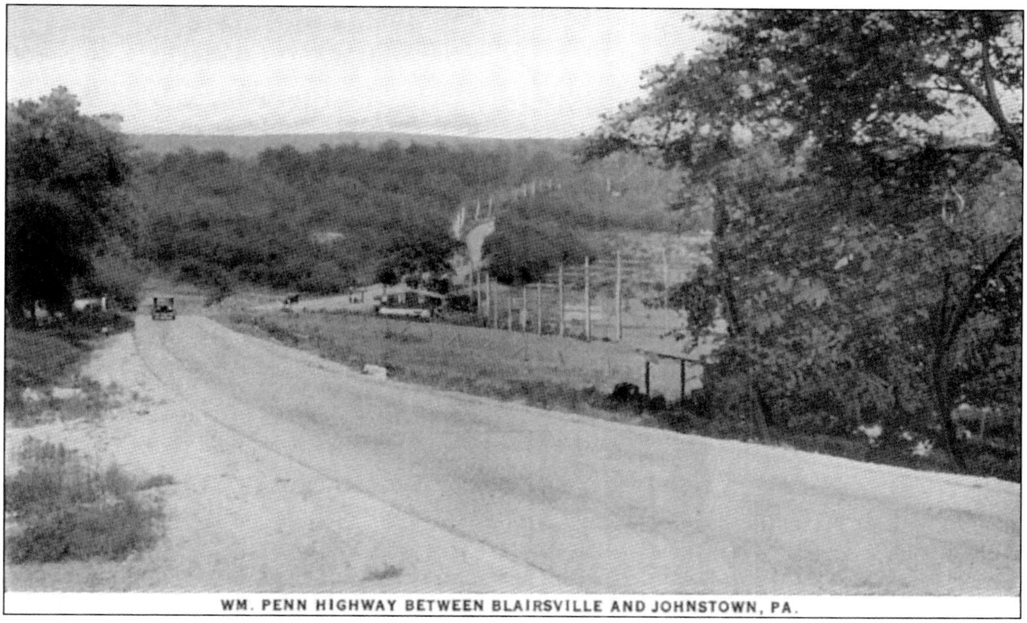

The William Penn Highway had several alternate alignments that motorists could follow as needed. One of these, shown in the 1920s, followed what is now state Route 56 along the Conemaugh River into the city of Johnstown, 10 miles to the south. It then returned northward along what is now William Penn Avenue and State Route 271 to rejoin the main highway at Mundy's Corner.

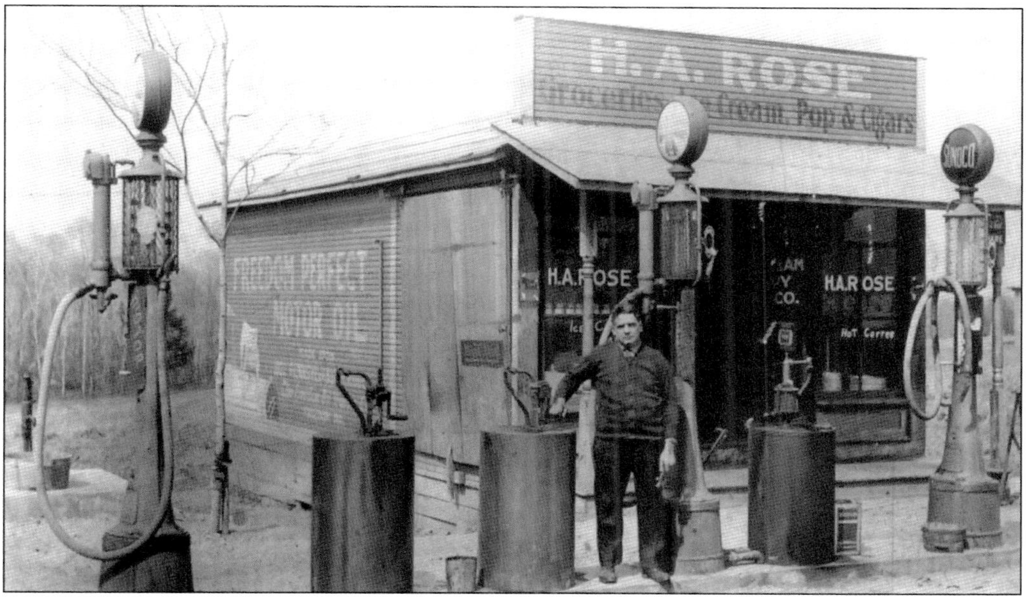

Mundy's Corner is a small community at what was originally the intersection of Route 22 and US Route 219, which continued several miles southward into Johnstown. H.A. Rose is shown here around 1930 outside of his small gasoline station along the William Penn Highway in Mundy's Corner. Here, he sold both Sunoco and Freedom brands of gasoline. Both routes have since been realigned onto modern highways, bypassing the community.

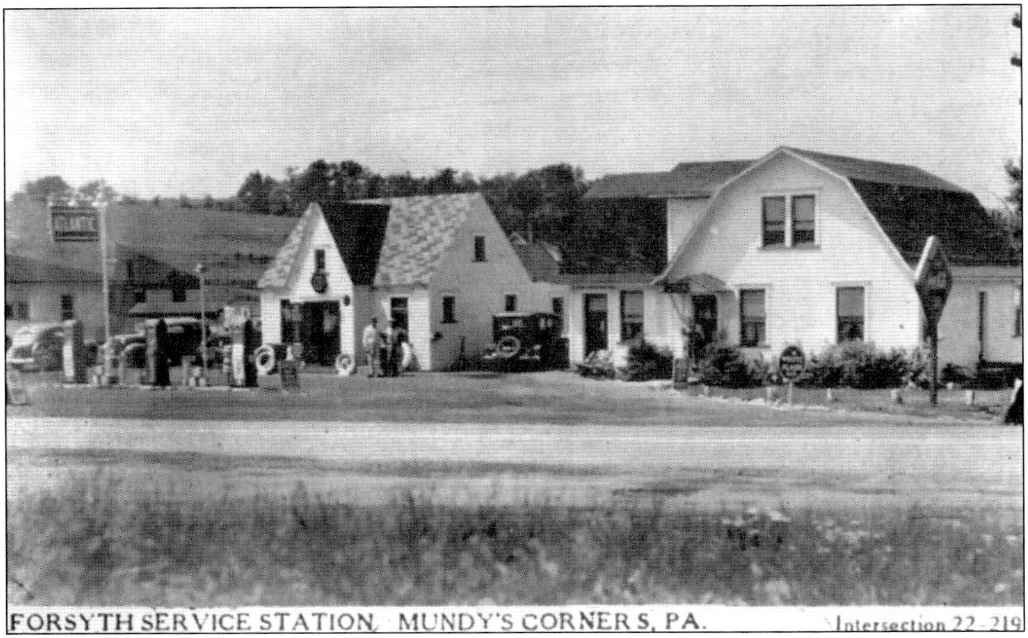

The Forsyth service station, shown here around 1940, stood along Route 22 in Mundy's Corner, near the intersection of Route 219. In addition to the sign for Atlantic gasoline, a sign for White Flash, Atlantic's primary brand, can also be seen, along with a large sign for Coca-Cola. Like many similar stations of the era, Forsyth also sold tires and featured a small lunchroom.

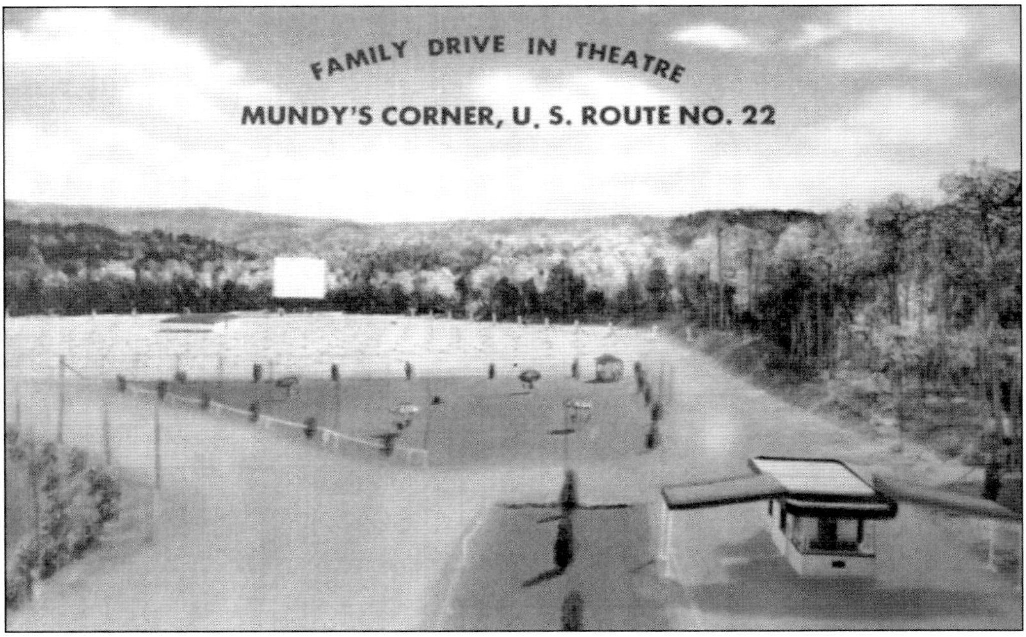

Mundy's Corner was also the site of a movie theater located along Route 22. The Family Drive In Theatre drew customers from nearby Ebensburg and Johnstown as well as the many small rural towns in the region. Like most drive-in theaters, it saw business peak in the 1960s, and the venue is no longer in operation.

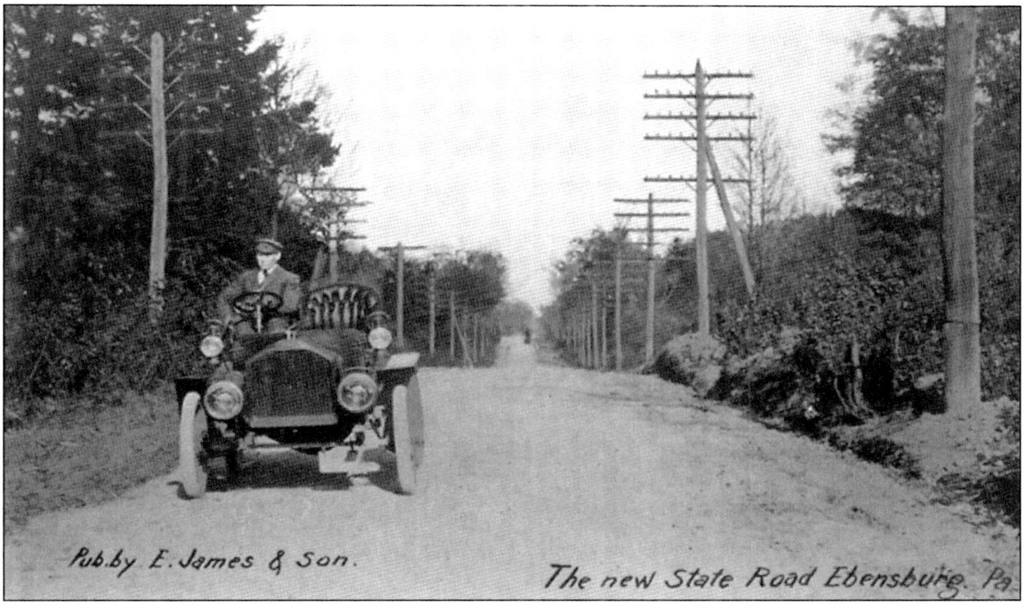

This postcard shows the new state road, which would soon be known as the William Penn Highway, near Ebensburg in 1916. Paved only with gravel, the road was just wide enough for two cars to pass. Long before the appearance of the many billboards, motels, restaurants, and gas stations that would later line much of the route, it seemed very isolated as it traveled through the sparsely populated mountain region of central Pennsylvania.

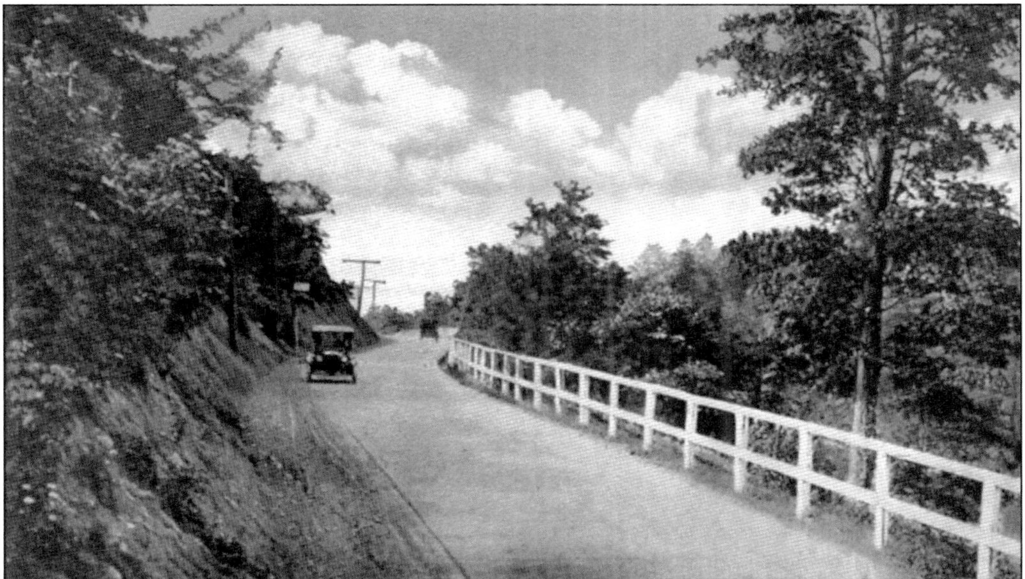

Shown here in the 1920s, the state road between Johnstown and Ebensburg was also known as the William Penn Highway. When the highway was established in 1916, the capital available from the company's private investors allowed for a great number of improvements, and soon wider roads, improved pavement, and guardrails appeared to improve safety. Today, the two cities are linked by limited-access divided highways.

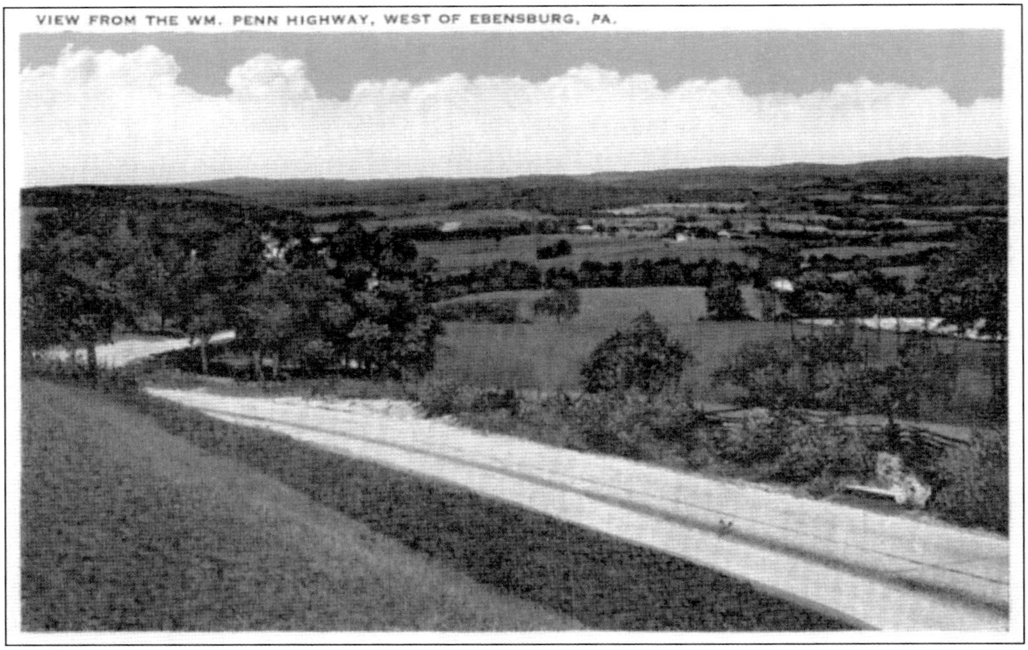

The rolling hills along the William Penn Highway just west of Ebensburg are shown here around 1930. Originally very isolated and rural in this area, the road passes through a busy commercial district today before crossing the modern limited-access highway that carries US Route 219 from Johnstown northward toward Buffalo.

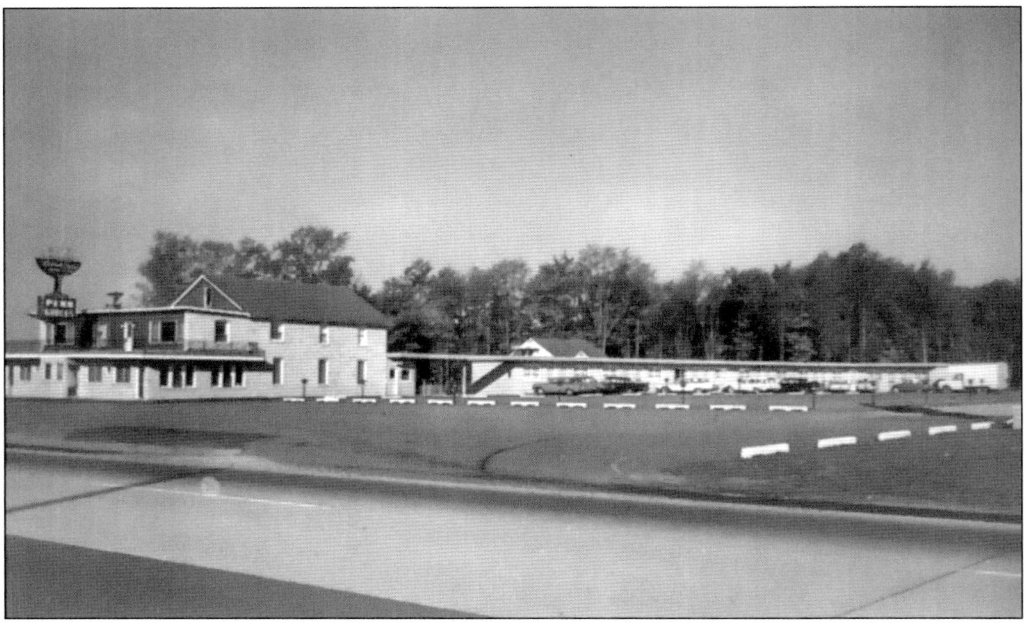

The Penn Gables Restaurant stands at 4588 Admiral Peary Highway (Route 22) on the west side of Ebensburg. One of the few early restaurants along the highway to remain in business, it is shown here in the 1960s. Originally, the restaurant had an adjacent motel, but this closed and was razed long ago.

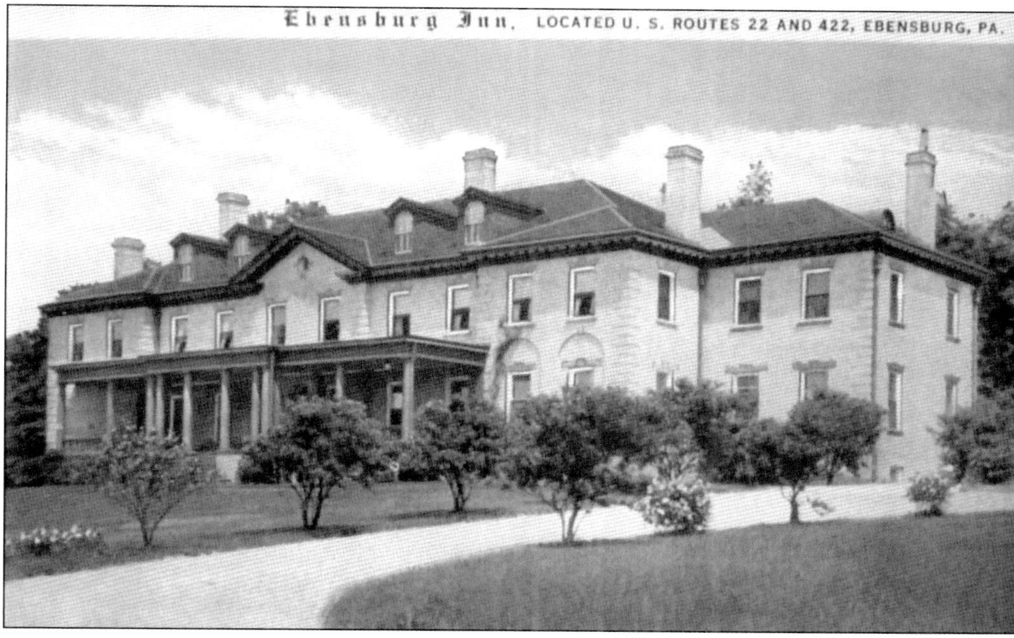

The Ebensburg Inn, shown above in the 1930s, operated for many years just west of the intersection of US Routes 22 and 422 on the west side of Ebensburg, providing some of the area's finest accommodations as well as sweeping views of the surrounding countryside. Built in 1900 by David Park, owner of a local steel company, the large hilltop mansion had been converted into a hotel by the 1930s. By the late 1950s, it had closed and was acquired in 1960 by the local Catholic diocese, which converted it and its surrounding 34-acre estate into what is now Bishop Carroll High School. Known today as Aquinas Hall, the stately home is surrounded by modern school buildings, as shown in the aerial view below.

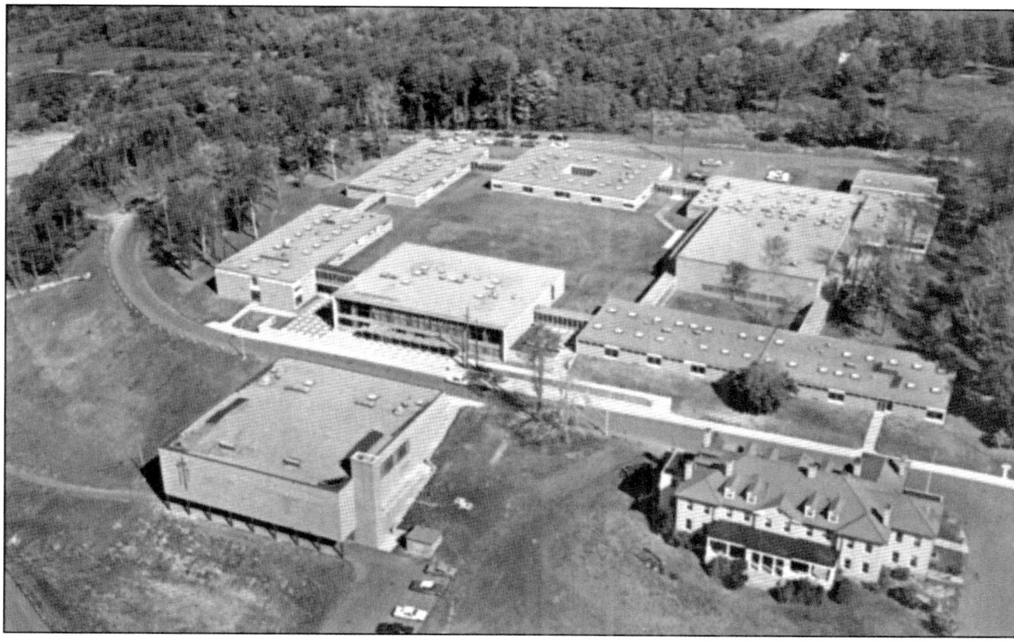

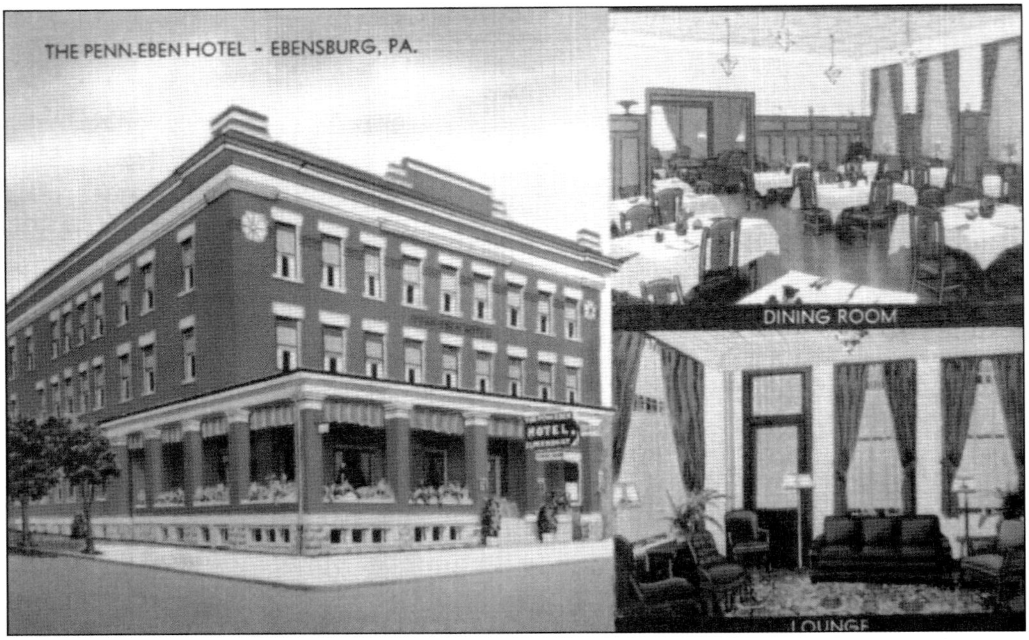

Pictured here around 1940, the Penn-Eben Hotel stood on the north side of West High Street (the original William Penn Highway) in Ebensburg, several blocks west of the town's center. The town's largest hotel, it featured 38 rooms, a formal dining room, and a sitting room. The hotel closed in the 1960s and the structure is no longer standing.

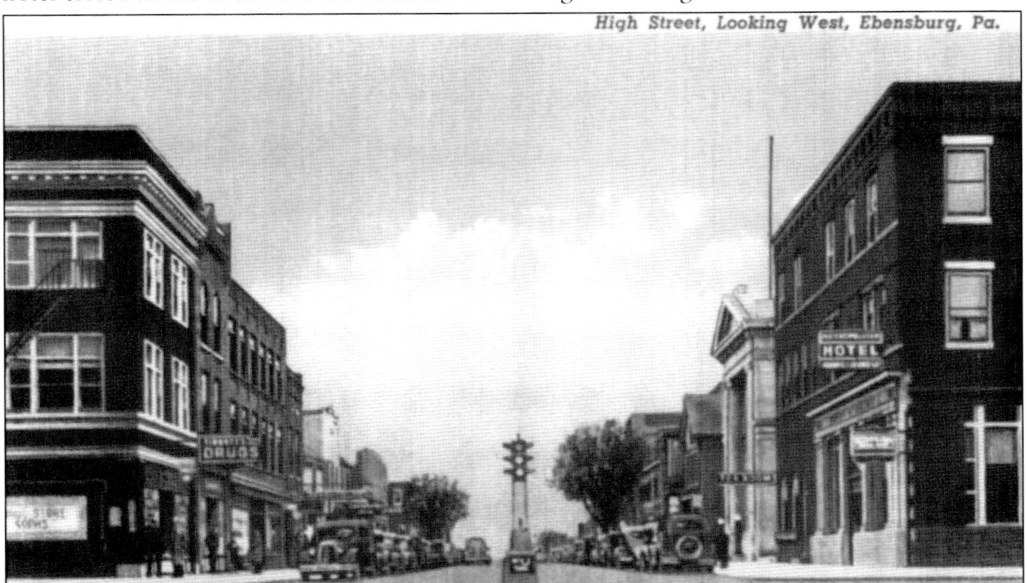

The intersection of Center and High Streets in Ebensburg is the center of town, and at one time it marked the eastern intersection of Routes 22 and 219. In this view looking west on High Street in the 1940s, the Metropolitan Hotel can be seen at right. Erected shortly after the turn of the century, the building remains standing today but has been extensively remodeled. Also note the traffic signal standing in the center of the intersection.

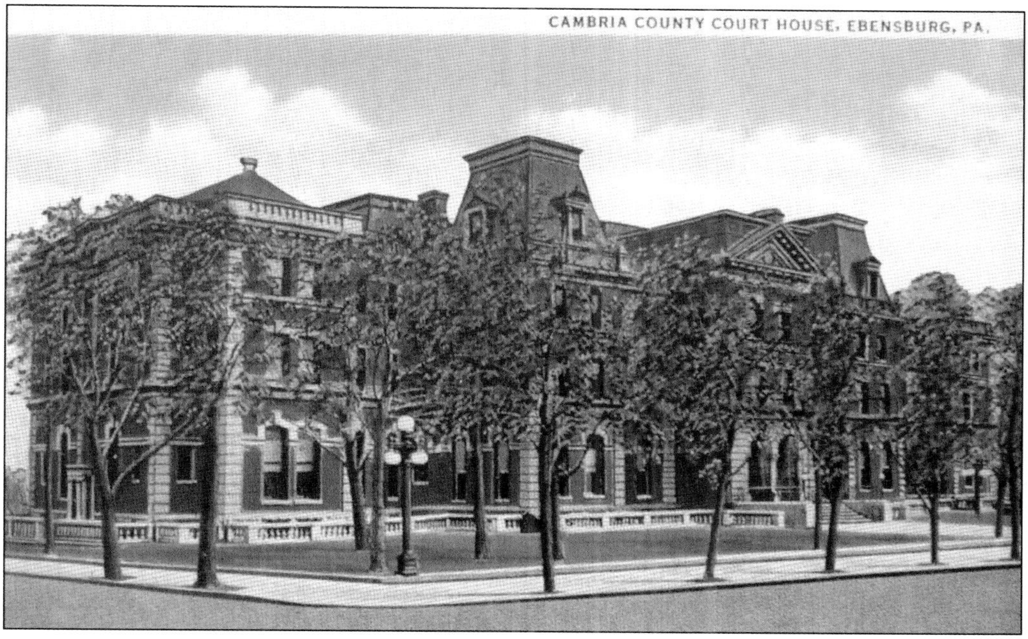

The Cambria County Courthouse stands atop a hill one block south of the center of Ebensburg and is visible from throughout the town. Built in 1880 in the Second Empire architectural style, it originally featured a tall clock tower, which was removed during an extensive renovation and expansion of the building in 1923.

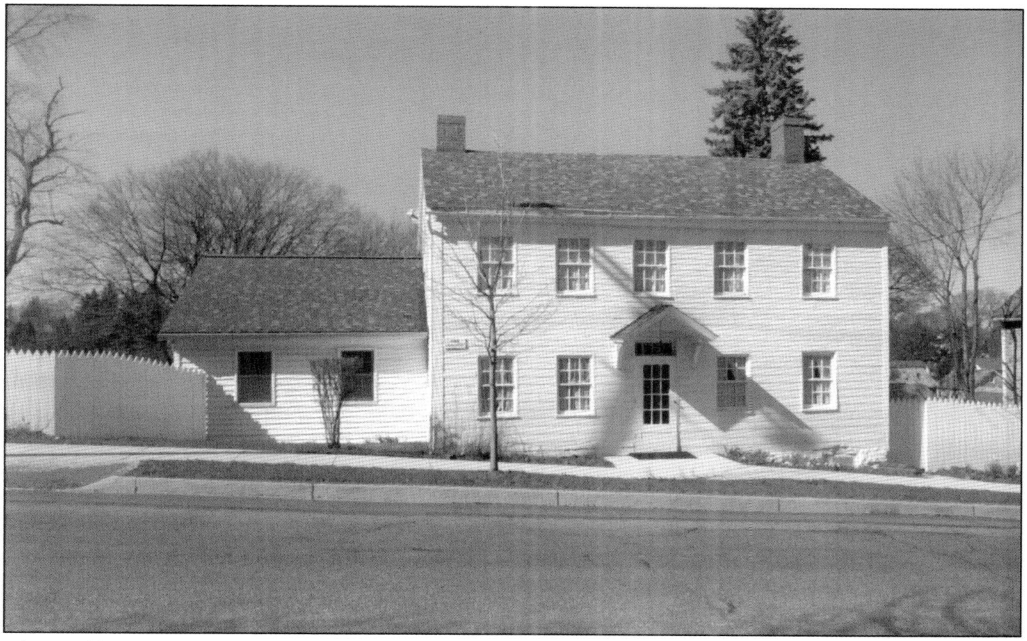

The William Penn Highway originally passed through Ebensburg as East and West High Street. Several blocks east of the town's center is this house, constructed by Welsh settler Hugh Roberts in 1799. Built as a true log cabin, it was later covered by clapboards and is Cambria County's oldest standing structure.

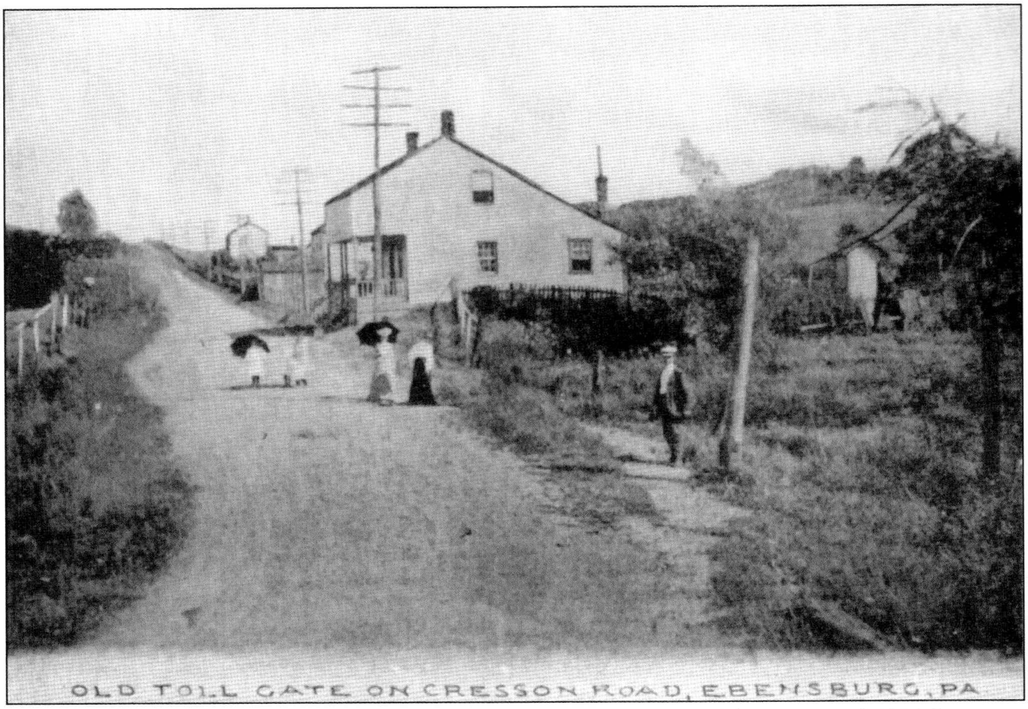

Pictured here around 1900 is a former tollhouse for the Northern Turnpike, situated along the William Penn Highway on the east side of Ebensburg in front of modern-day Lake Rowena. Built in 1820, the tollhouse remained in operation until 1870 and was destroyed by fire in 1943. A monument stands at the site today.

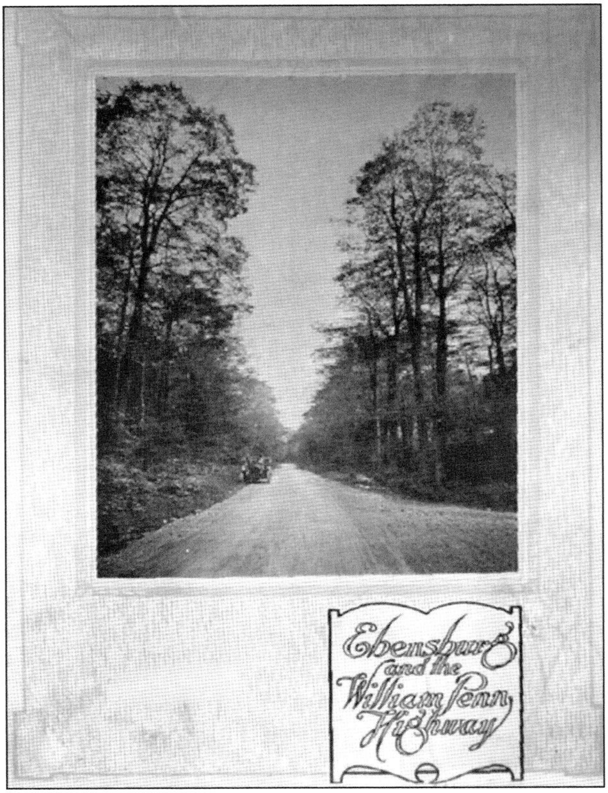

This photograph of the new William Penn Highway comes from a booklet produced in 1916 to encourage use of the new road in the area around Ebensburg. Despite most of the early highway having only gravel pavement, it was a dramatic improvement from the previous Northern Turnpike, which was unreliable and, in some cases, entirely impassable during the harsh winter season. (Courtesy of the Cambria County Historical Society.)

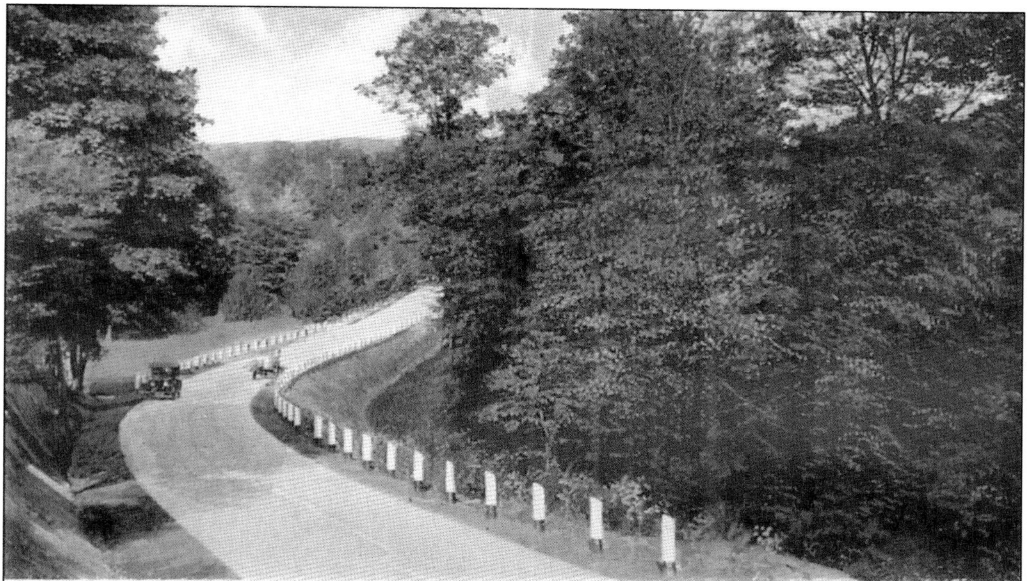

SCENE ON WM. PENN HIGHWAY BETWEEN EBENSBURG AND LORETTO, PA.

This image from the 1920s shows the rolling hills encountered by the original William Penn Highway and Route 22 as it traveled six miles from Ebensburg to Loretto on what is now known as Manor Drive. The highway then turned south on St. Joseph Street to travel toward Cresson. This entire alignment was eliminated in 1934 in favor of Admiral Peary Highway.

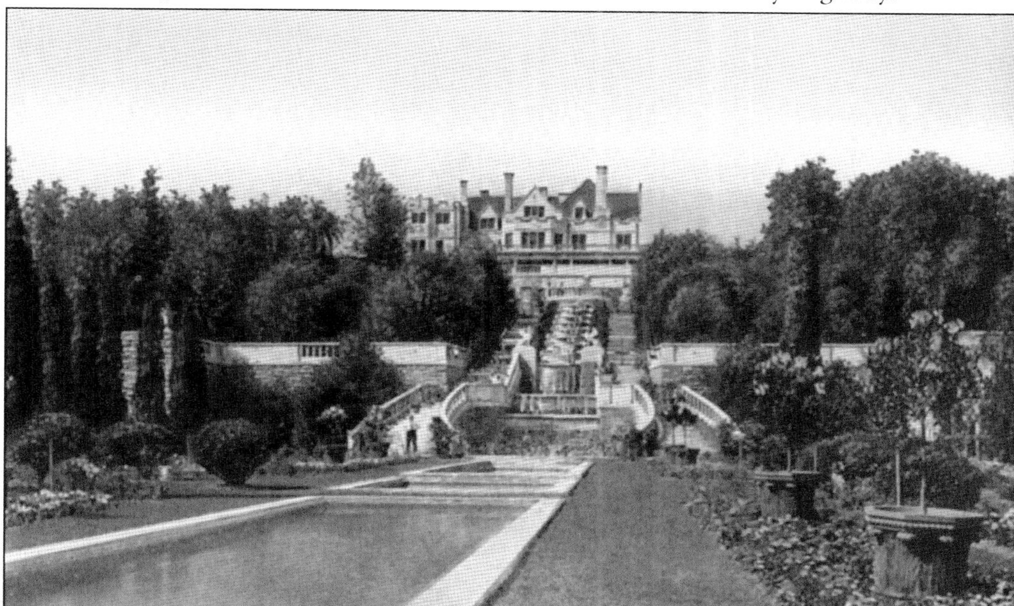

CHARLES M. SCHWAB SUMMER HOME, LORETTO, PA. ON WM. PENN HIGHWAY.

Until 1934, the William Penn Highway directly passed the 44-room summer home of Charles M. Schwab, president of the US Steel Corporation, in Loretto. Known as Immergrun, the mansion stands atop a high hill overlooking St. Francis University. Featuring opulent gardens on its 1,000 acres, the home was later sold and today serves as the Mount Assisi Friary, in association with the university.

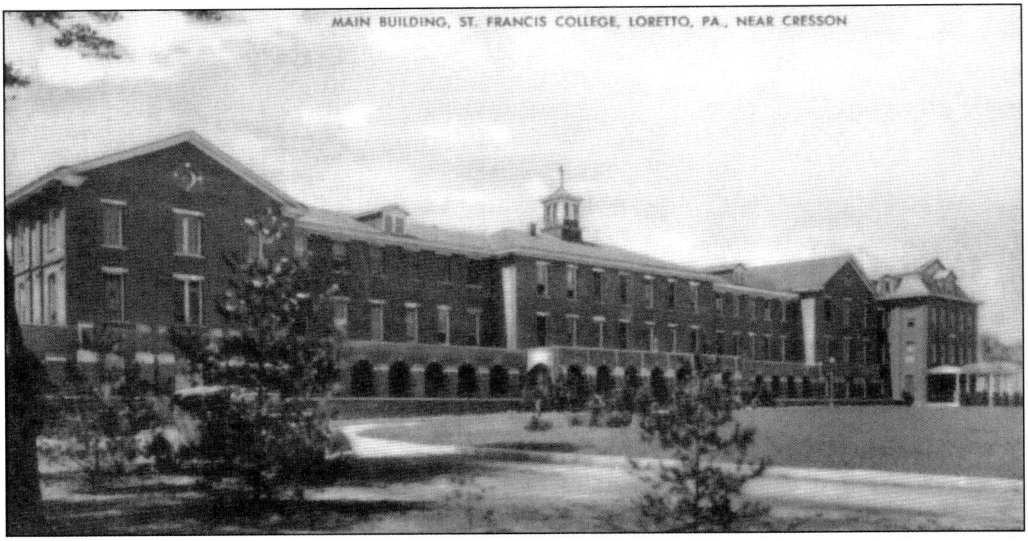

St. Francis University was founded in the town of Loretto in 1847 as a Catholic liberal arts college. Sitting on a 600-acre campus, it currently has more than 2,400 students. This early postcard shows the college's main building, situated along the original course of the William Penn Highway, which traveled through the small town. In 1931, five years after being designated as Route 22, the highway was moved several miles south to what is today known as Admiral Peary Highway.

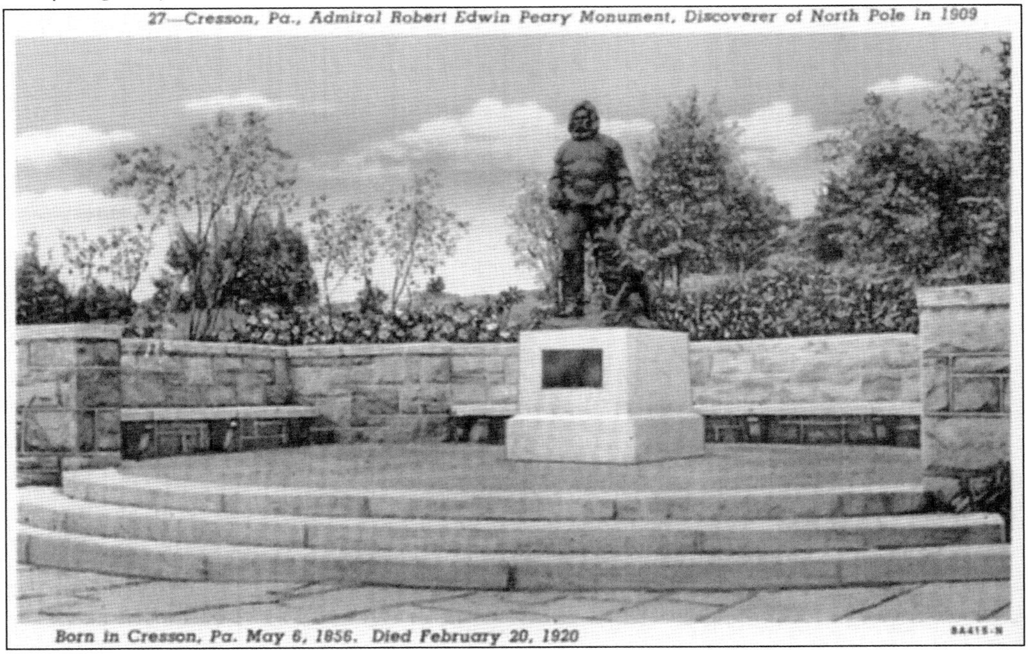

Adm. Robert Peary was born in Cresson in 1856, and he is widely credited as being the first explorer to reach the North Pole (although this has been debated by many scientists since that time). He is commemorated locally by the naming of a 12-mile stretch of former Route 22 as Admiral Peary Highway, as well as the erection of this statue in Cresson, across from Mount Aloysius College.

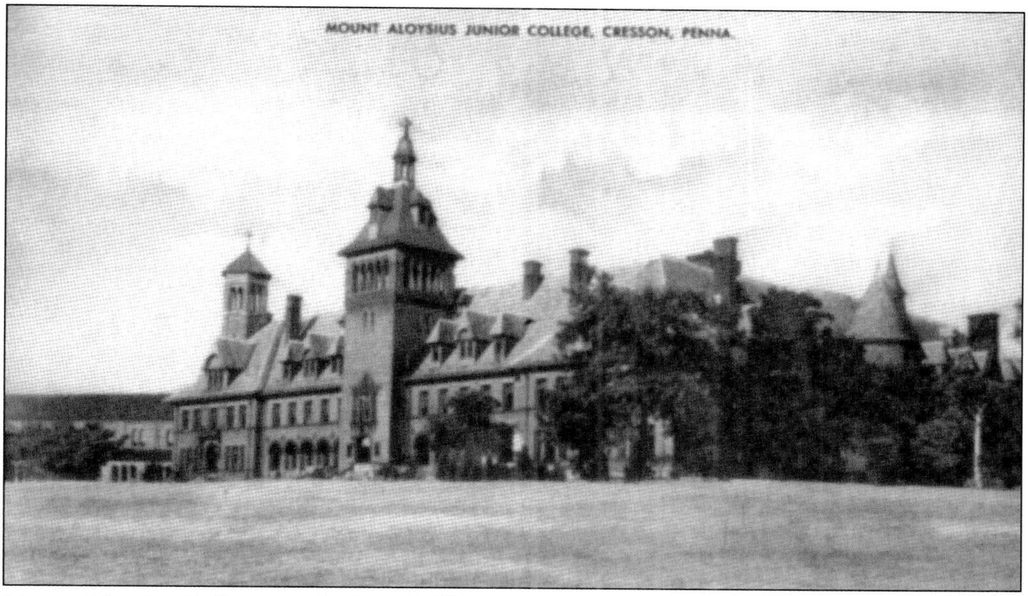

Mount Aloysius College stands along William Peary Highway (Old Route 22) on the west side of Cresson. Founded in 1853 in nearby Loretto by a group of nuns from the Sisters of Mercy, it moved to its current location in 1897. The complex covers 193 acres and consists of 12 buildings, the most notable of which is the main administration building shown here. More than 2,000 students attend the college today.

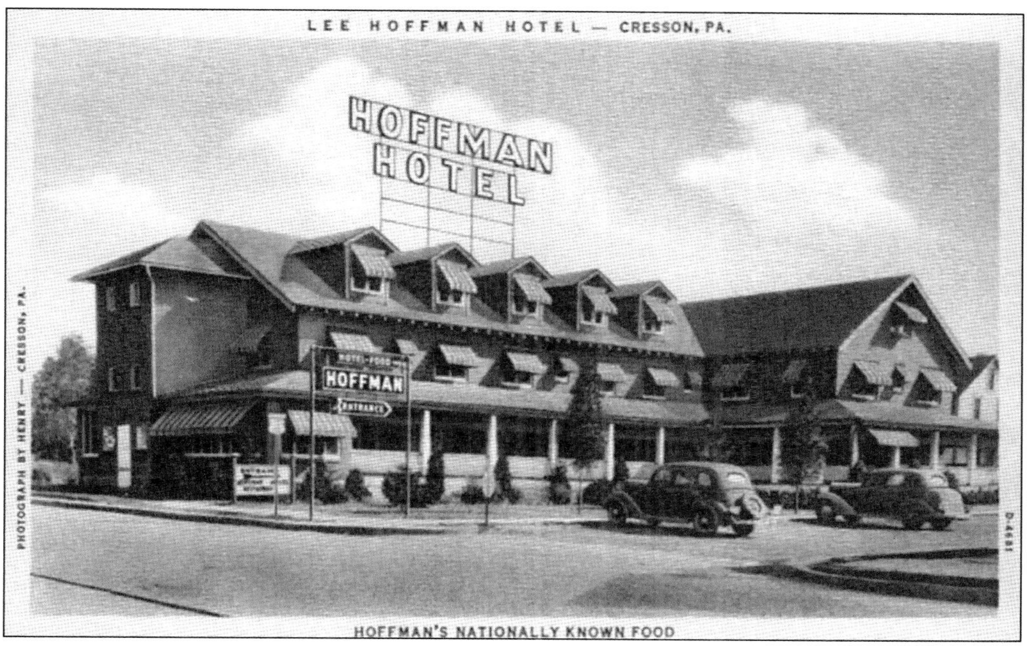

The Lee Hoffman Hotel, shown here around 1940, was located near Route 22 in Cresson. It was one of several hotels operated by Hoffman along the William Penn and Lincoln Highways in central Pennsylvania. Known for its fine food, the hotel's restaurant was recommended by Duncan Hines in some of its advertising. The hotel is no longer standing.

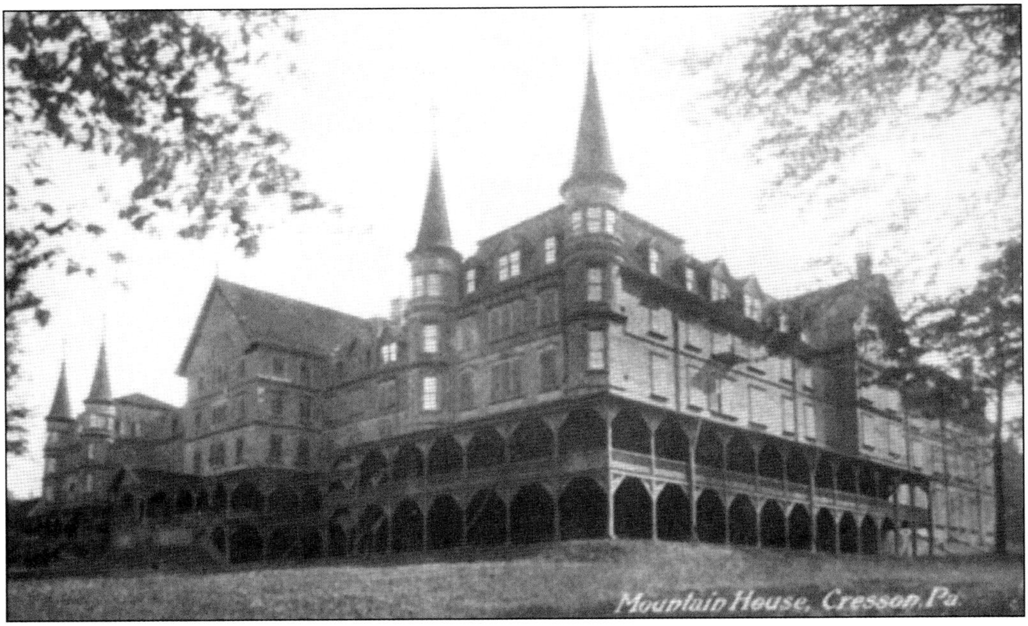

Admiral Peary Highway passes two blocks north of the former site of the Mountain House resort in Cresson. Built in 1880–1881 by the Pennsylvania Railroad, the massive Victorian building stood five stories in height and had accommodations for up to 900 guests; the complex was surrounded by 400 acres of wooded property. Despite its opulence, it was not successful as a business and was razed in 1916.

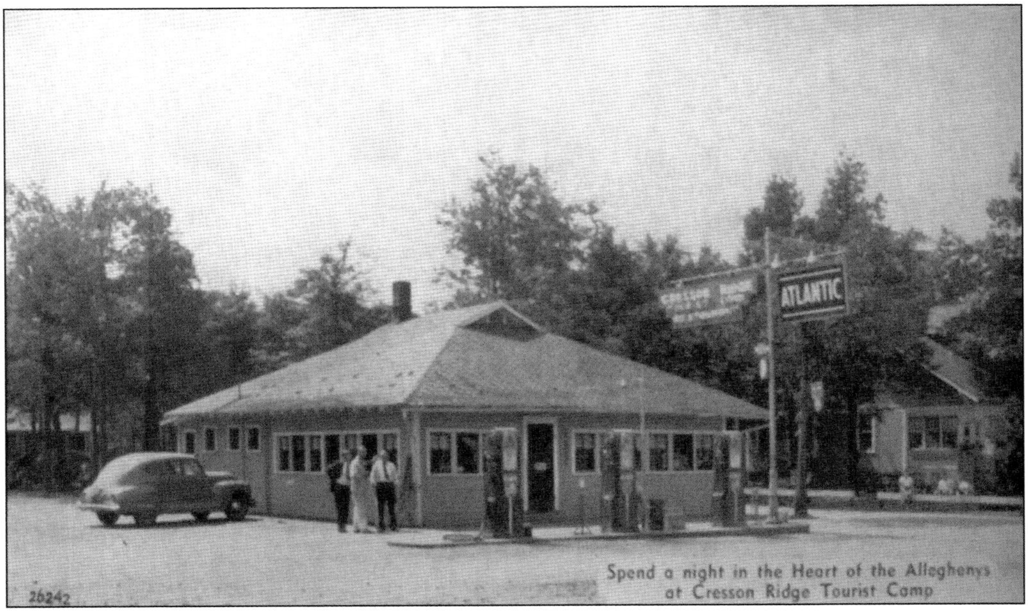

The Cresson Ridge Tourist Camp stood atop Cresson Mountain, the highest point along Route 22. The easternmost ridge of the Allegheny Mountains, it forms part of the Eastern Continental Divide. The camp featured an Atlantic gasoline station and tourist cabins; although the camp closed long ago, a few remnants of the cabins were still standing as of 2015.

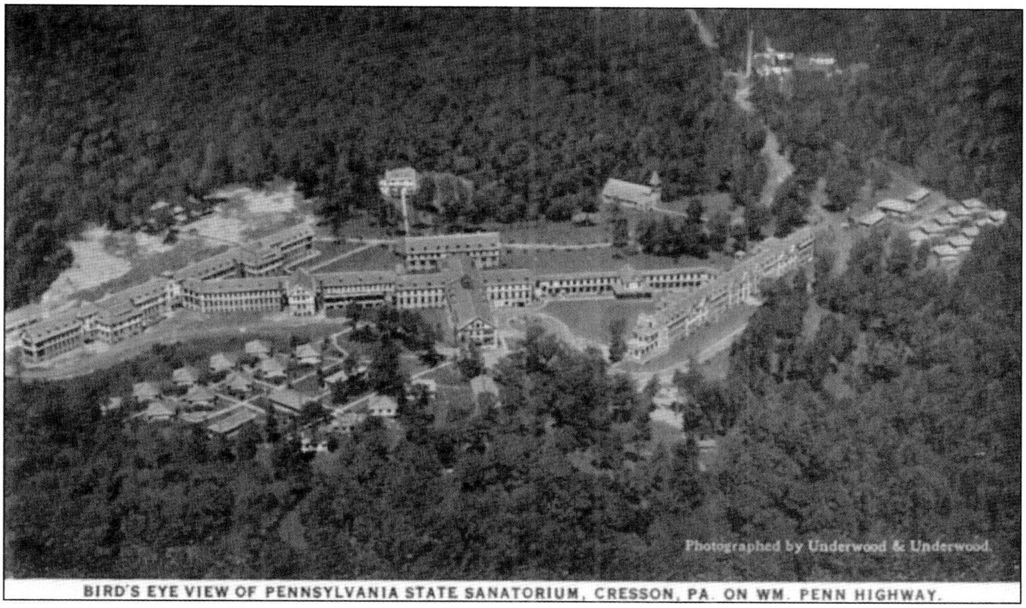

BIRD'S EYE VIEW OF PENNSYLVANIA STATE SANATORIUM, CRESSON, PA. ON WM. PENN HIGHWAY.

The Cresson Tuberculosis Sanatorium was built just south of Route 22 between 1912 and 1916, on land donated by philanthropist Andrew Carnegie. The site stood at an elevation of just over 2,400 feet (the highest point along all of Route 22) at the top of Cresson Mountain. Its location made it ideal for the location of a tuberculosis hospital, where patients were isolated for extended stays while being exposed to fresh mountain air to help their recuperation in the days before proper medication was available. The 500-acre complex featured numerous large Tudor-style buildings to house patients, and it remained in operation until 1956. It was then used as a hospital for patients with mental and physical challenges until being converted into a medium-security men's prison in 1983. It closed in 2013, but many of the buildings remain standing today.

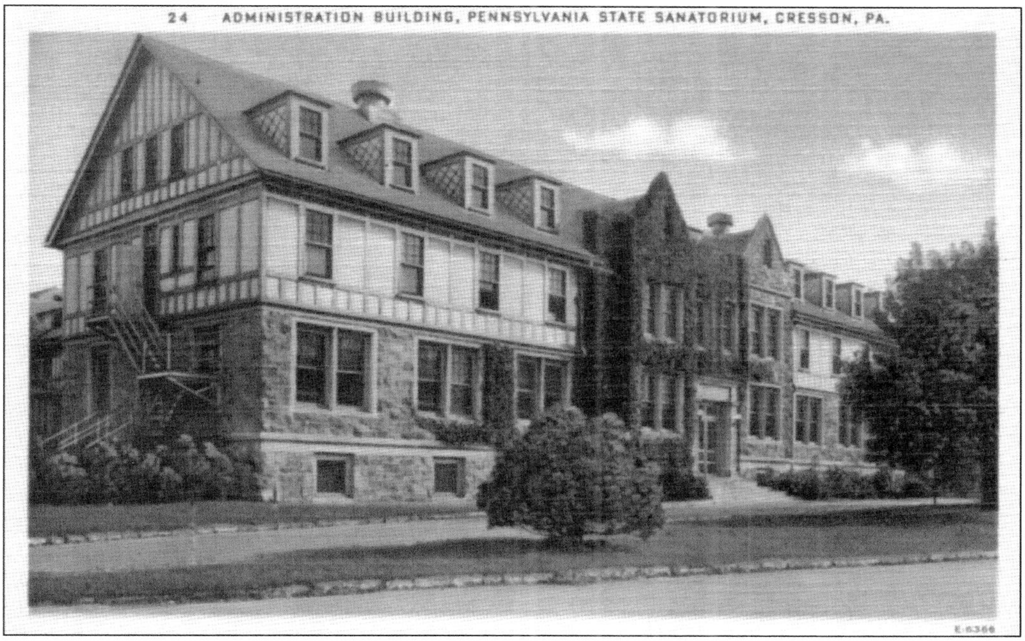
24 ADMINISTRATION BUILDING, PENNSYLVANIA STATE SANATORIUM, CRESSON, PA.

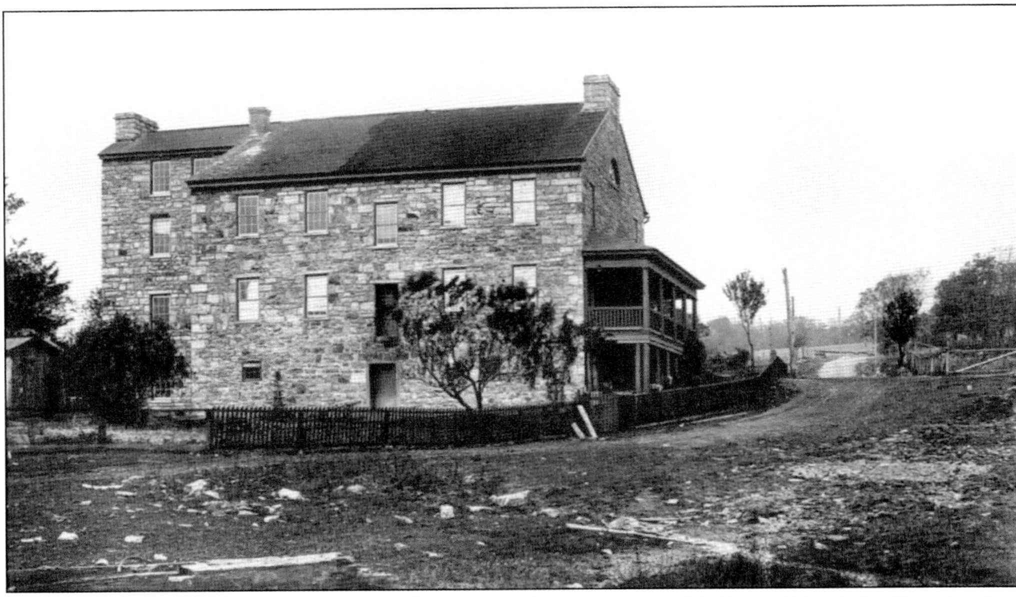

This three-story stone structure was built by Samuel Lemon around 1830 and faced the Huntingdon, Cambria, and Indiana Turnpike (and later the Allegheny Portage Railroad) at the summit of the Allegheny Mountain Ridge. Shown above around 1900, it was known as the Lemon House, home to a tavern and inn for travelers. It remained in the Lemon family until 1903, when it began a series of ownership changes while remaining occupied. In 1966, it was incorporated into the Allegheny Portage Railroad National Historic Site, which operates it today as a museum, shown below. The building is easily visible from Old Route 22, which passes several hundred feet to its south.

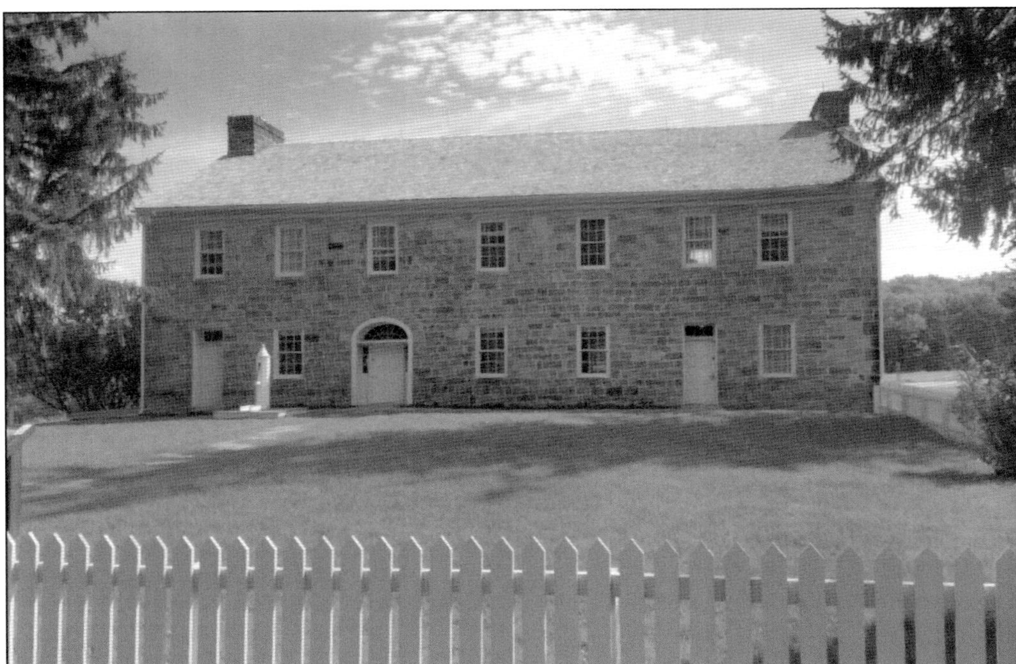

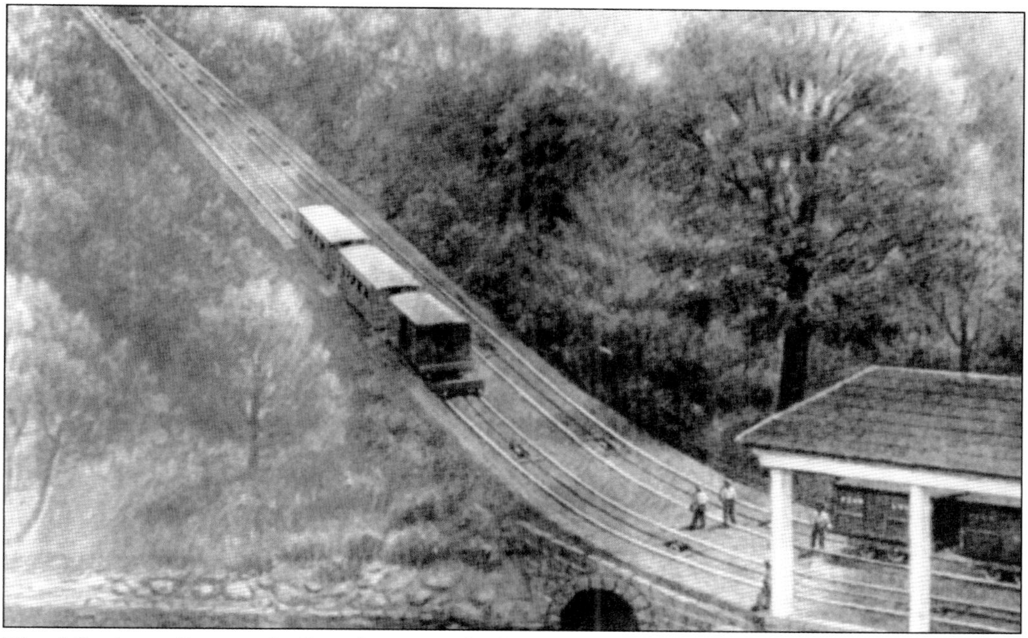

The Allegheny Portage Railroad consisted of 10 inclines and planes crossing the 36 miles of mountains between Hollidaysburg and Johnstown. Shown here are prints of two drawings of Inclined Plane No. Six, made in the 1830s by local artist George Storm. Above, the railcars have been disconnected from the locomotive and are attached to the long rope or cable that would then pull them up the incline to the engine house, pictured below. A locomotive would then pull the cars across another plane until reaching the next incline. When large volumes of freight were being transported along the canal, the boats themselves were loaded onto railcars and pulled upward, also shown below.

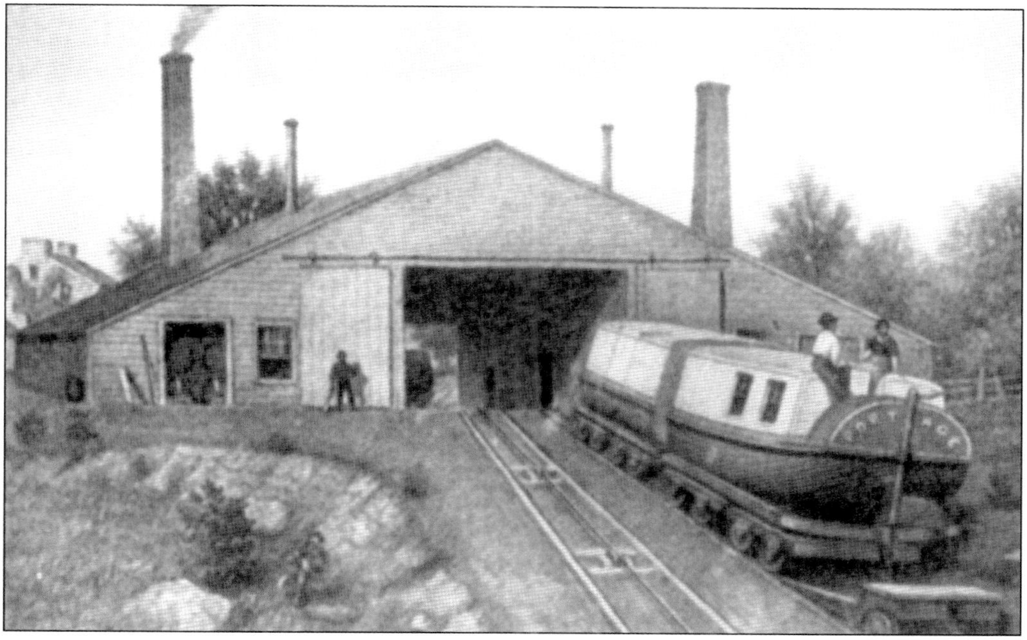

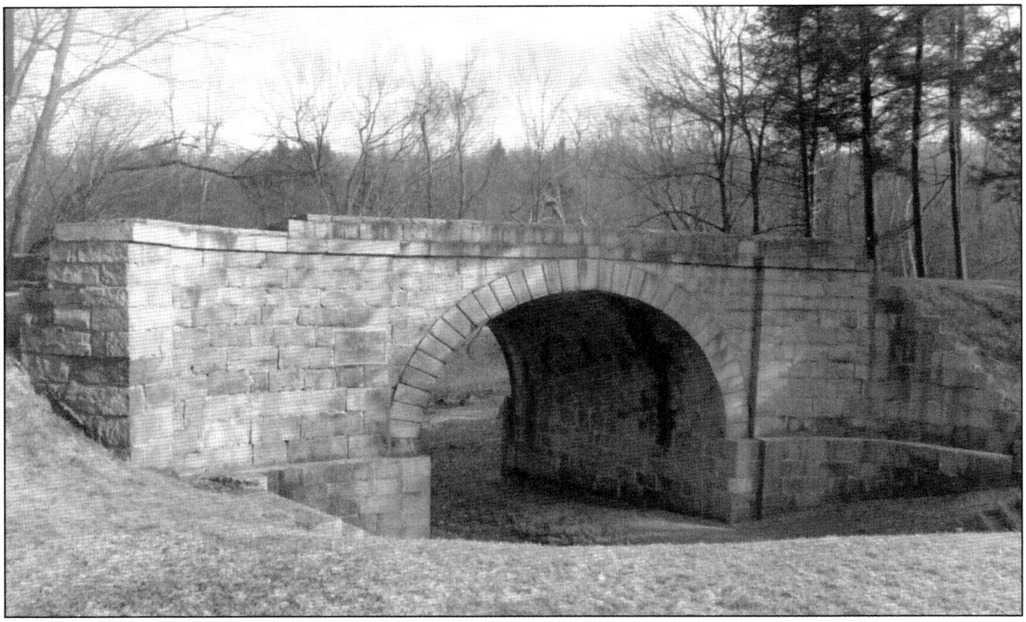

Known as the Skew Arch Bridge, the stone structure shown above (as it appears today) was built in 1834 for the Huntingdon, Cambria, and Indiana Turnpike (or the Northern Turnpike) to cross the Allegheny Portage Railroad at the top of the Allegheny Front. Built in the shape of a parallelogram to make the turn easier for teams of horses, it was somewhat of an engineering marvel at the time. It remained in use by the William Penn Highway until 1922, when the road down the mountain was divided into eastbound and westbound segments. The bridge has been preserved and is part of the national historic site today. The monument shown below was built next to the bridge in 1934 to commemorate the 100th anniversary of the Allegheny Portage Railroad.

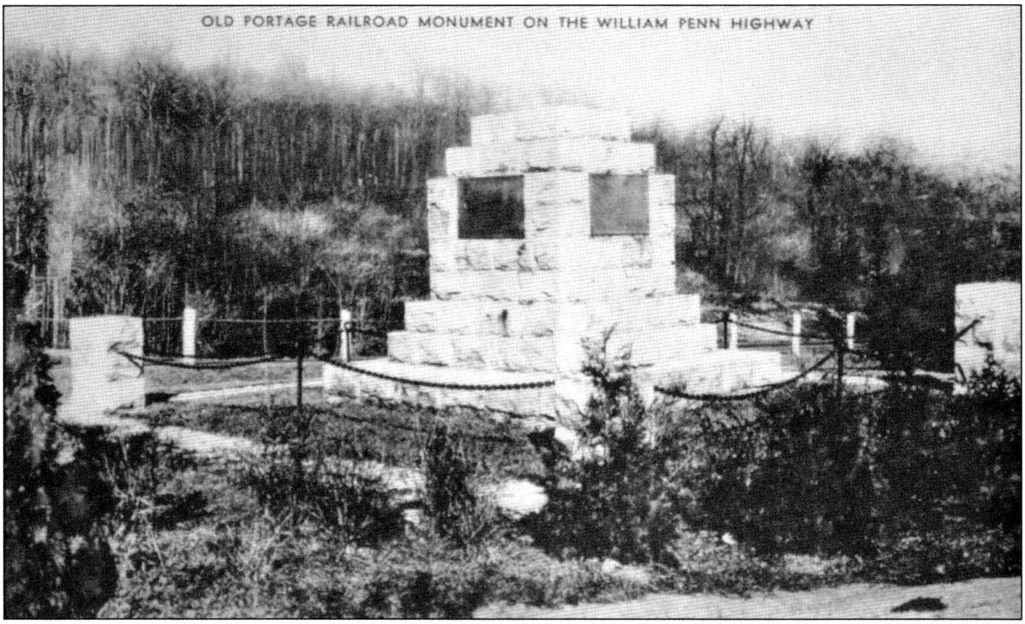

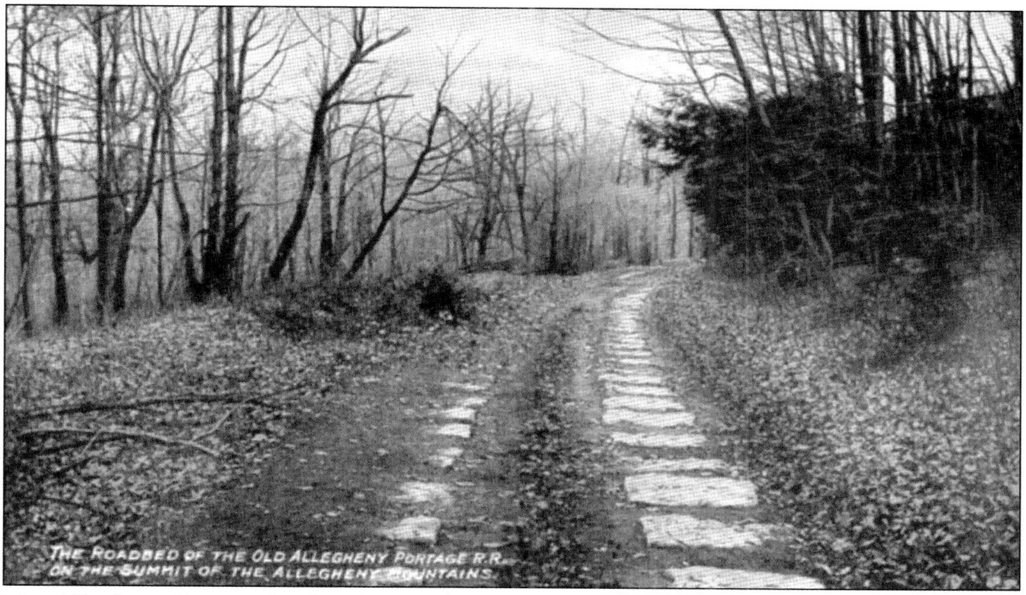

The Allegheny Portage Railroad opened in 1834 as an extension of the Pennsylvania Canal, pulling boats up the long grade of the Allegheny Front on rail lines, enabling them to continue on their journey between Harrisburg and Pittsburgh. The railroad, which operated for roughly 20 years before being replaced by the New Portage Railroad nearby, traveled through the hollow formed by Blair Run, close to where the eastbound lanes of Route 22 were later constructed. After the railroad was removed, stones like those shown above were all that remained until the construction of the road in the early 20th century. In the 1960s, the National Park Service rebuilt a portion of the original railroad at the top of the mountain, with a visitor center and a replica of Engine House No. 6 shown below.

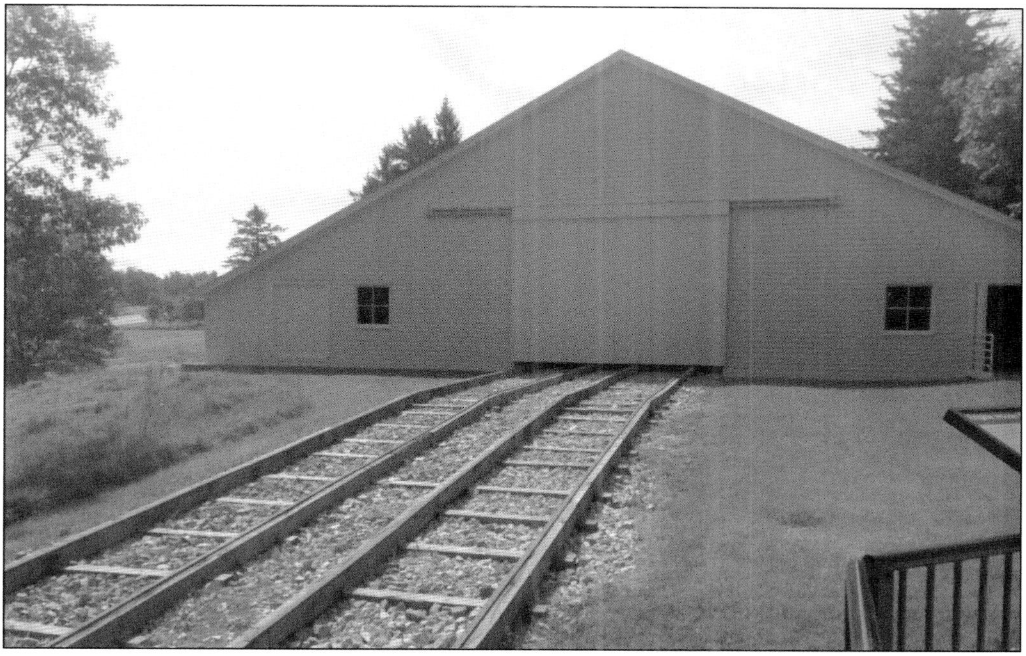

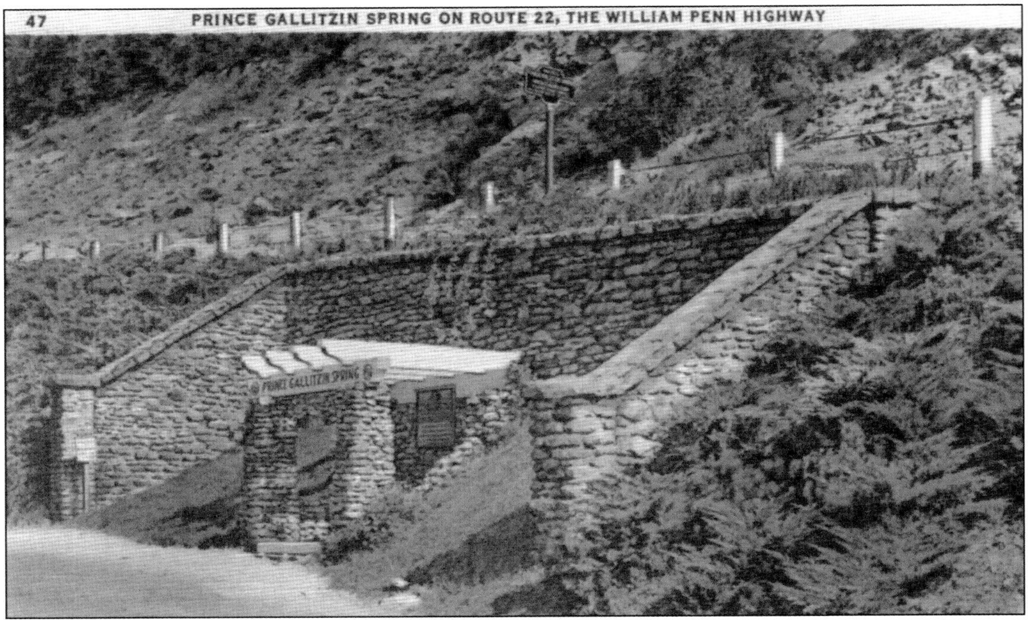

The Prince Gallitzin Spring was known to the earliest travelers on the road through Blair Gap in the 1800s. After becoming designated as Route 22 in the 1920s, the road was improved in many areas. Here, the modern road was built above and behind the spring, while preserving it and the stonework around it. A small parking area represents the original highway.

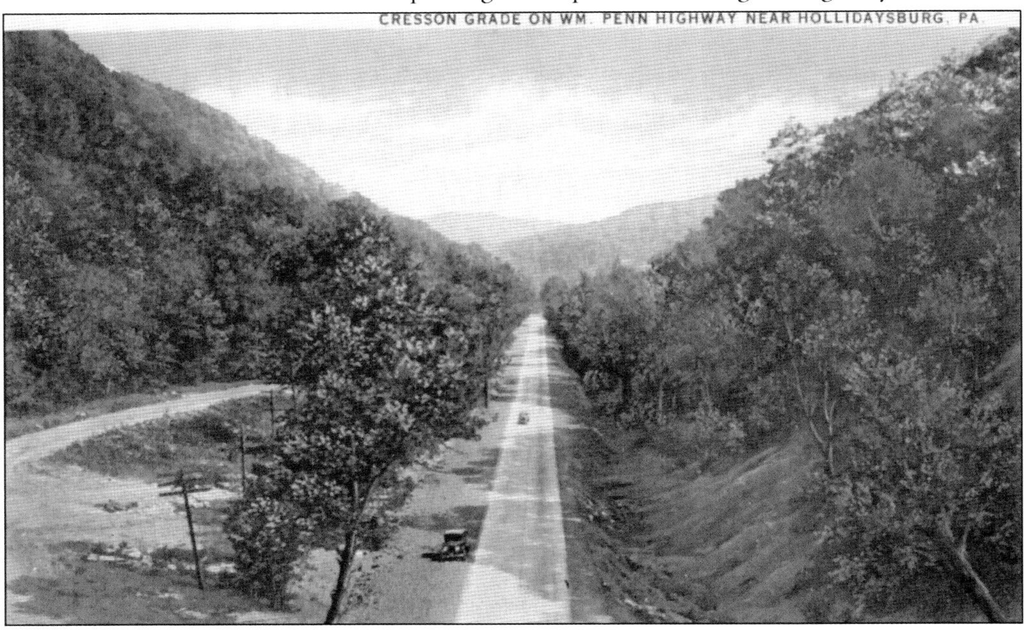

This is a view of the Cresson Grade along the original William Penn Highway from the 1930s. In this view looking westward, the road is ascending the mountain, eventually reaching an elevation of 2,430 feet, the highest point along the entire highway. Through much of the grade, the road is split into eastbound and westbound lanes. In 1983, this entire section was bypassed by a modern expressway, traveling roughly one mile to the north.

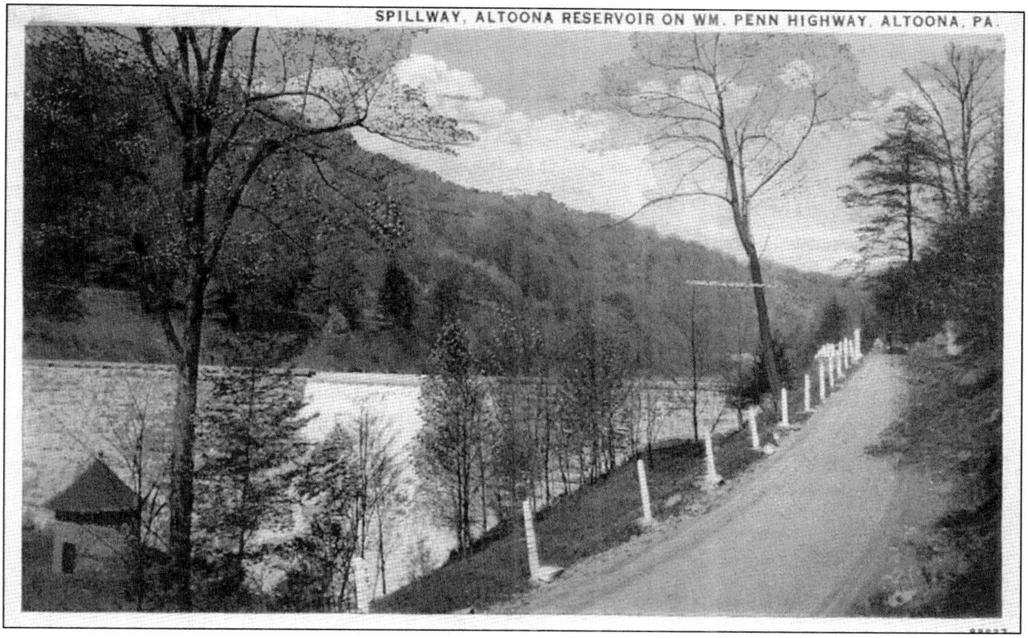

Just below the Prince Gallitzin Spring is a stone dam, built in 1907 to create the Blair Run Reservoir. At four acres in size, it is the smallest of several reservoirs that exist along the course of the small stream to supply water to the city of Altoona. The reservoir lies between the eastbound and westbound alignments of Route 22, roughly halfway down the long hill. In the image above, the William Penn Highway is shown in the early 1920s, before the road was paved with asphalt. The image below is from the 1930s, offering a different view of the reservoir.

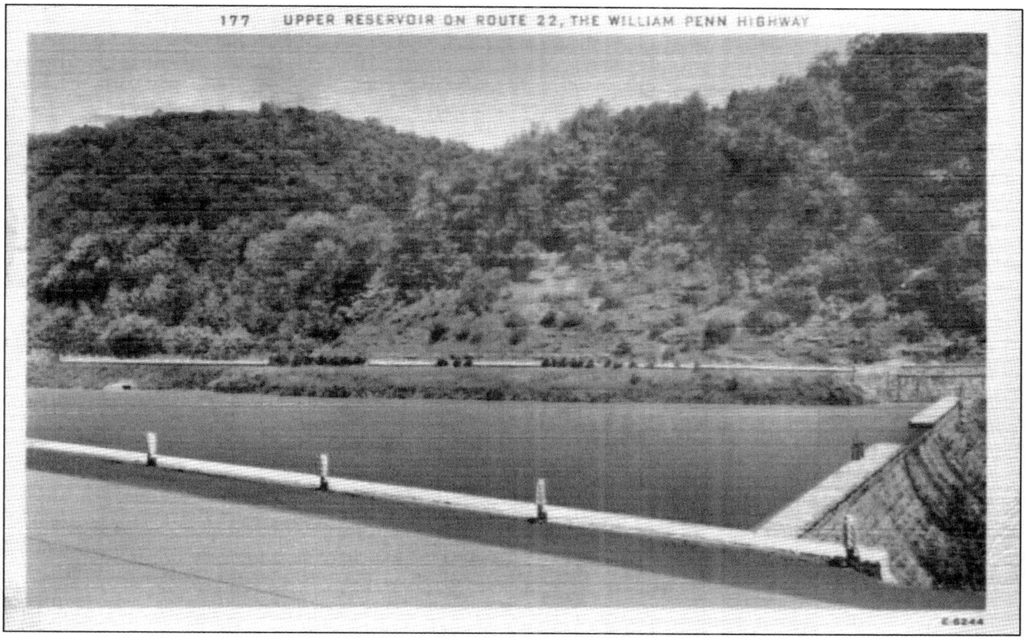

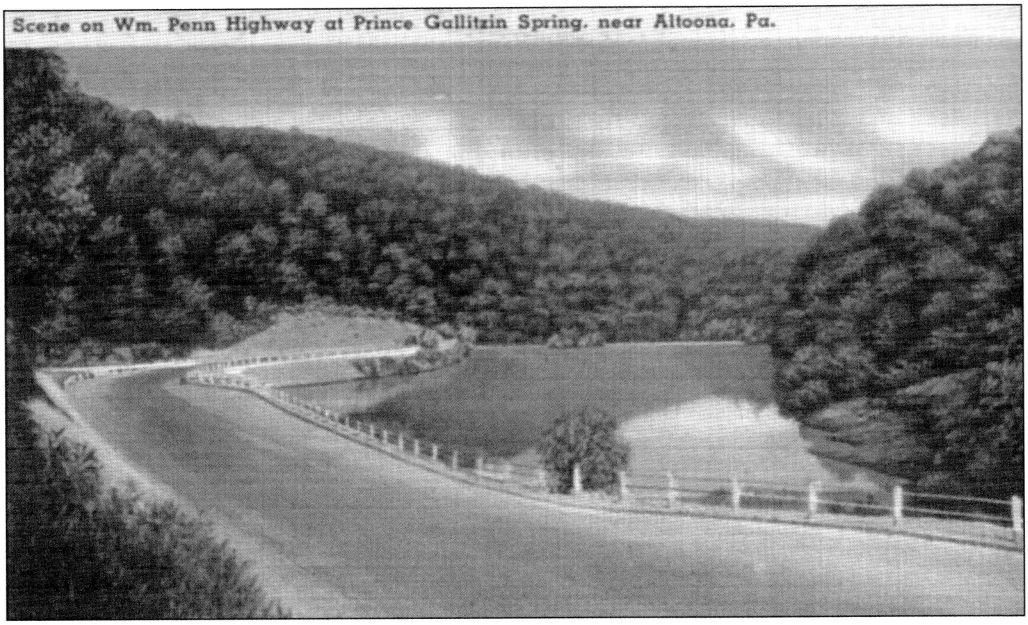

The heavily wooded three-mile trek down the eastern side of the Allegheny Front (sometimes referred to as Cresson Mountain) is one of the most scenic segments of the entire William Penn Highway. As a result, it has been the subject of numerous postcards over the years, like those shown here, as the road passes two of the reservoirs along Blair Run. Beginning in 1922, the highway was split into an eastbound (downhill) alignment, following the course of the former Allegheny Portage Railroad's inclined planes, and a westbound (uphill) alignment, following the course of the former Huntingdon, Cambria, and Indiana Turnpike. Although the highway was later bypassed by the modern Route 22 highway to the north, the road retains the bidirectional alignment today.

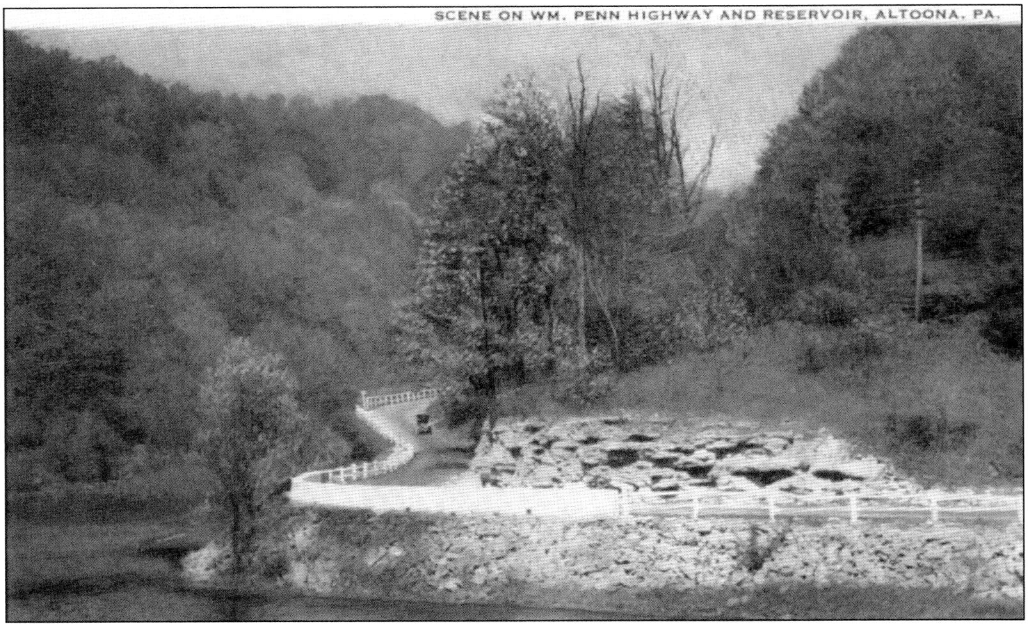

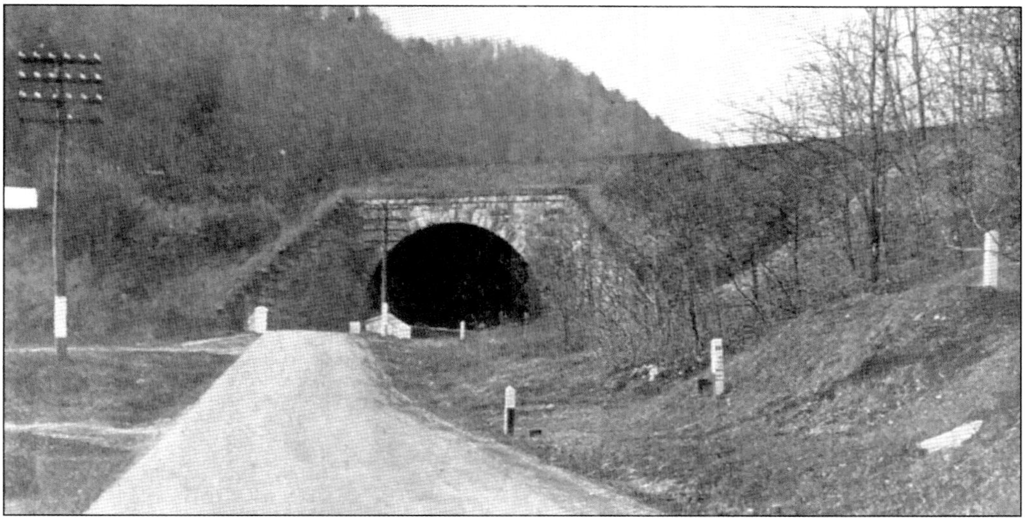

The New Portage Railroad was built in 1854 to replace the original Allegheny Portage Railroad. Although this new system was soon purchased by the Pennsylvania Railroad as an alternative line to its own nearby track up the mountainside, it sat idle for many years before reopening in 1904. At that time, this large stone railroad bridge (shown above in 1916, from a William Penn Highway brochure) was built at the base of the Cresson Grade, crossing what would soon become the William Penn Highway. Forming part of a huge arc known as the Muleshoe Curve, the bridge (shown below as it appears today) remains standing, although railroad traffic ended in 1981. The rails have since been removed, and its right-of-way is used today as a hiking trail. (Above, courtesy of the Cambria County Historical Society.)

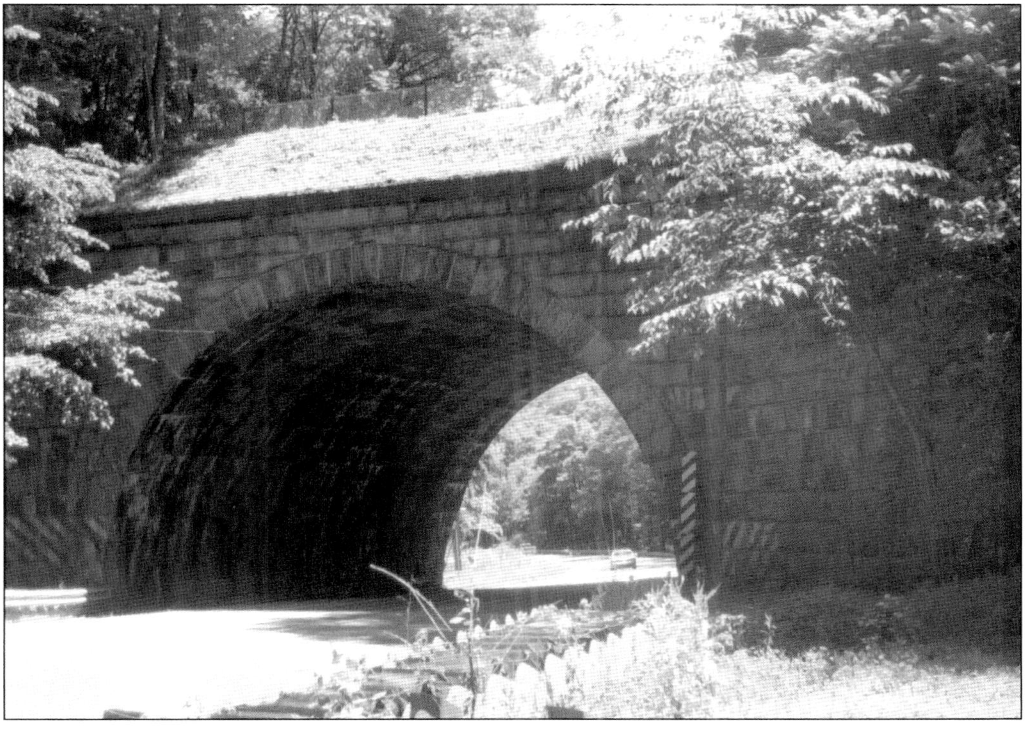

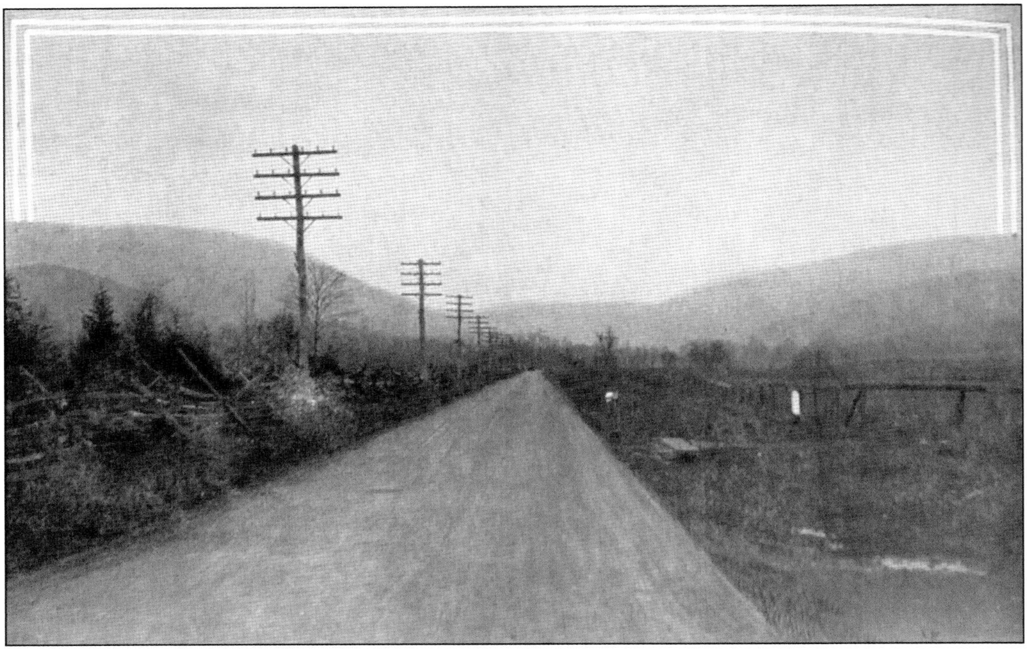

This is a view of the newly improved road that would soon become the William Penn Highway in 1916, looking westward from the town of Duncansville toward Cresson Ridge and the Allegheny Front. Other than a few scattered farms, this area was largely devoid of any commercial establishments at the time. (Courtesy of the Cambria County Historical Society.)

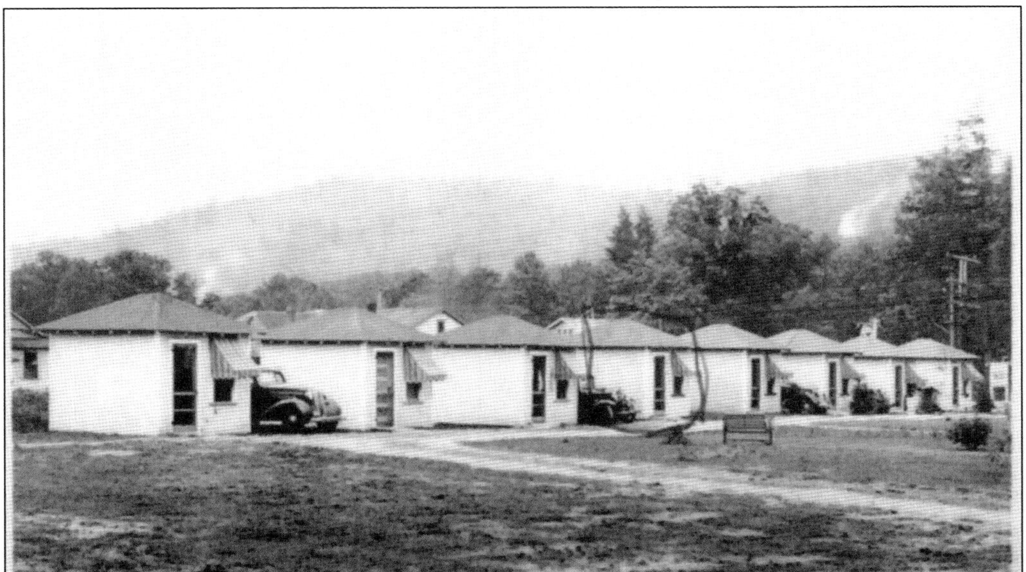

At the base of the Cresson Grade, a series of small motor courts and cabins appeared in the 1930s, as traffic along the William Penn Highway (today known as Old Route 22) began to increase. The Rolling Rock Cabins are pictured here in the late 1930s; the cabins eventually gave way to an actual motel at the site.

Five

Through the Juniata Valley

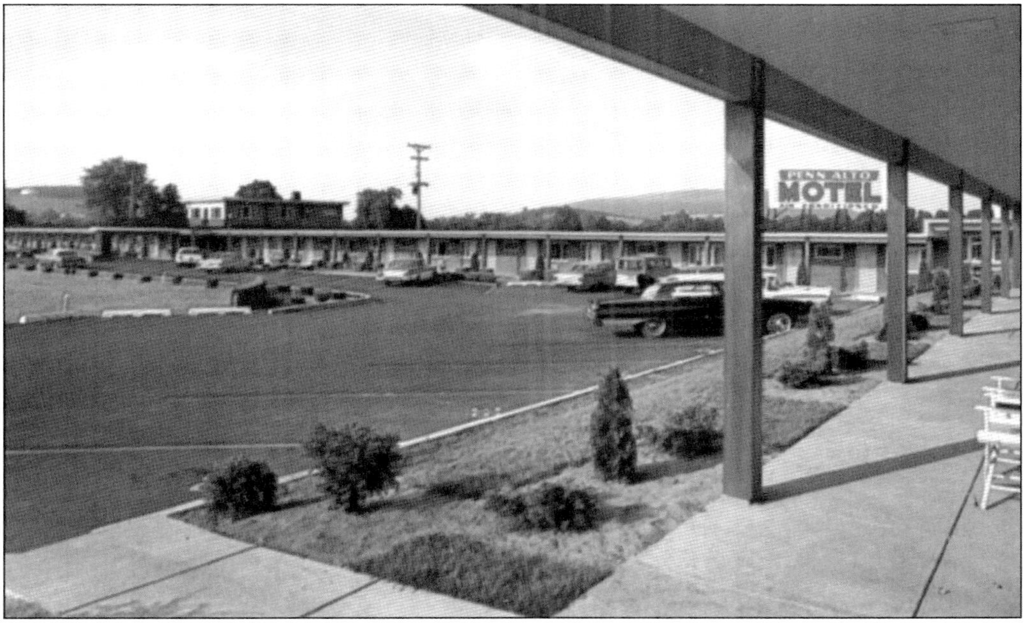

Opened in 1920, the huge Hotel Penn-Alto was downtown Altoona's premier luxury hotel. By the 1950s, it was also providing a different level of lodging near the junction of Routes 22 and 220 in Duncansville, five miles south of Altoona. The affiliated Penn Alto Motel was a 38-room facility without the luxurious trappings of a traditional hotel. However, all rooms did have tile showers, air-conditioning, telephones, radios, and television.

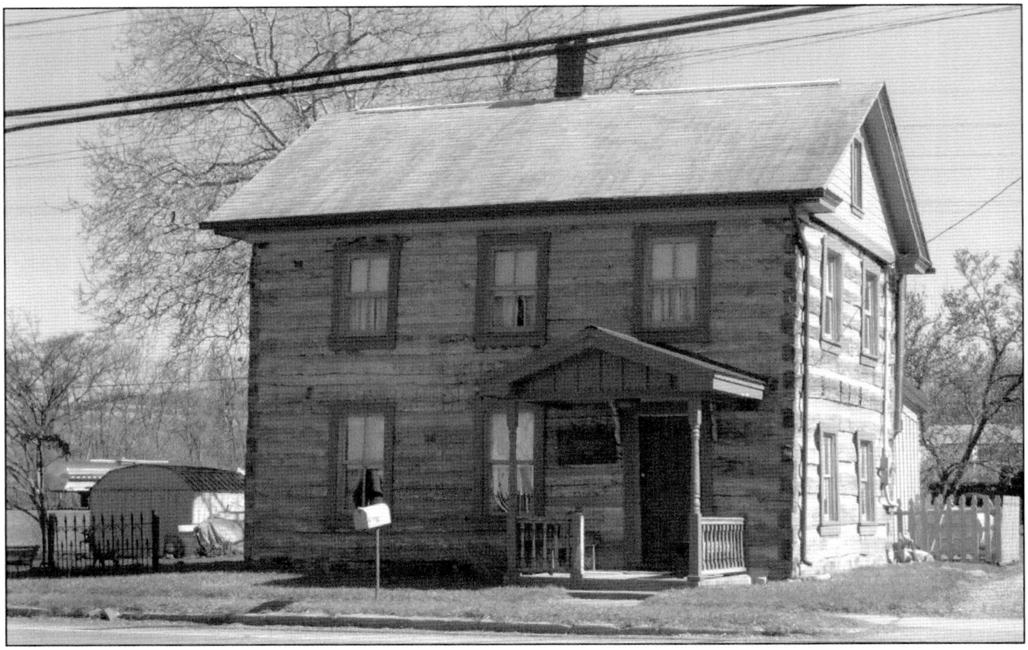

The Jacob Walters Homestead stands along Route 22 in Duncansville. The log structure was built in 1820, the same year as the opening of the Huntingdon, Cambria, and Indiana Turnpike, an early predecessor of the William Penn Highway. Shown as it appears today in its restored form, the home is one of numerous log structures still standing along the highway.

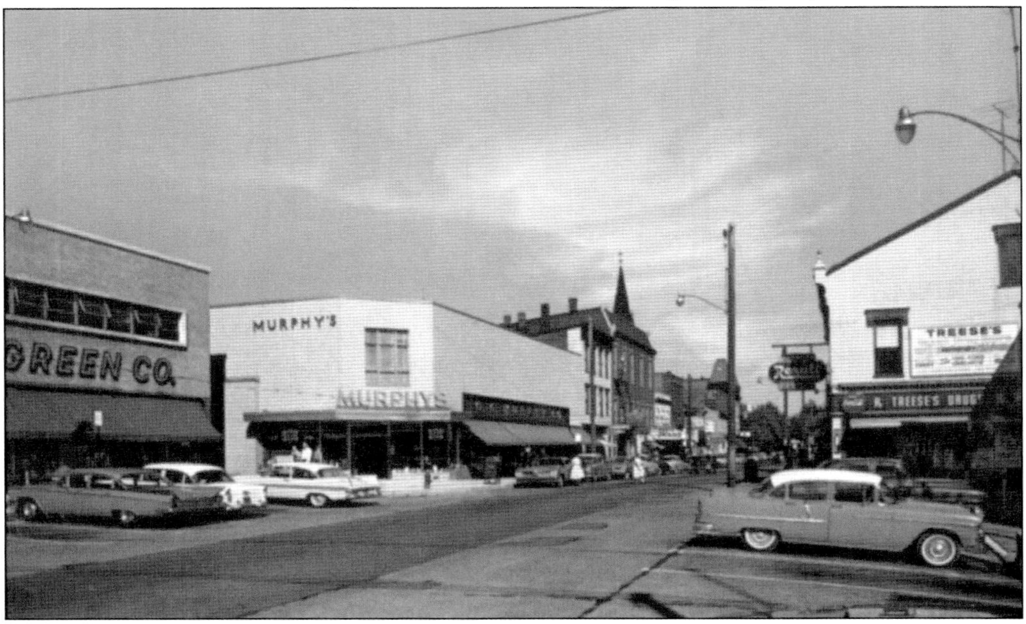

Allegheny Street carried Route 22 through the center of Hollidaysburg until the 1930s, when it was moved two blocks south to Blair Street, where it remains today. In this view from about 1960, the street is lined with small businesses such as a Rexall Drug Store, across the street from a G.C. Murphy Department Store.

On Allegheny Street (the original alignment of Route 22) at the center of Hollidaysburg is the ornate Blair County Courthouse. Resembling a church more than a government building, it was built in 1875 in the Gothic Revival architectural style and features a tall bell tower that is visible throughout the area.

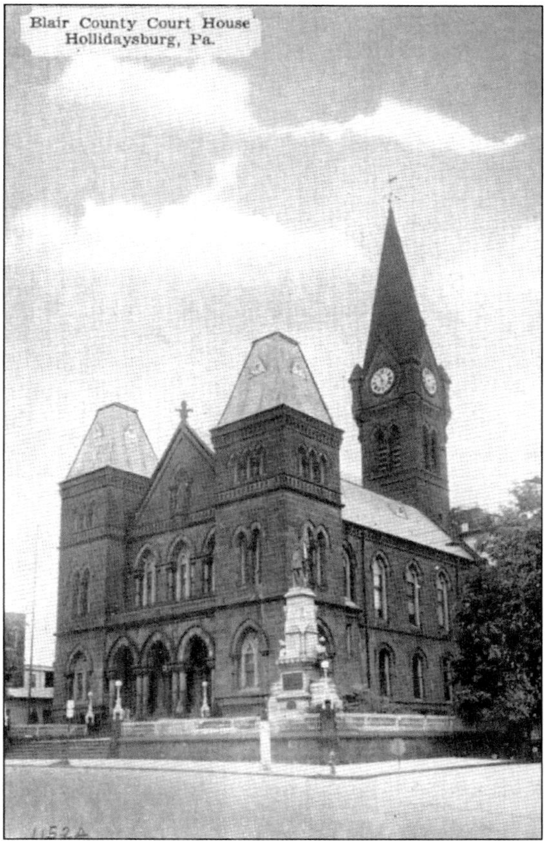

This is a westward aerial view of Hollidaysburg in the 1930s, with the William Penn Highway in the foreground. The towers of the city hall and a church give the small town an impressive skyline. In the distance is the south end of the long ridge known as Brush Mountain, which towers over most of the area with a peak elevation of more than 2,500 feet.

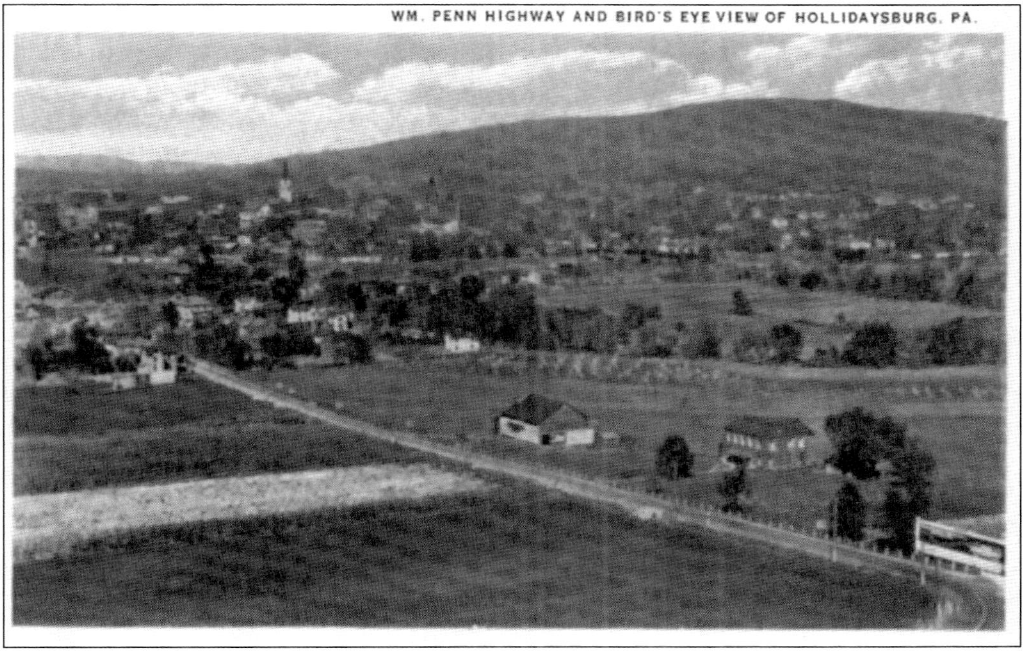

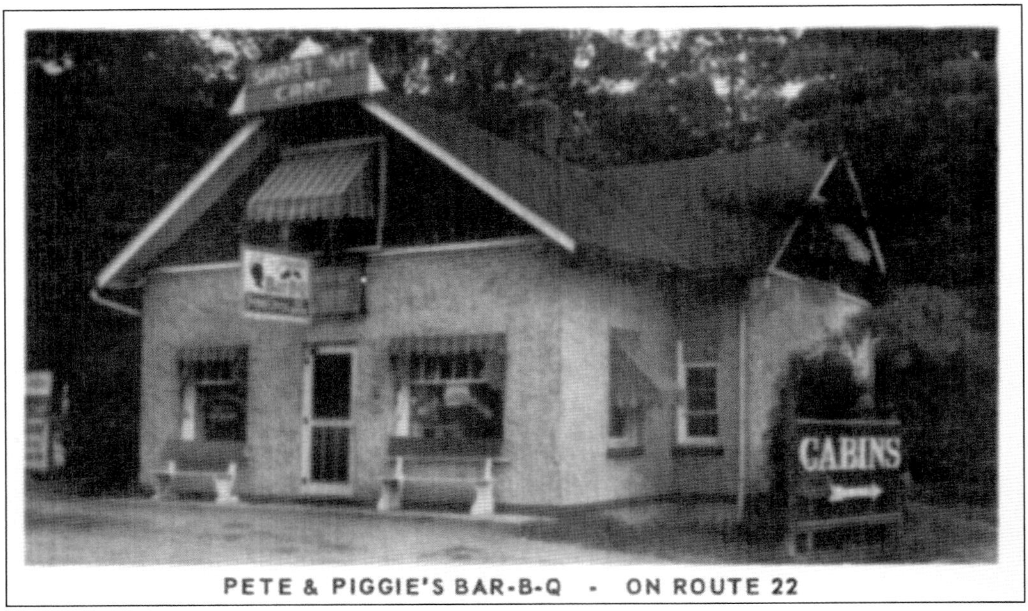

Standing 10 miles east of Hollidaysburg along a very rural stretch of Route 22, the building shown above was originally constructed in the 1930s as the Short Mountain Camp, featuring cabins for travelers, a small restaurant, and an Esso gas station. By the 1960s, it had been converted into Pete & Piggie's Bar-B-Q restaurant, featuring "the highest pies in the U.S.A., 8 inches high." Although the restaurant was advertised widely in the region, Pete & Piggie's is no longer in business today. However, one painted sign (shown below) remains visible on the side of a barn just east of Hollidaysburg as of this writing.

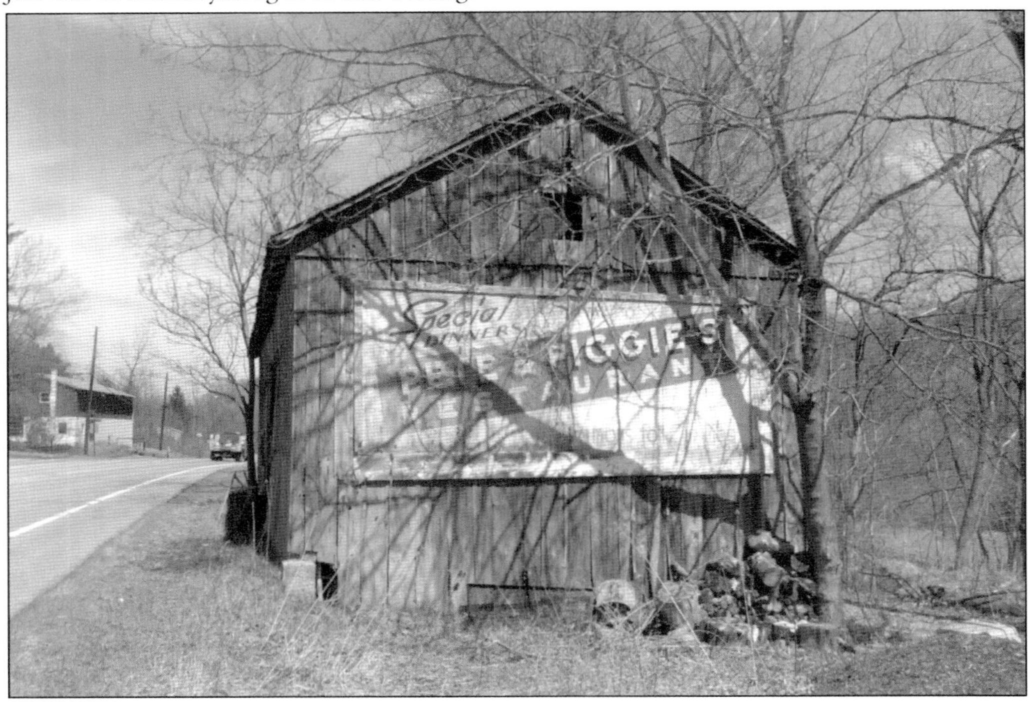

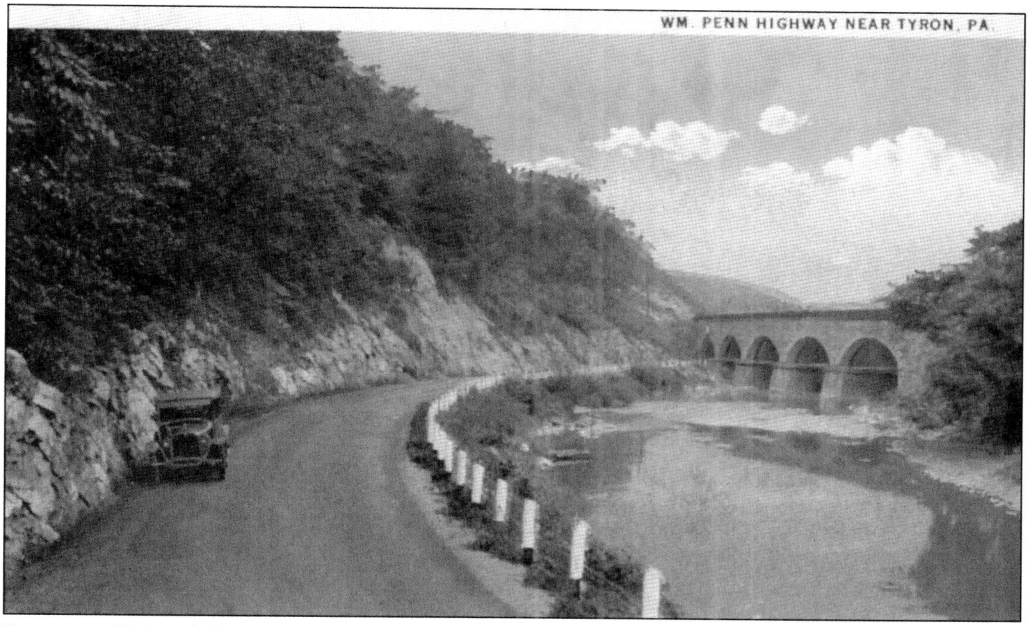

Between 1916 and 1926, the William Penn Highway traveled from Loretto directly eastward to Altoona, then northward to the borough of Tyrone, before connecting to its modern alignment near Water Street. This scene from the 1920s shows a segment of the highway passing beneath a stone railroad bridge near Tyrone.

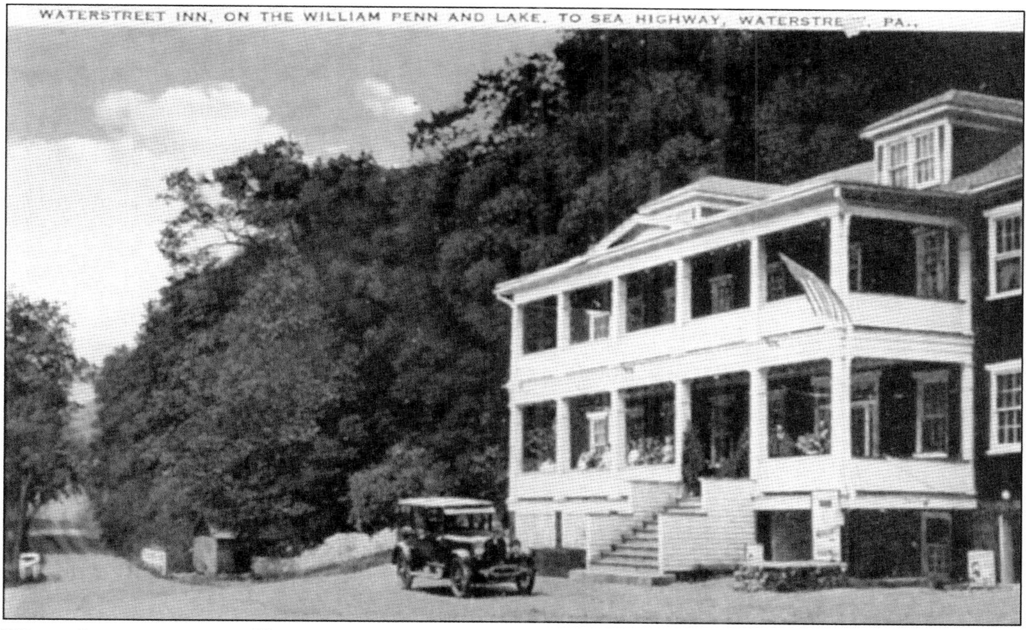

Water Street was a small community at the intersection of Route 22 and State Route 453, so named for a nearby water gap between Short and Tussey Mountains. The gap was so narrow that early settlers were forced to travel along the sandy bottom of the Juniata River, forming a so-called Water Street. This hotel, seen in the 1920s, was along what is now known as Shaffersville Road.

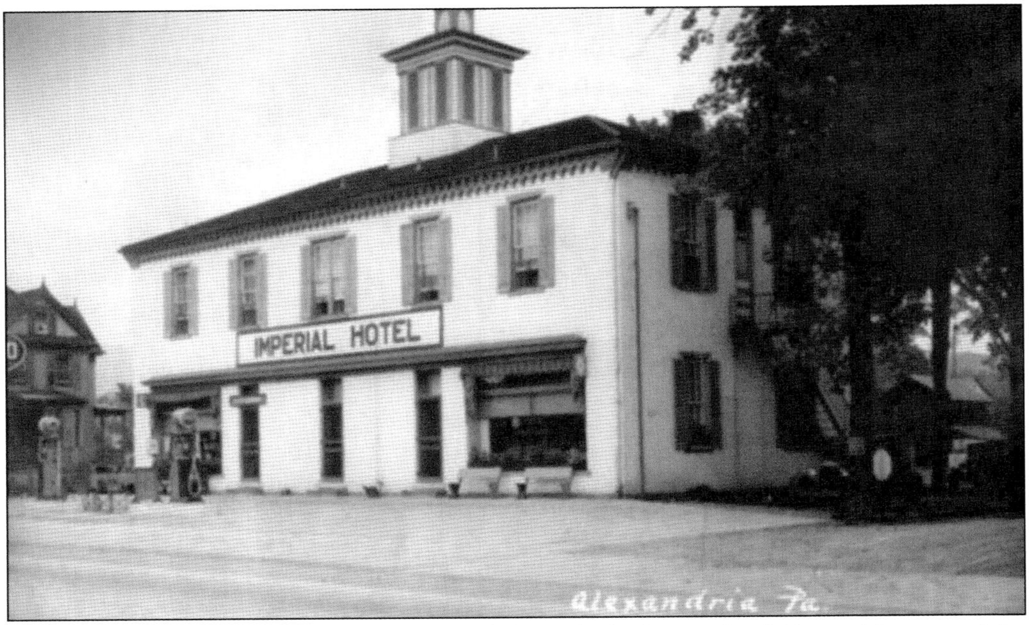

The original William Penn Highway passed through the borough of Alexandria, one of the region's earliest known settlements. Established in 1744 by Indian trader John Hart, it was known as the Hartslog settlement until 1791. Pictured here around 1930 are the Imperial Hotel and Amoco filling station along Main Street. By the mid-1930s, shortly after being designated as Route 22, the highway was moved onto a new and more direct alignment to the south, bypassing Alexandria altogether. The loss of traffic led to the hotel's closing, after which the building was converted into a private residence. It is shown below as it appears today.

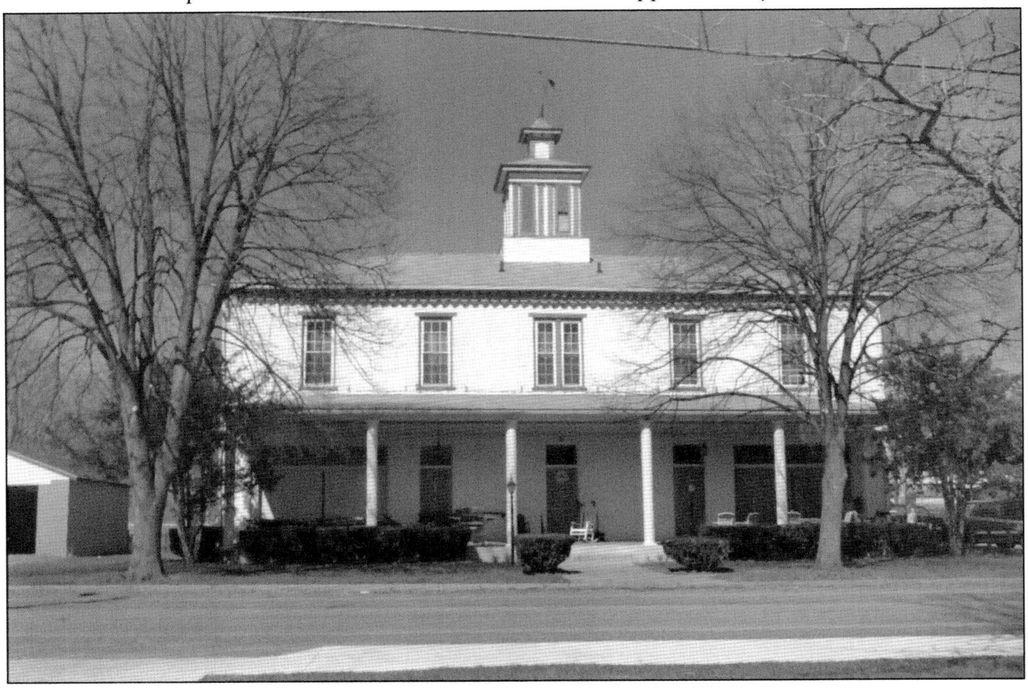

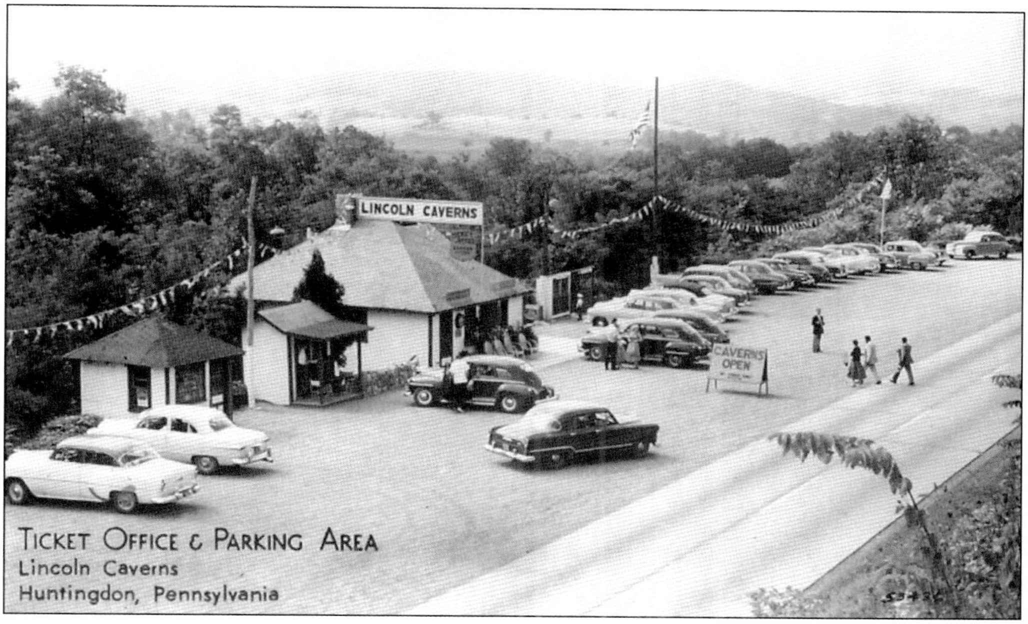

Above is the parking area for Lincoln Caverns, just west of Huntingdon, in the mid-1950s. Discovered in May 1930 while improvements were being made to nearby Route 22, the caverns were opened to the public shortly thereafter, along with the adjacent Whisper Rocks, discovered in 1941. Purchased by Myron Dunlavy shortly after opening, the site was previously known as Hi-Way-May Caverns, then as the William Penn Caverns; it was renamed Lincoln in 1937. Owned and operated by the same family since that time, it is one of the most-visited attractions in central Pennsylvania, with schoolchildren visiting regularly from throughout the region. Below is a view of the original entrance to the caverns, directly off the highway. It was later moved to a site more protected from passing traffic.

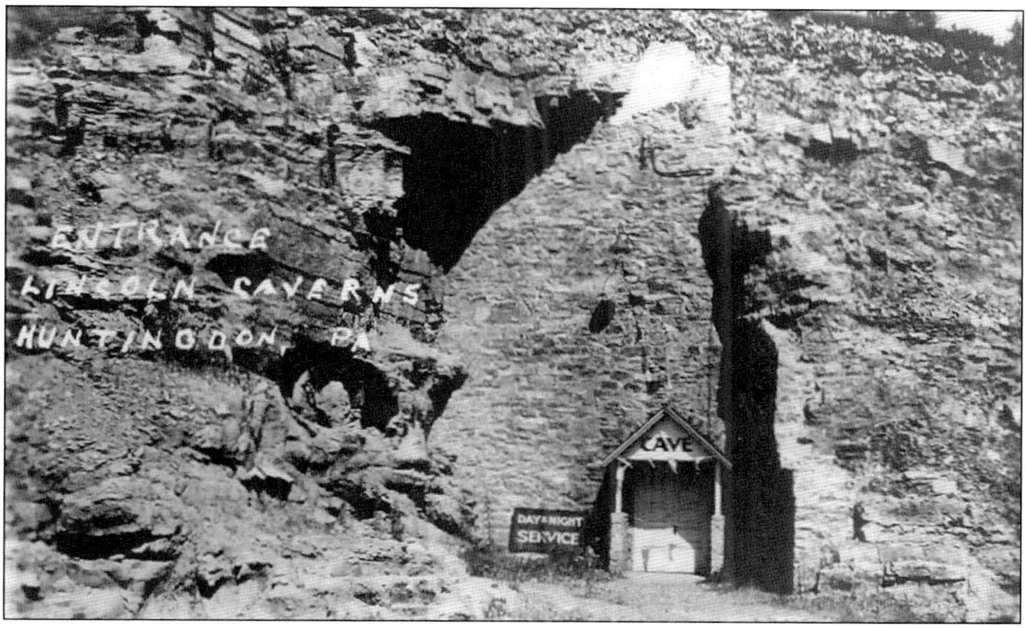

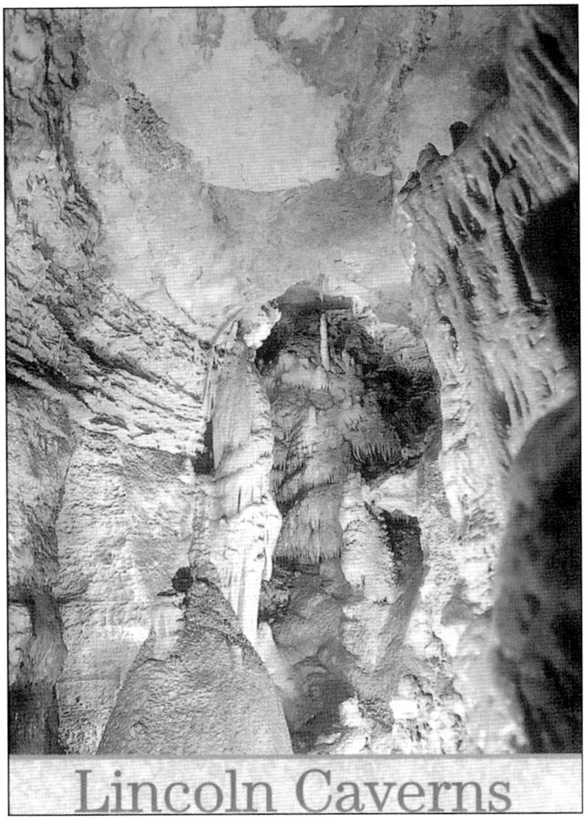

Shown here are two postcard views of the interior of Lincoln Caverns (and the cavern known as Whisper Rocks, higher in the same hillside). A tour of the caverns gives a thorough lesson in geology; stalactites and stalagmites are actively forming at all times due to the continuous flow of water through the rocks and the precipitation of calcium and other minerals to create a wide variety of formations. Hour-long tours of the caverns remain available on a seasonal basis, allowing visitors to see thousands of formations and crystals in the narrow passageways and underground rooms. The site also has a large gift shop featuring an extensive array of rocks and gemstones.

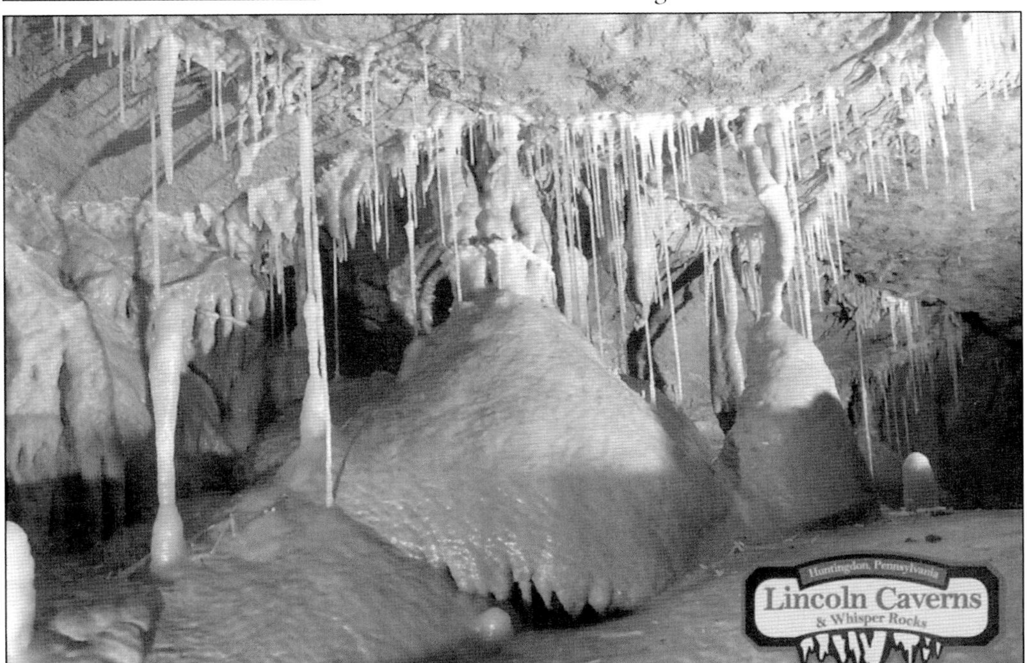

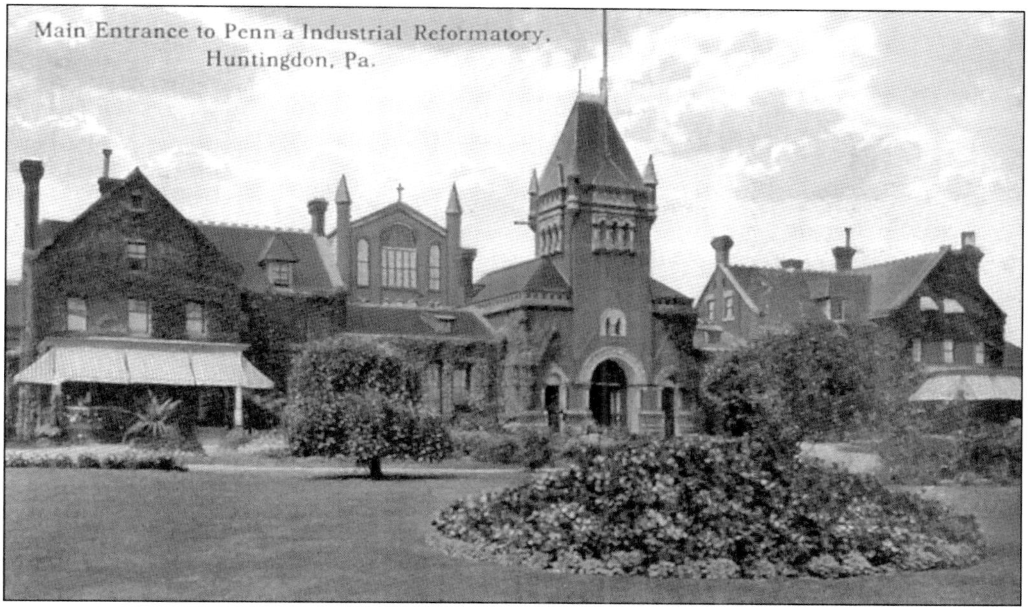

Standing at the intersection of Pennsylvania Avenue and Pike Street (the original William Penn Highway), the State Correctional Institution at Huntingdon is a close-security prison. Built in 1889 as the Huntingdon Reformatory for Young Offenders, it retains many of its imposing Victorian architectural features. It remains surrounded by crop fields, a relic of the days when teenagers and young men were taught to farm as a vocation.

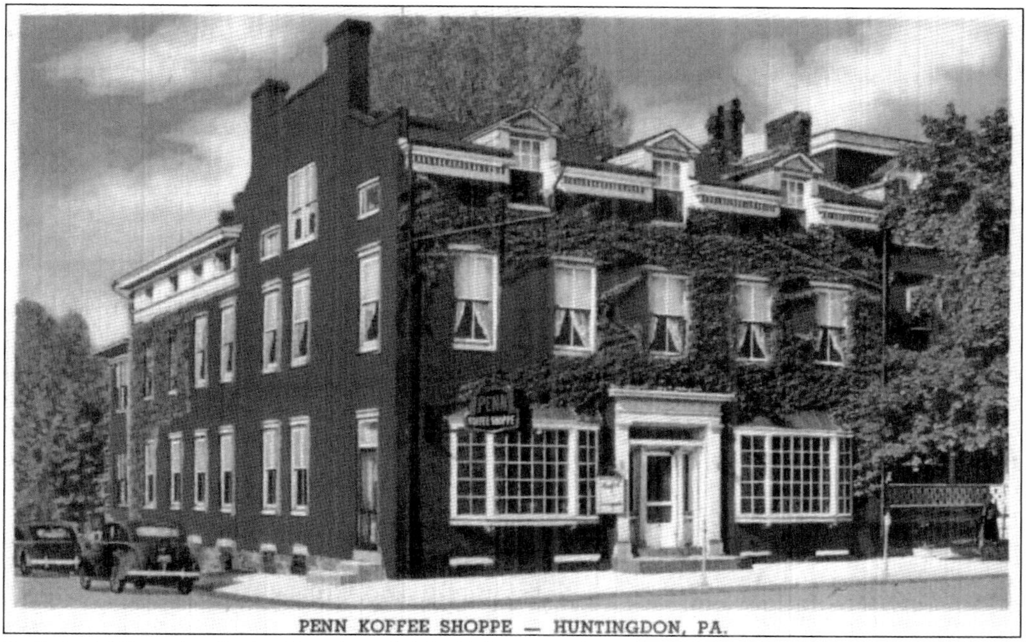

Built in 1842 as the Gwin Mansion, this building stood at 500 Penn Street in Huntingdon, three blocks west of the county courthouse. By the 1940s, when this postcard was made, the former home was occupied by the Penn Koffee Shoppe, and later it housed the Town House Restaurant. The building is no longer standing.

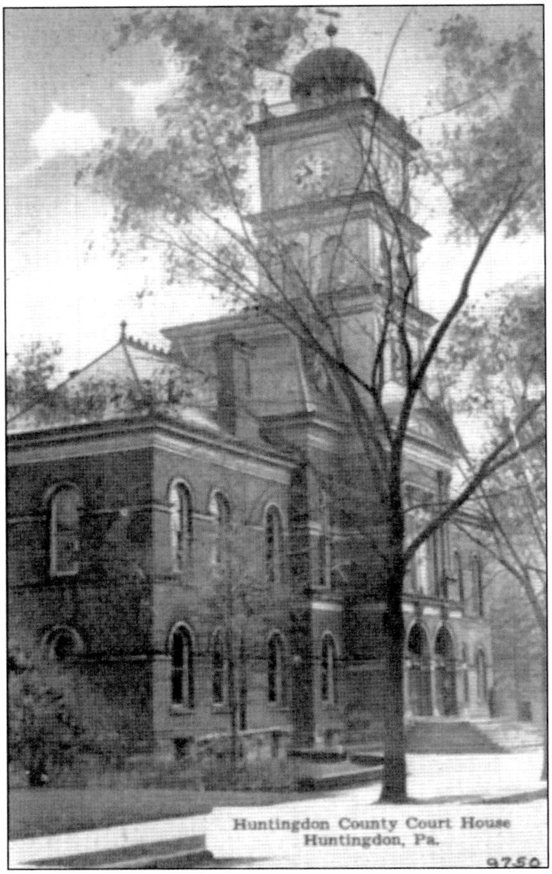

Shown here is a postcard view of the Huntingdon County Courthouse in Huntingdon, postmarked in 1927. Located on Penn Street (formerly the William Penn Highway and Route 22), the structure was built in 1883 in the French Renaissance architectural style. While most of the building looks the same today, much of the clock tower was rebuilt in later years, with many of the ornate features being removed.

This aerial view of Huntingdon in the 1950s shows the original alignment of Route 22 on the right side, traveling through the middle of town as Penn Avenue. On the left side of the view is its current alignment, still known today as William Penn Highway. Built in the 1940s, the modern highway is lined with more commercial establishments than the original road.

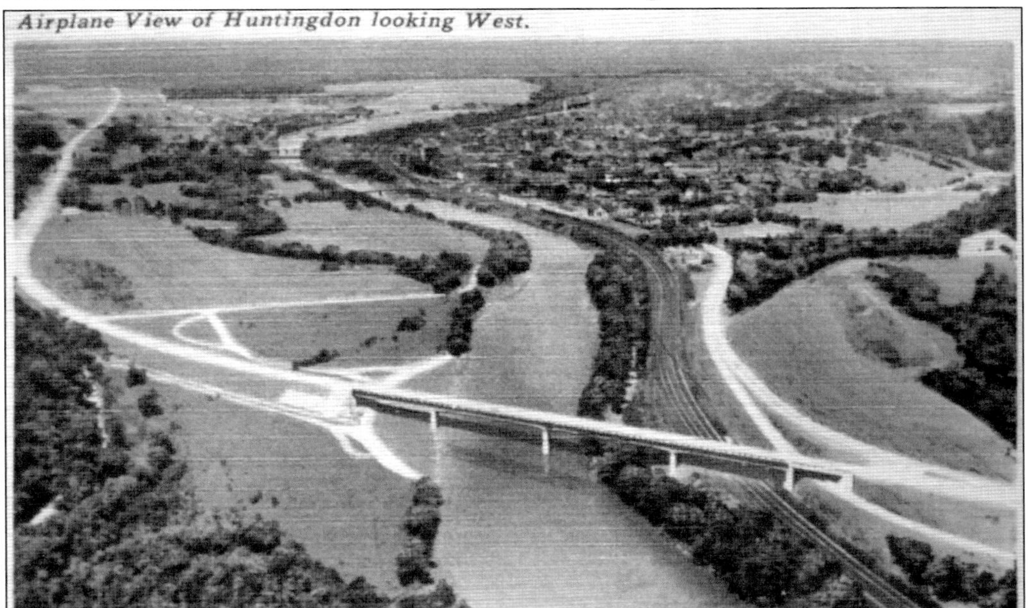

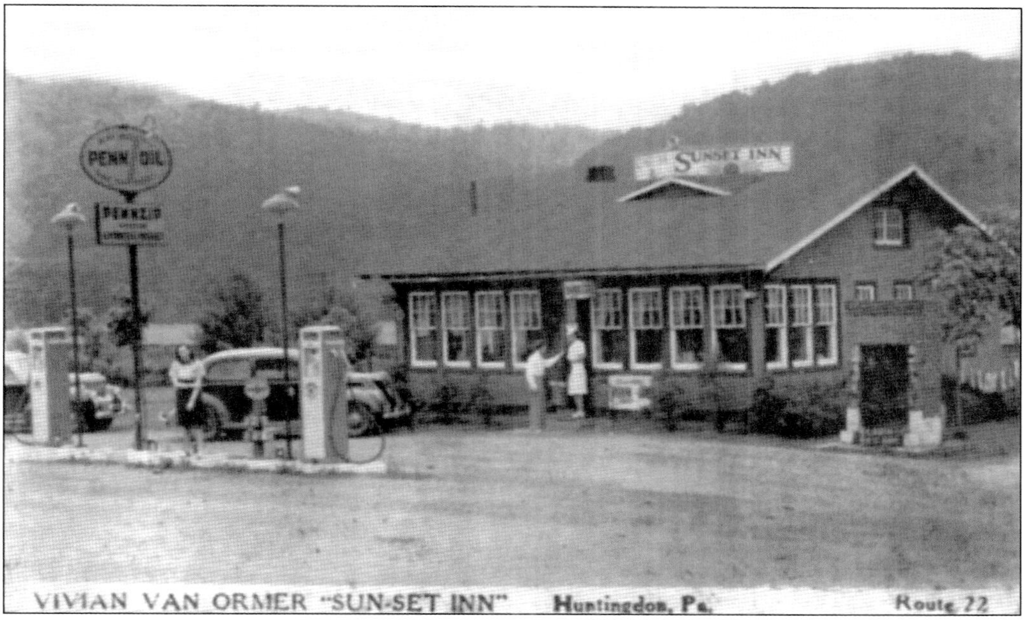

Owned by Vivian Van Ormer, the Sunset Inn was another roadside stop in Huntingdon. Shown here around 1940, it was primarily a Pennzoil gasoline station with a small lunchroom, featuring barbecue. It also advertised restrooms and cabins for overnight stays. As was the case with many of these small gas stations, the owner resided in the back portion of the station.

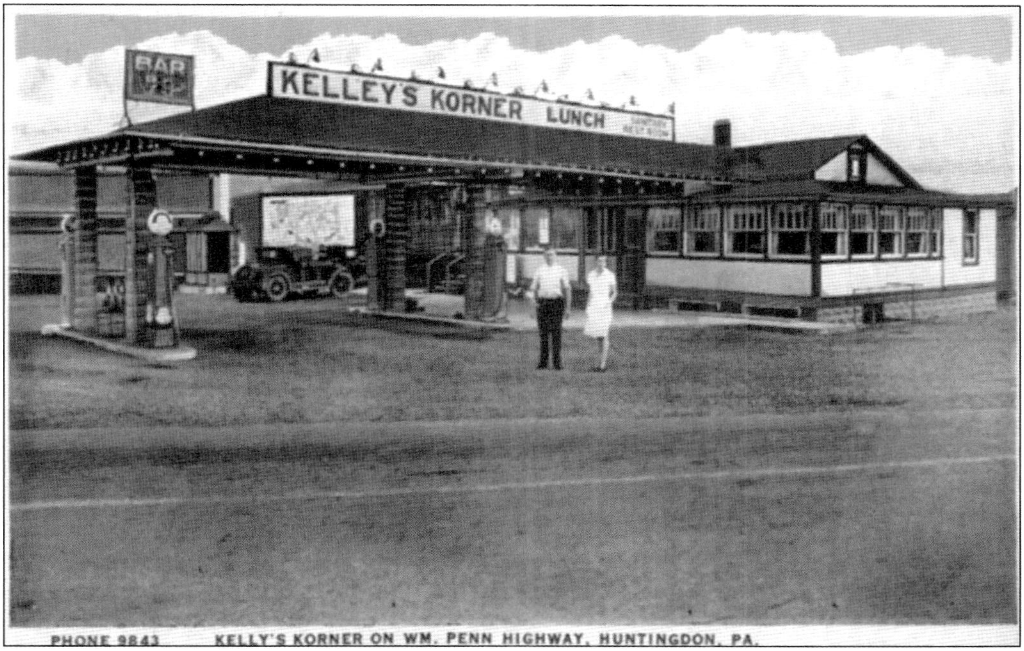

Pictured here around 1935, Kelley's Korner was another early gas station along the William Penn Highway in Huntingdon. It also offered a lunchroom, bar, and as noted on the sign, a sanitary bathroom, in an era when such things were not to be taken for granted. As was often the case at that time, the proprietors are seen here posing in front of their establishment.

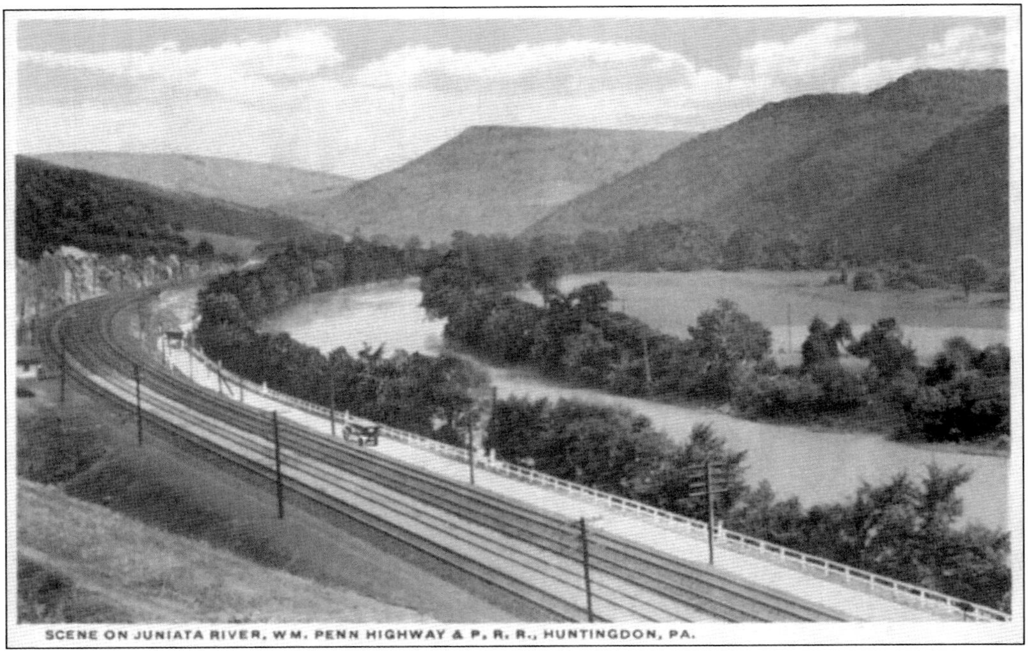

This is a scene showing the recently paved William Penn Highway traveling eastward from Huntingdon, between a main line of the Pennsylvania Railroad and the Juniata River, about 1930. Between 1832 and 1895, the Pennsylvania Canal also ran parallel to the road between Hollidaysburg and Harrisburg. Numerous ridges line the Juniata River through this area, some reaching peaks of more than 2,000 feet.

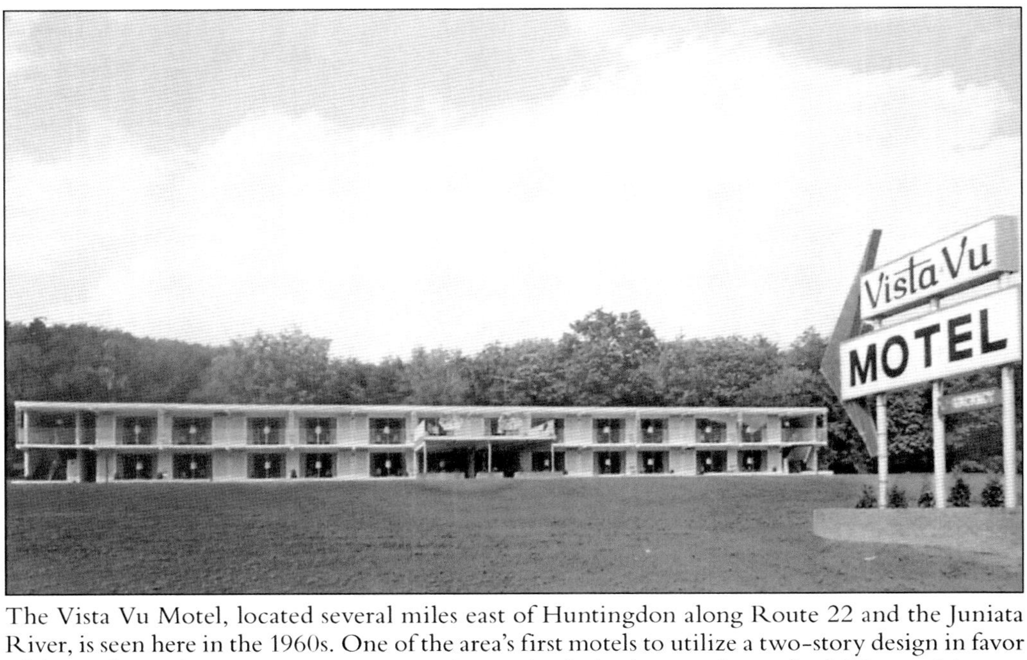

The Vista Vu Motel, located several miles east of Huntingdon along Route 22 and the Juniata River, is seen here in the 1960s. One of the area's first motels to utilize a two-story design in favor of the traditional one-story motor court, it remains in business today as the Millstone Manor.

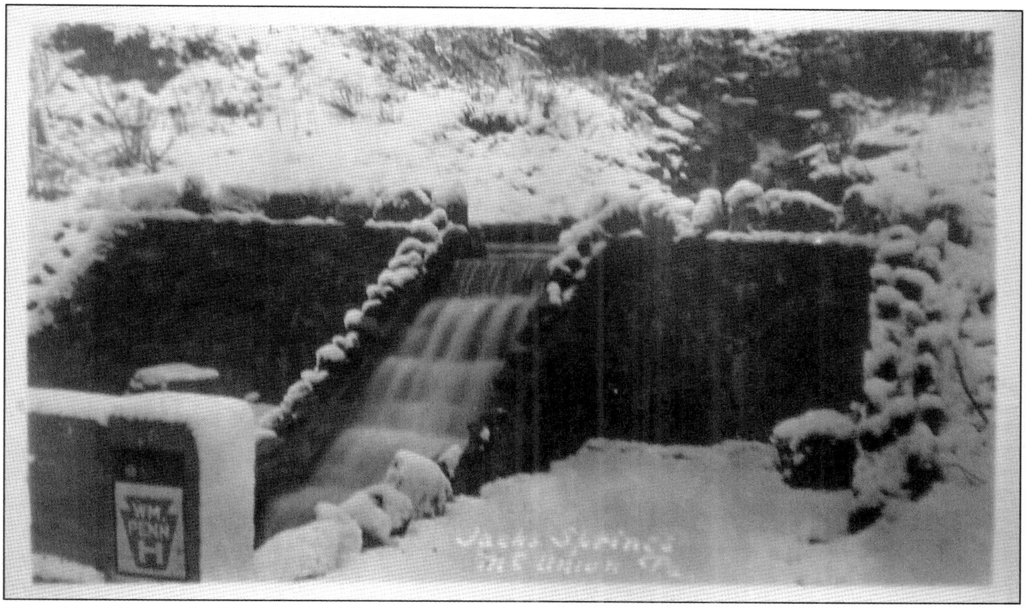

Traveling through the Appalachian Mountains, drivers would occasionally encounter springs where fresh water could be obtained. One such site was Jacks Spring near Mount Union. Of particular interest in this postcard from about 1930 is the appearance of the William Penn Highway sign. White, red, and blue in color, these steel signs were posted along the highway to guide tourists in the days when detailed maps were few and far between.

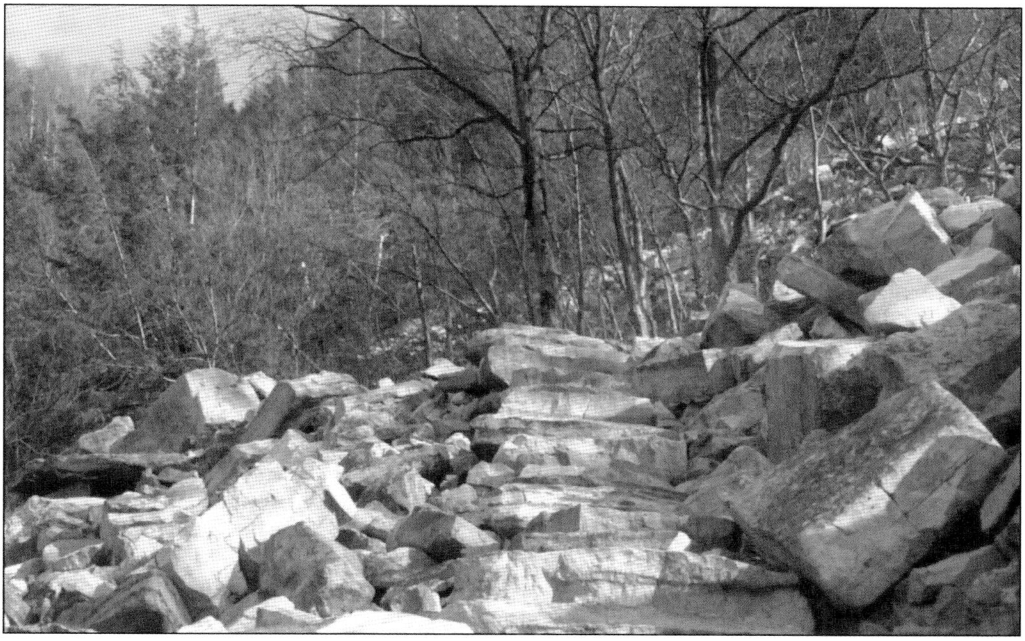

Roughly nine miles east of Huntingdon is a water gap known as Jacks Narrows. Rising nearly 1,000 feet from the valley on the north side of Route 22 here is a trail known as the Thousand Steps. The steps were carved out of rock in the early 20th century to allow workers to ascend and descend daily to work in a large stone quarry at the top of Jacks Mountain.

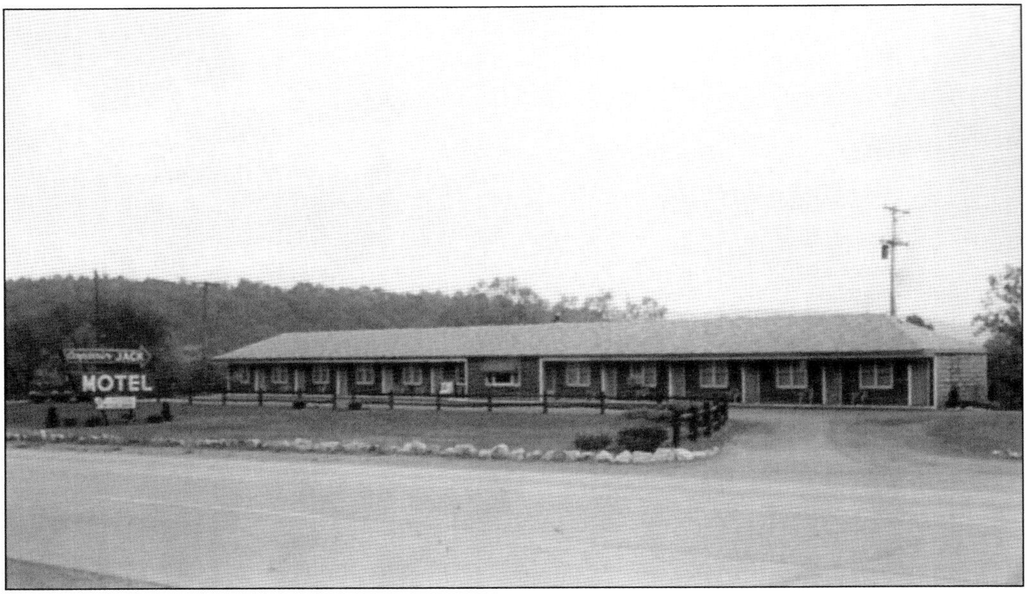

Captain Jack's Motel operated along Routes 22 and 522 just east of Mount Union, in a picturesque setting directly along the Juniata River. Shown in the 1970s, the motel offered telephone and cable television in each room, along with tile baths, air-conditioning, free picnic grounds, and a restaurant and gas station next door.

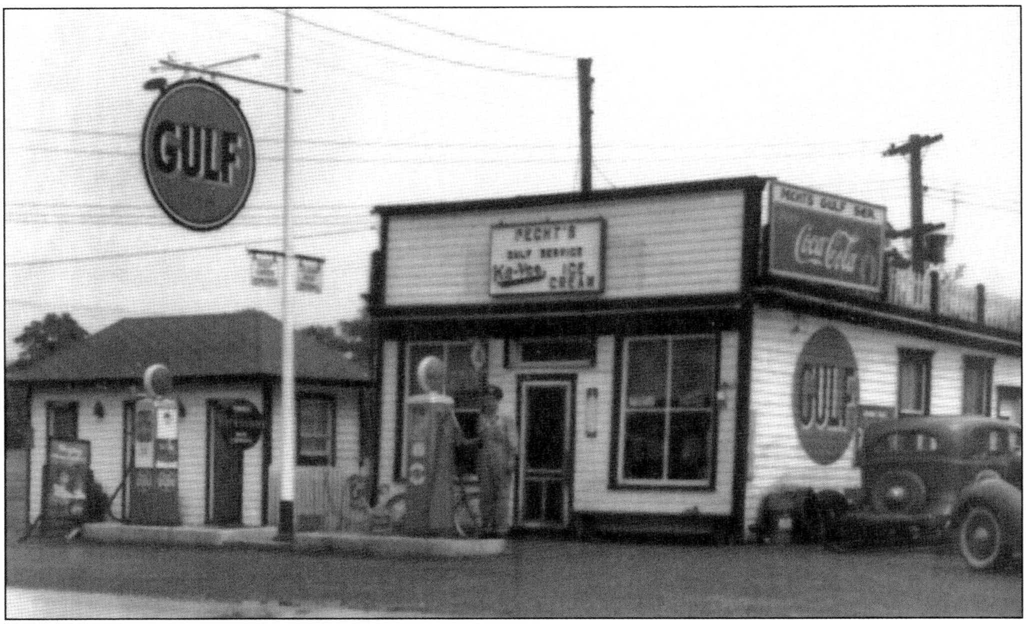

Pecht's service station in the village of McVeytown, between Mount Union and Lewistown, is seen here in the 1940s. Besides Gulf gasoline, the station also displayed signs for Coca-Cola, 7-Up, Firestone tires, and local Ka-Vee ice cream. The original course of the William Penn Highway traveled somewhat north of this, through the village of Airydale. After being designated as Route 22, it was realigned through McVeytown in 1928.

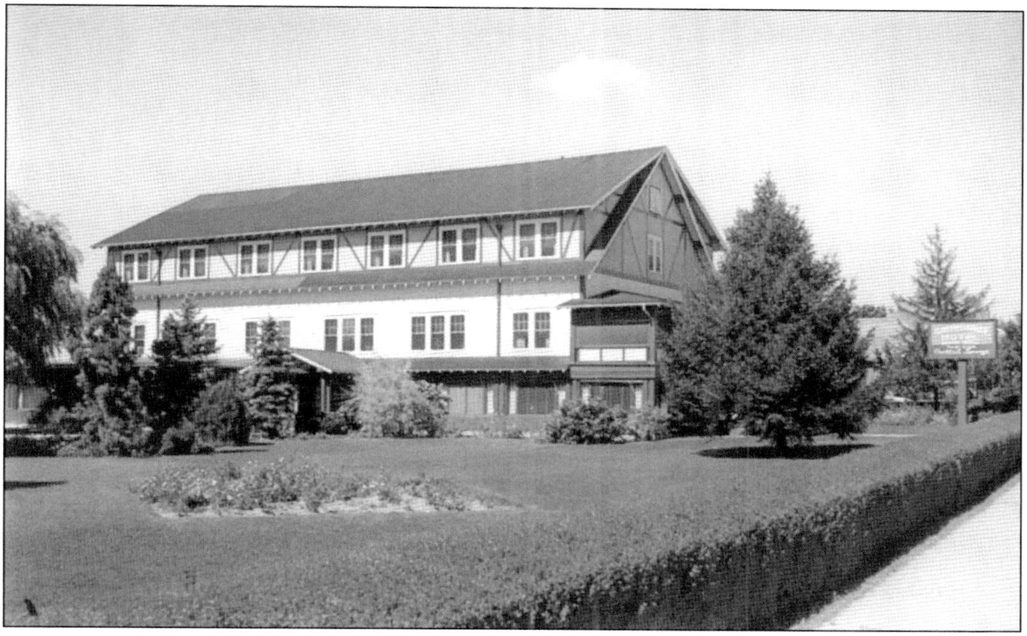

Shown above is a 1930s view of the Green Gables Hotel, which operated at 900 South Main Street (on the original course of the William Penn Highway and Route 22) in Lewistown. Built in 1931, it featured 22 rooms, a large rustic lobby with plush furniture that is shown below, and a screened-in porch with wicker furniture. A later annex provided an additional 20 rooms to the site, but the hotel eventually closed after a new highway bypass around the city reduced traffic through downtown. New owners renovated it in the late 2000s, but within a few years it had closed again and stands vacant as of 2014.

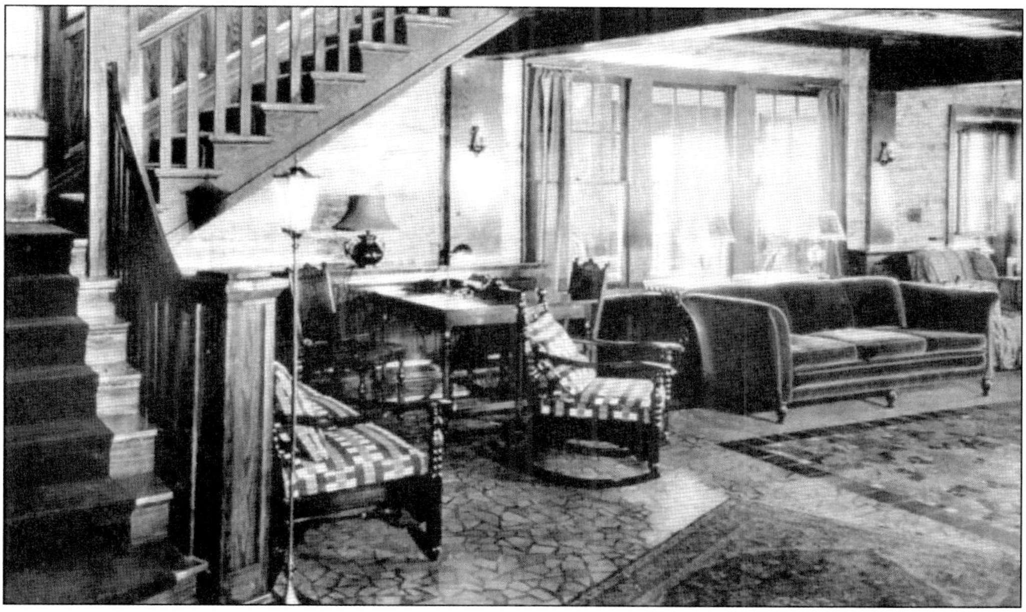

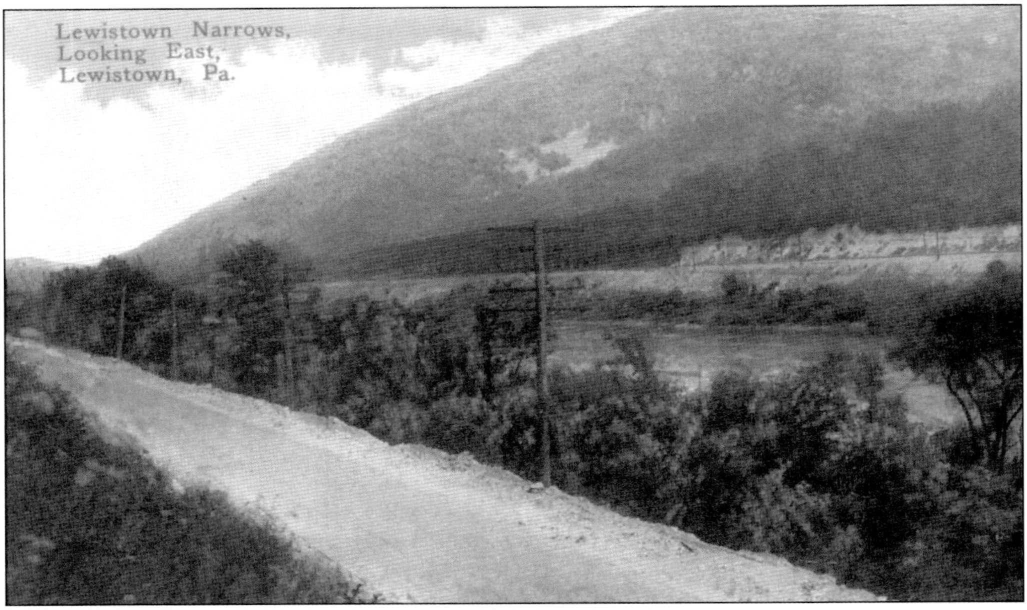

One of the most scenic sections of the William Penn Highway, the Lewistown Narrows is a narrow water gap in the ridge known as Shade Mountain, several miles east of Lewistown. Due to the lack of alternative routes through the area, it has been used by Native Americans, early settlers, the canal, the highway, and the railroad. Being the primary highway between Harrisburg and both State College and Altoona, the highway carries between 20,000 and 50,000 cars daily. However, due to the limited space, it still had just two lanes, with a passing lane as late as 2002, making it one of the state's most dangerous road segments. A massive reconstruction project built the road into a far safer, limited-access highway by 2007. The road is shown above in the 1920s, prior to being paved, and below in the 1950s.

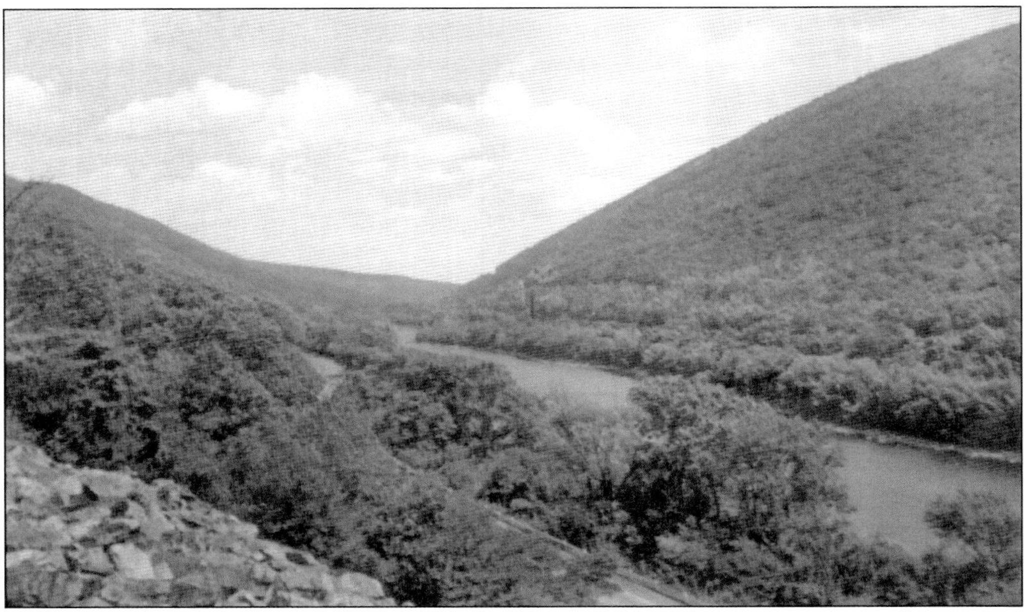

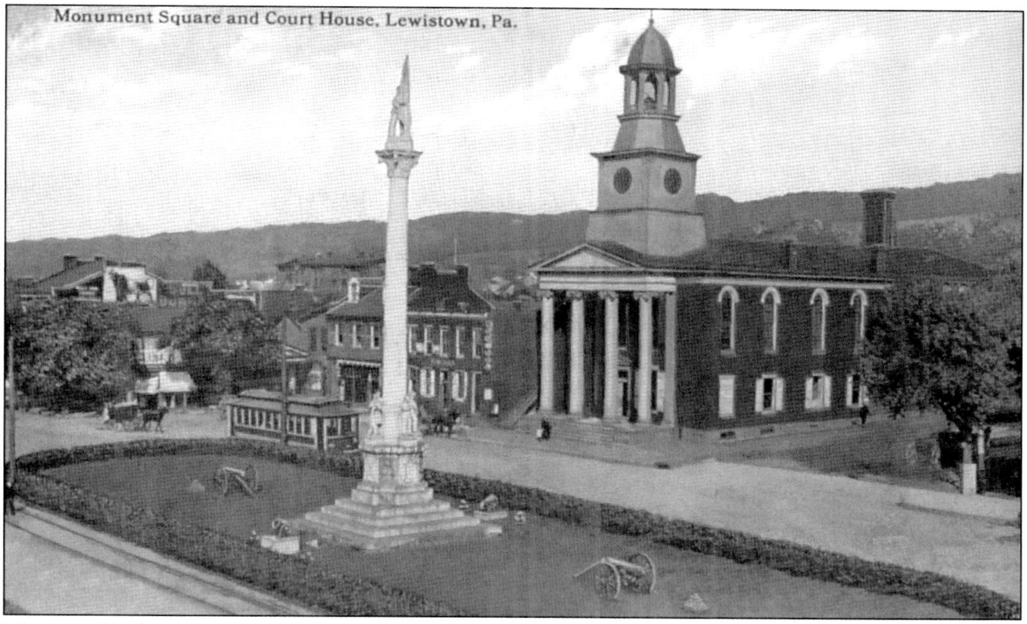

This view of Lewistown from about 1915 shows Monument Square, across from the Mifflin County Courthouse. The 64-foot-tall Soldiers and Sailors Monument in the center of the square was built in 1906 and includes one stone from President Lincoln's tomb that was built into the base. The square is along the original course of the William Penn Highway and Route 22; today, the route bypasses downtown on a modern highway.

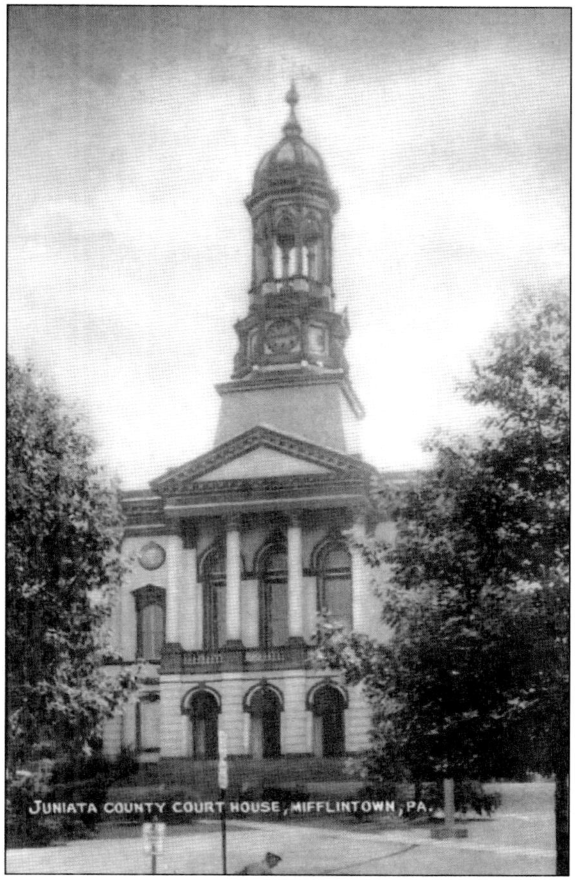

Sparsely populated and rural, Juniata County stands between Lewistown and Harrisburg. Route 22 in this area has been a limited-access divided highway since the 1970s, but the original William Penn Highway traveled along Main Street in the county seat of Mifflintown. Shown here is the county courthouse, built in 1873, facing Main Street.

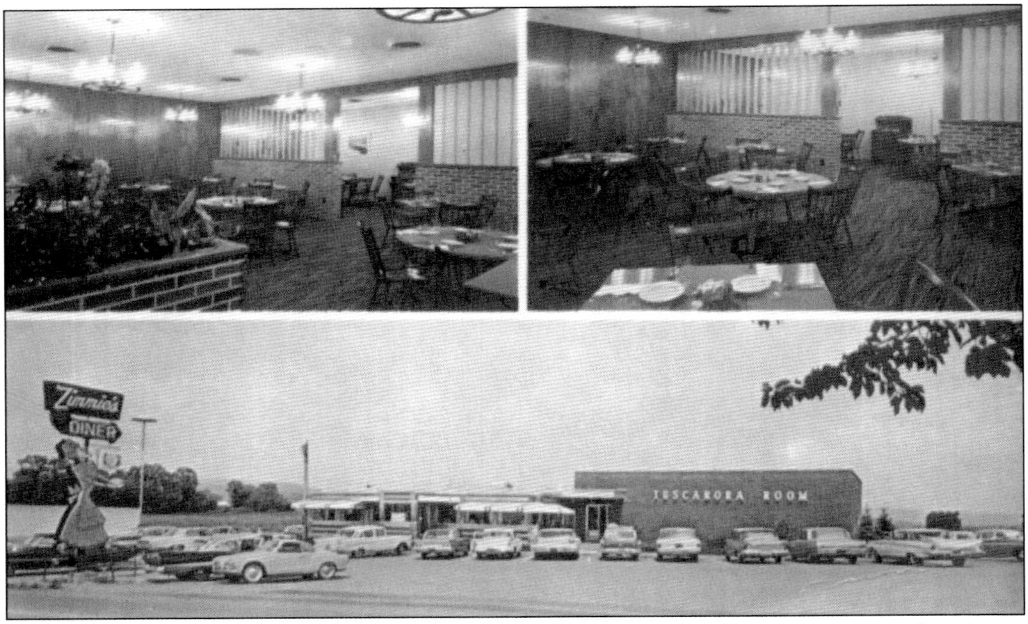

Although somewhat west of the area traditionally known for its Pennsylvania Dutch culture, Zimmie's Diner in Mifflintown specialized in that style of food. By the early 1960s, when this postcard was made, the restaurant had added the Tuscarora banquet room, named for the mountain ridge by the same name nearby.

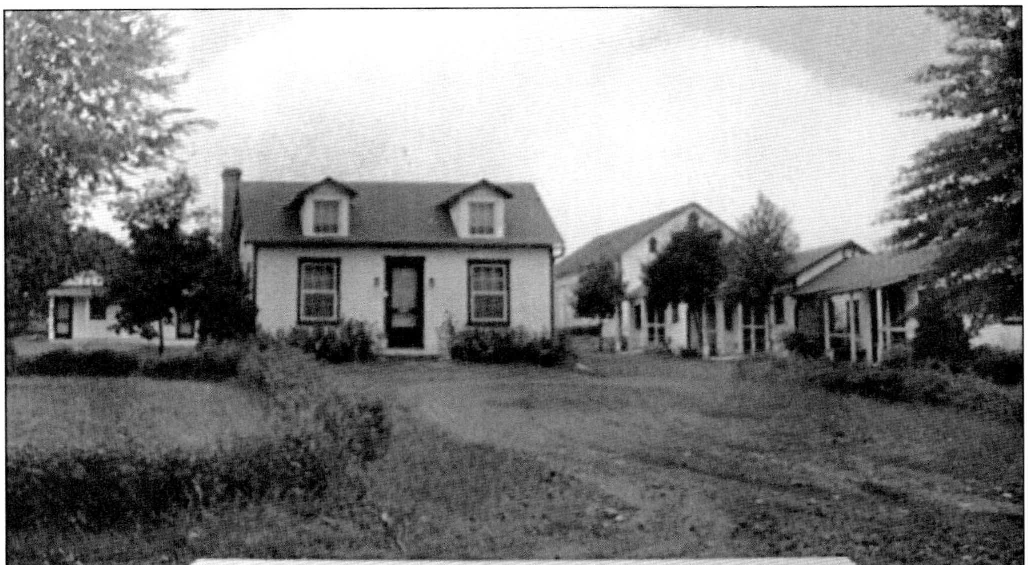

The Colonial Village, shown in the 1940s, was established with the construction of a few tourist cabins on an existing farm; note the barn in the background and the owner's residence in the foreground. With relatively few places to stay in the rural and sparsely populated area of Millerstown in central Pennsylvania, these basic amenities were no doubt a welcome sight for some travelers along the William Penn Highway.

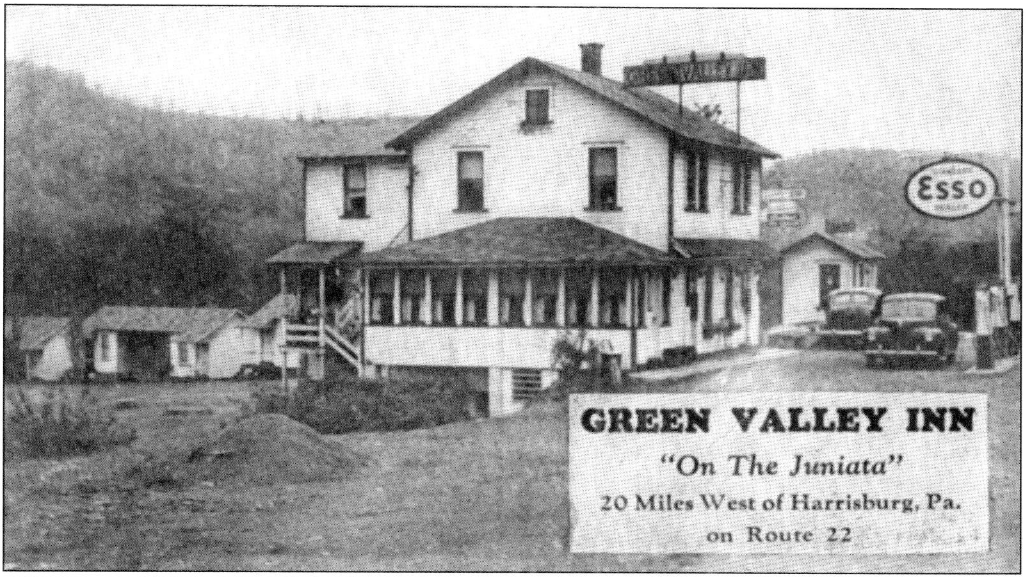

The Green Valley Inn, shown here in the 1940s, stood along the William Penn Highway and the Juniata River, several miles west of its confluence with the Susquehanna. Selling Esso gasoline, the inn also had a small restaurant that served Sealtest ice cream as well as small cabins in the back for overnight stays. Establishments like this had largely disappeared from the road by the 1970s.

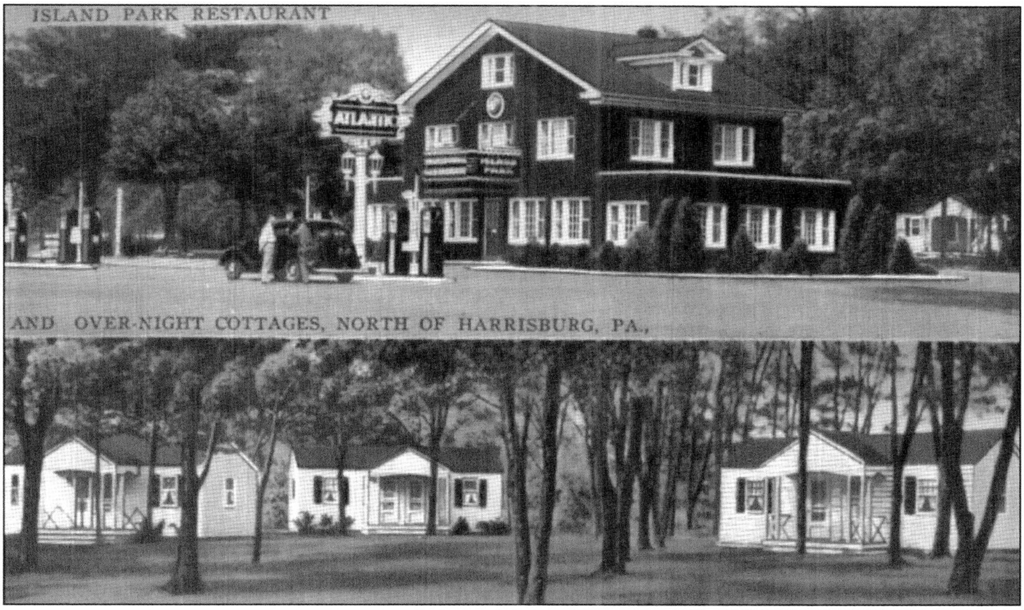

Just west of the Susquehanna River stood the Island Park Restaurant and Cottages and its adjacent Atlantic gas station, shown here in the 1940s. Located in the small locality named Benvenue near the confluence of the Juniata and Susquehanna Rivers, the establishment was along a brief stretch of highway that once carried US Routes 11, 15, 22, and 322.

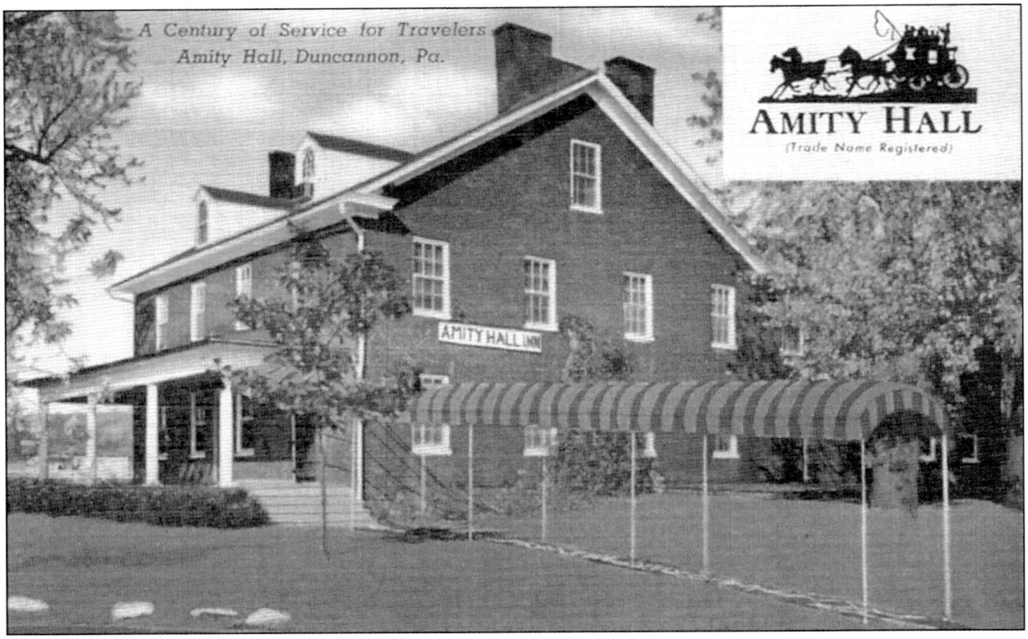

The William Penn Highway was dotted with old hotels, dating to its early days as the Northern Turnpike and its proximity to the canal. One of the oldest hotels was known as Amity Hall, built in 1828 around the time of the canal's opening. Its location was ideal for an early inn, being at the confluence of the Juniata and Susquehanna Rivers as well as the intersection of the William Penn Highway and the Susquehanna Trail, another early highway. The hotel and restaurant remained open in the 1940s, as seen in these postcards, with a nearby Esso gas station. After a succession of ownership changes, the restaurant closed in the 1980s, and the building was destroyed by arson in 2009.

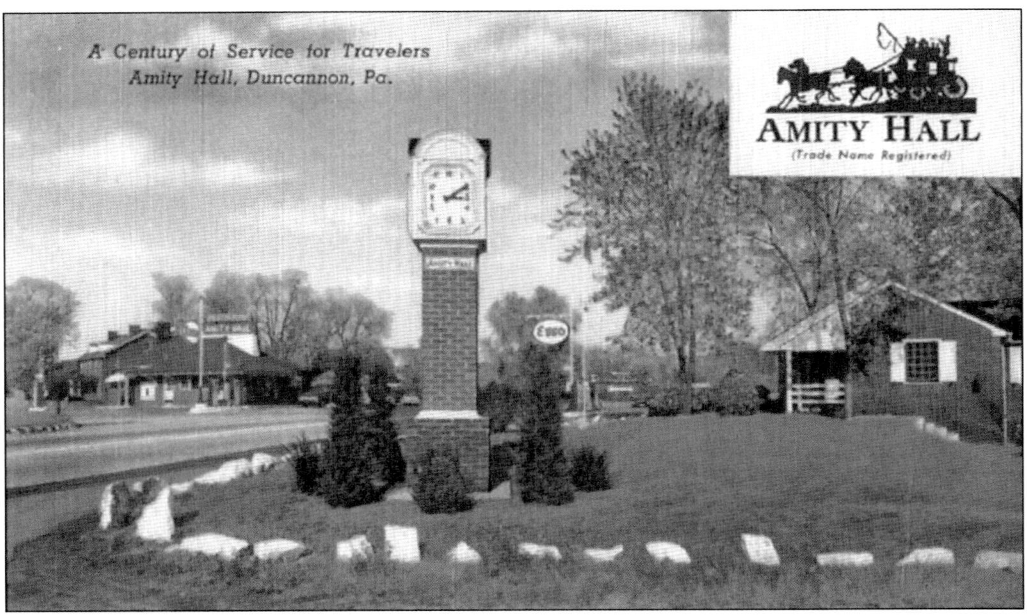

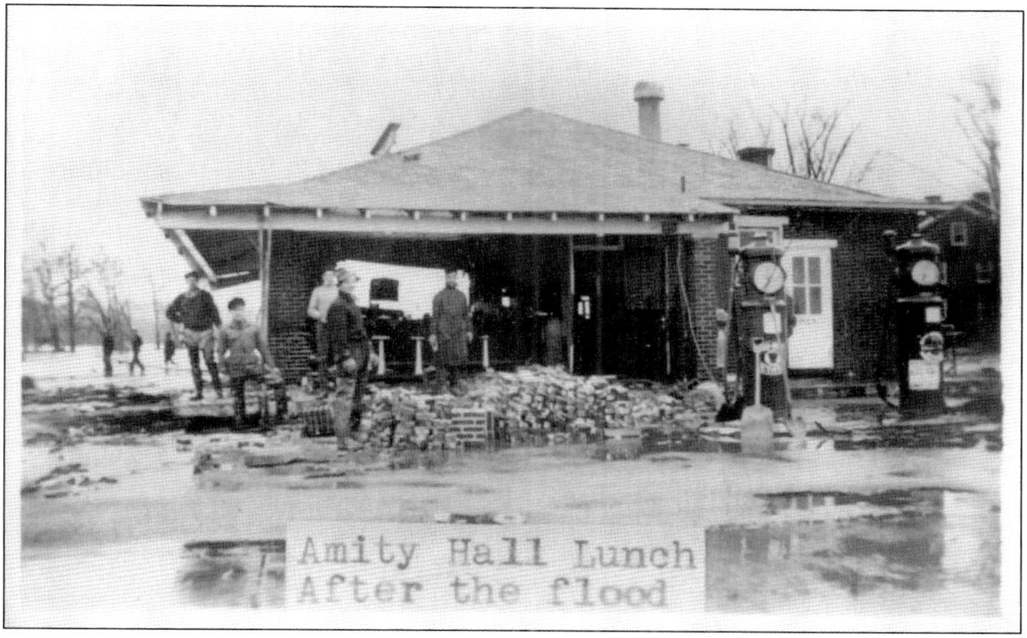

Amity Hall's location at the confluence of two rivers made it susceptible to flooding, as evidenced by this postcard view of damage to the gas station after the devastating St. Patrick's Day Flood of 1936. Harrisburg's second-worst flooding disaster, the storm left more than 150 people dead in 16 states and caused roughly $300 million in damage. Note the uncommon clock-face gas pumps at the station.

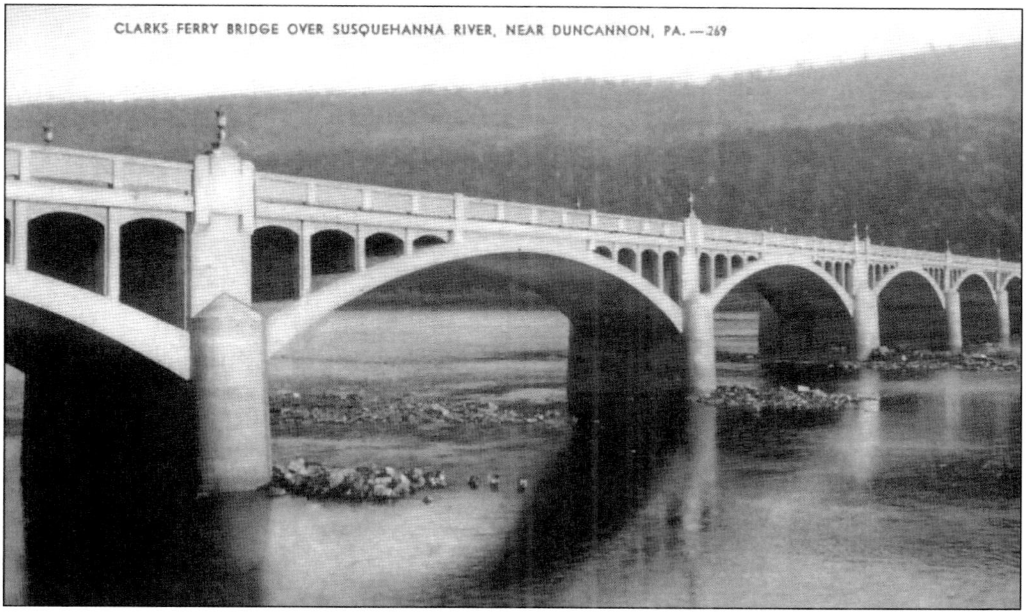

Route 22 travels in conjunction with US Route 322 for more than 50 miles between Lewistown and Harrisburg. The highway crosses the Susquehanna River at a location originally known as Clarks Ferry. The concrete arched bridge shown here was built in the 1930s to replace the original narrow toll bridge and in later years was replaced by a wider, modern steel girder bridge.

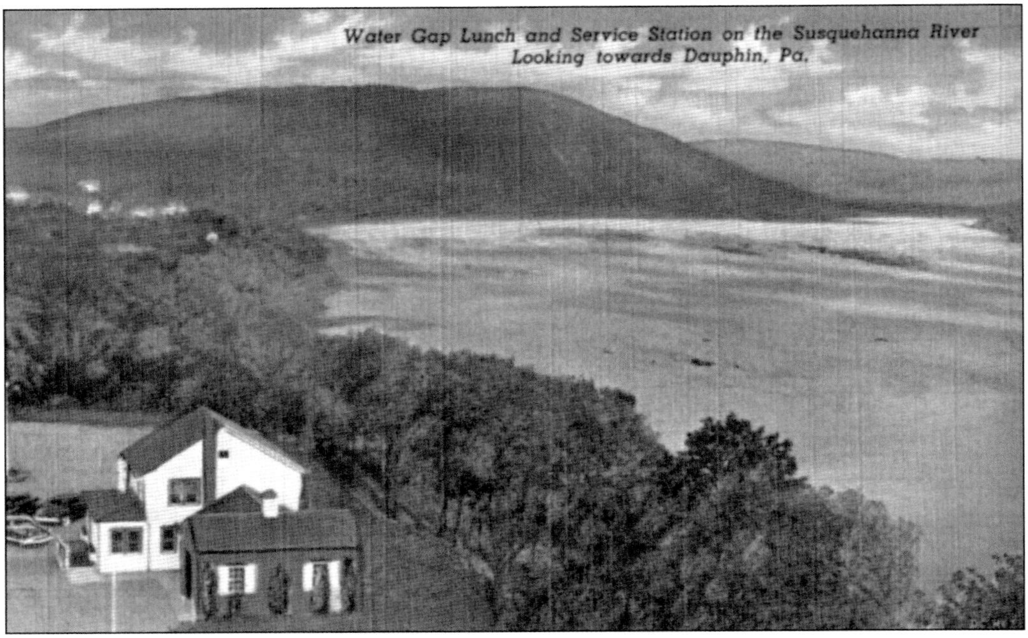

The portion of the William Penn Highway between the Clarks Ferry crossing and Harrisburg provides many scenic views of the Susquehanna River, the three water gaps through which it flows, and several surrounding ridges (particularly Blue Mountain, Cove Mountain, and Peters Mountain). Shown here in the 1940s are two views of the road, looking southward at the Water Gap Service Station (above) and northward (below). By this time, the road had been widened to four lanes, noted here as a superhighway. Since that time, the road has been upgraded further to a limited-access highway all the way into Harrisburg.

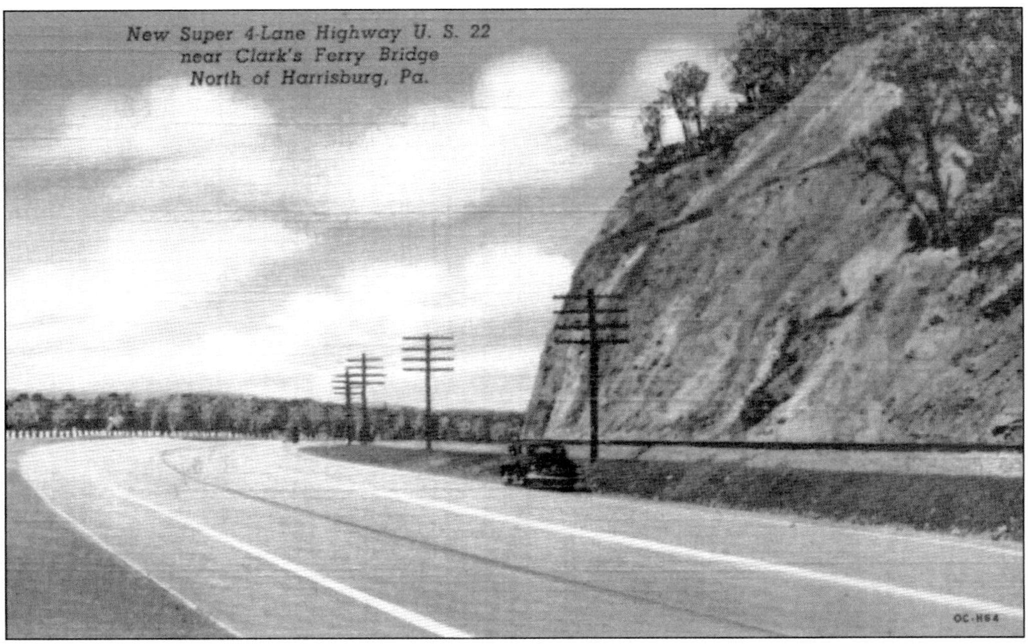

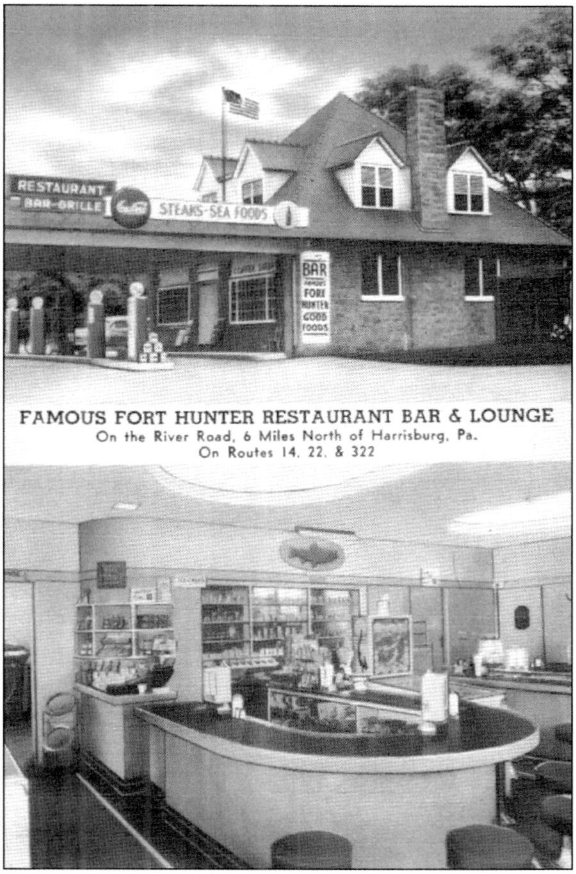

Pictured here around 1940 (right), the Fort Hunter Park service station operated along the William Penn Highway six miles north of Harrisburg. Standing within sight of the Susquehanna River, the station was named after nearby Fort Hunter, a blockhouse used by the British between 1755 and 1763 to protect settlers against attacks by Native Americans. Like many of the other early gas stations along the highway, this one featured a lunchroom and cabins for overnight stays. Gasoline is no longer sold at the site (below), although the vacant and well-preserved stone building remains standing today. Although this segment of the original highway, known as North Front Street, no longer carries Route 22, a sign is visible in the background showing access to Routes 22 and 322 on the modern highway nearby.

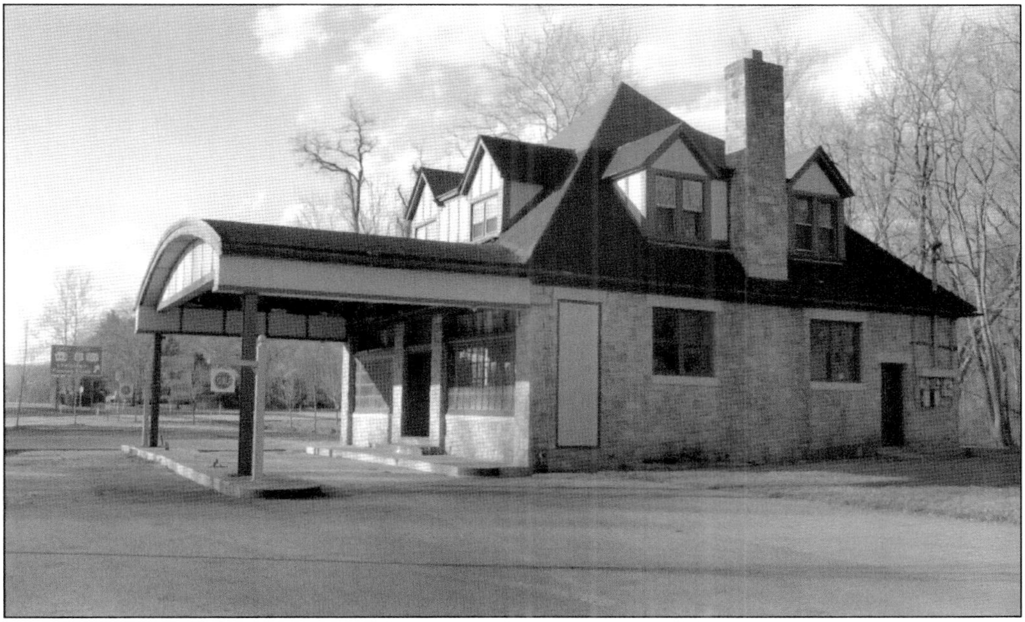

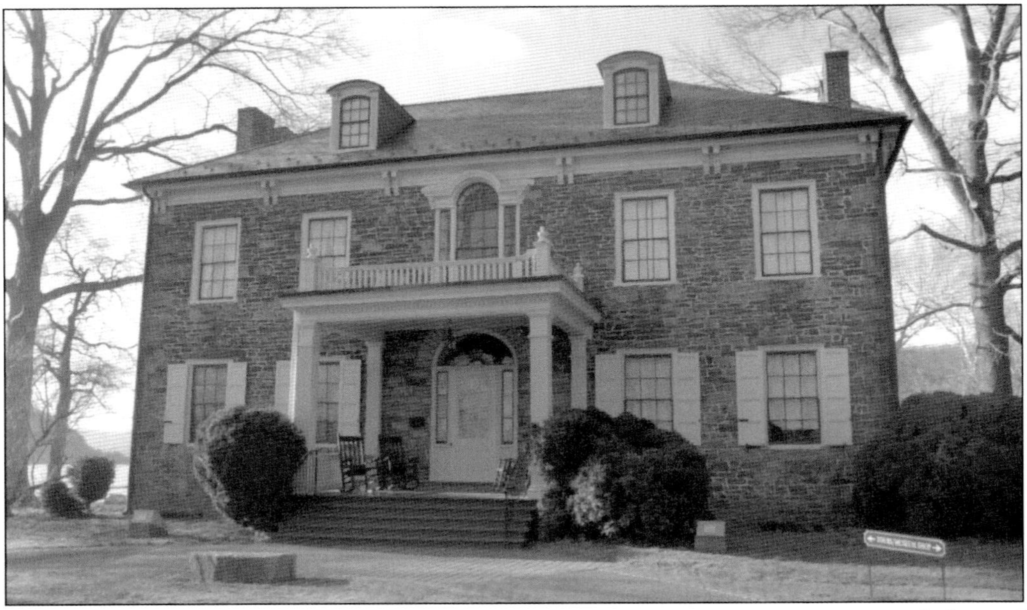

Six miles north of downtown Harrisburg along North Front Street is Fort Hunter Park, located at the site of a blockhouse established by the British in 1755. Although the fort was abandoned in 1763, its name has persisted and is associated with more recent structures. One of these is the McAllister Mansion (shown here) built in 1786 at the center of a plantation, several buildings of which remain standing.

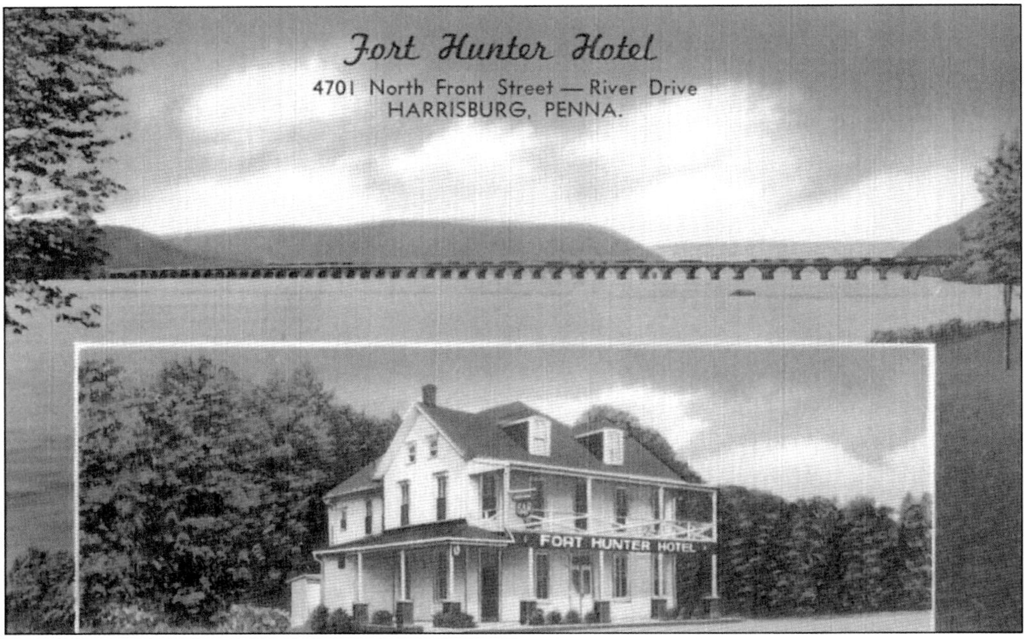

The Fort Hunter Hotel operated in a large former residence at 4701 North Front Street (Route 22), on the north side of Harrisburg. The site, across the street from the Susquehanna River, was just a quarter of a mile south of the Rockville railroad bridge. Pictured here in the 1940s, the hotel is no longer standing.

Six

Harrisburg to Allentown before 1931

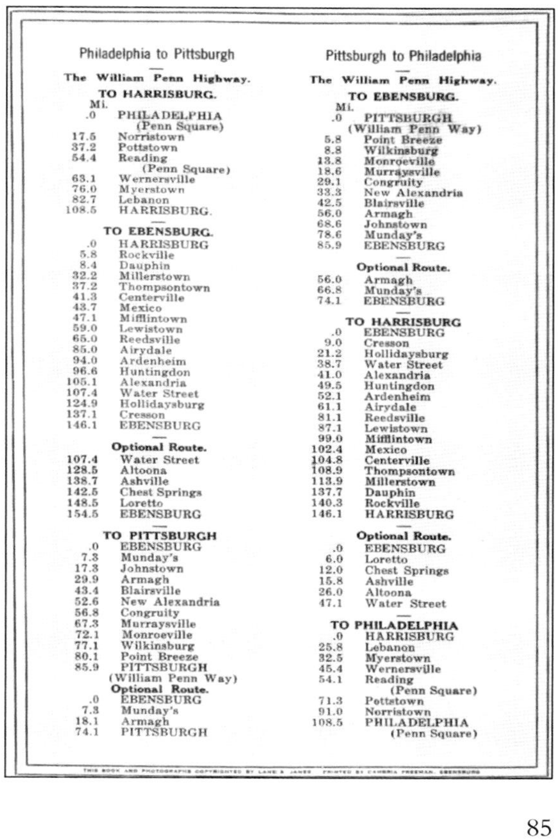

Philadelphia to Pittsburgh

The William Penn Highway.

TO HARRISBURG.

Mi.	
.0	PHILADELPHIA (Penn Square)
17.5	Norristown
37.2	Pottstown
54.4	Reading (Penn Square)
63.1	Wernersville
76.0	Myerstown
82.7	Lebanon
108.5	HARRISBURG.

TO EBENSBURG.

Mi.	
.0	HARRISBURG
5.8	Rockville
8.4	Dauphin
32.2	Millerstown
37.2	Thompsontown
41.3	Centerville
43.7	Mexico
47.1	Mifflintown
59.0	Lewistown
65.0	Reedsville
85.0	Airydale
94.0	Ardenheim
96.6	Huntingdon
105.1	Alexandria
107.4	Water Street
124.9	Hollidaysburg
137.1	Cresson
146.1	EBENSBURG

Optional Route.

Mi.	
107.4	Water Street
128.5	Altoona
138.7	Ashville
142.5	Chest Springs
148.5	Loretto
154.5	EBENSBURG

TO PITTSBURGH

Mi.	
.0	EBENSBURG
7.3	Munday's
17.3	Johnstown
29.9	Armagh
43.4	Blairsville
52.6	New Alexandria
56.8	Congruity
67.3	Murraysville
72.1	Monroeville
77.1	Wilkinsburg
80.1	Point Breeze
85.9	PITTSBURGH (William Penn Way)

Optional Route.

Mi.	
.0	EBENSBURG
7.3	Munday's
18.1	Armagh
74.1	PITTSBURGH

Pittsburgh to Philadelphia

The William Penn Highway.

TO EBENSBURG.

Mi.	
.0	PITTSBURGH (William Penn Way)
5.8	Point Breeze
8.8	Wilkinsburg
13.8	Monroeville
18.6	Murraysville
29.1	Congruity
33.3	New Alexandria
42.5	Blairsville
56.0	Armagh
68.6	Johnstown
78.6	Munday's
85.9	EBENSBURG

Optional Route.

Mi.	
56.0	Armagh
66.8	Munday's
74.1	EBENSBURG

TO HARRISBURG

Mi.	
.0	EBENSBURG
9.0	Cresson
21.2	Hollidaysburg
38.7	Water Street
41.0	Alexandria
49.5	Huntingdon
52.1	Ardenheim
61.1	Airydale
81.1	Reedsville
87.1	Lewistown
99.0	Mifflintown
102.4	Mexico
104.8	Centerville
108.9	Thompsontown
113.9	Millerstown
137.7	Dauphin
140.3	Rockville
146.1	HARRISBURG

Optional Route.

Mi.	
.0	EBENSBURG
6.0	Loretto
12.0	Chest Springs
15.8	Ashville
26.0	Altoona
47.1	Water Street

TO PHILADELPHIA

Mi.	
.0	HARRISBURG
25.8	Lebanon
32.5	Myerstown
45.4	Wernersville
54.1	Reading (Penn Square)
71.3	Pottstown
91.0	Norristown
108.5	PHILADELPHIA (Penn Square)

This mileage chart from 1916 shows distances between locations on the William Penn Highway between Philadelphia and Pittsburgh. The optional alignments through Altoona and Johnstown are also shown here. Charts like this would need to be rewritten nearly every year when segments of the route were realigned or improved. (Courtesy of the Cambria County Historical Society.)

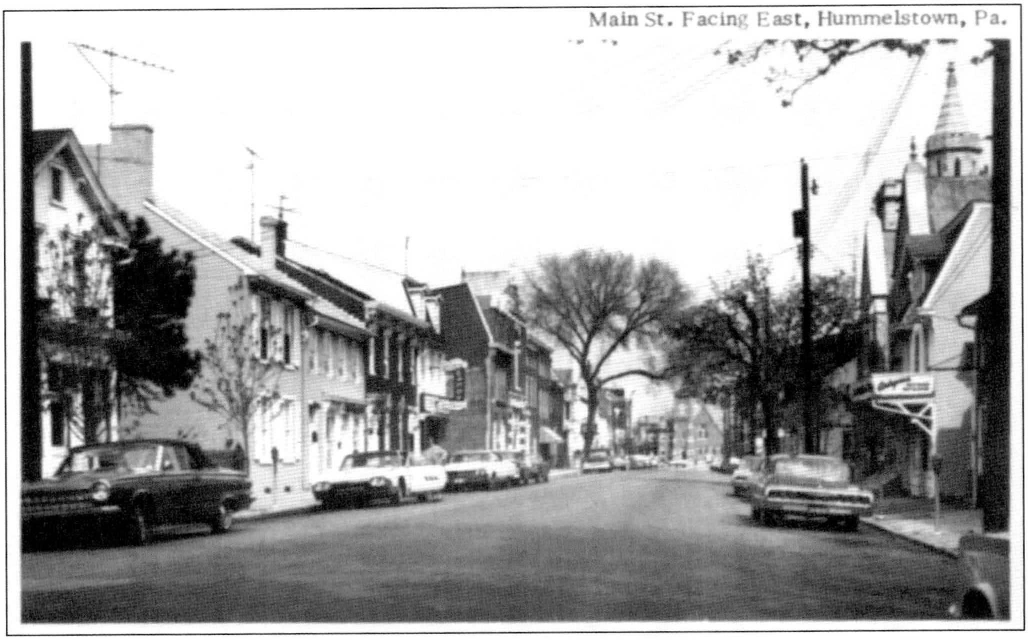

Standing between Harrisburg and Hershey along the original course of the William Penn Highway is the borough of Hummelstown. First settled in 1762, it has a modern population of more than 4,000 residents. Main Street, shown in this view facing eastward in the 1960s, carried the highway until it was realigned in 1931.

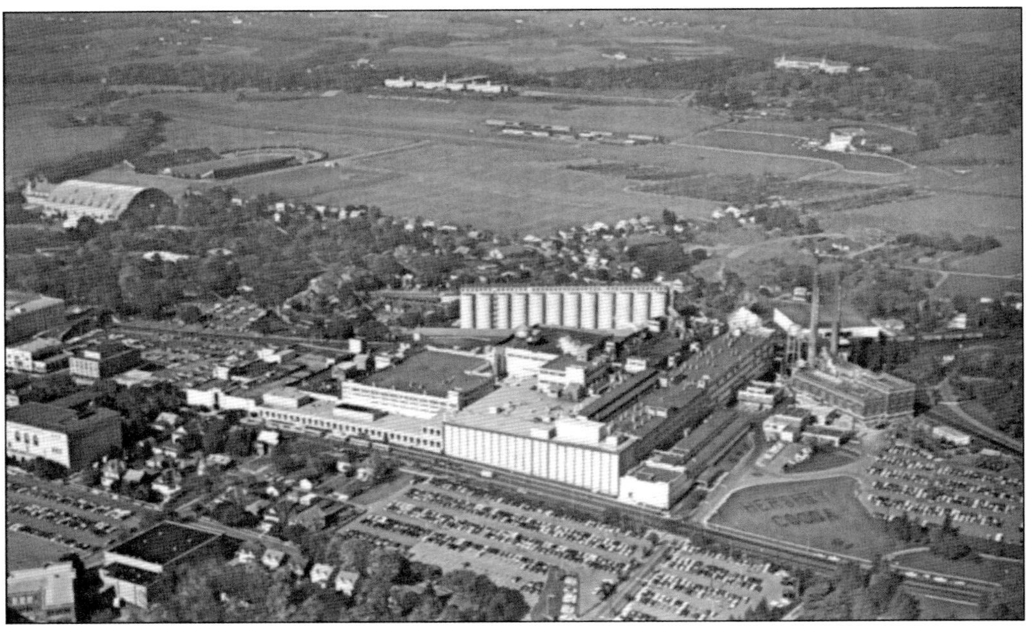

Hershey is the home of the world-famous chocolate company of the same name. This aerial view of the company's main factory in the 1970s shows East Chocolate Avenue in the foreground. Designated today as US Route 422, it was the original alignment of the William Penn Highway and Route 22 until the realignment of 1931.

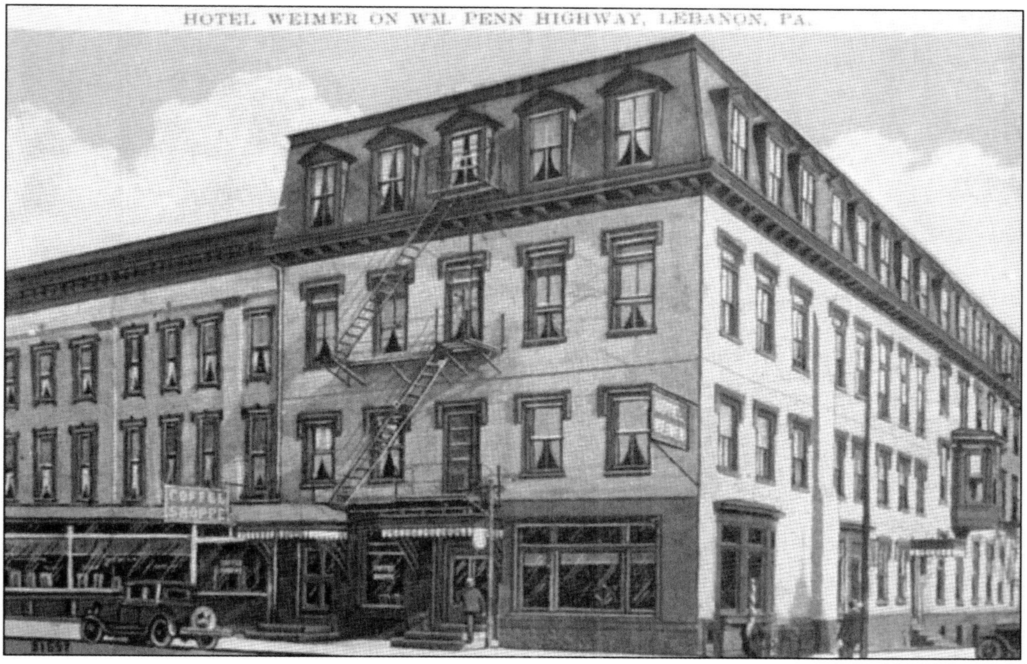

The city of Lebanon is the Lebanon County seat and was originally a Native American community resettled by Europeans in the early 1700s. The original William Penn Highway continued through the city along Cumberland Street (today carrying Route 422) until 1931. In the process, it passed the Hotel Weimer, shown here around 1930.

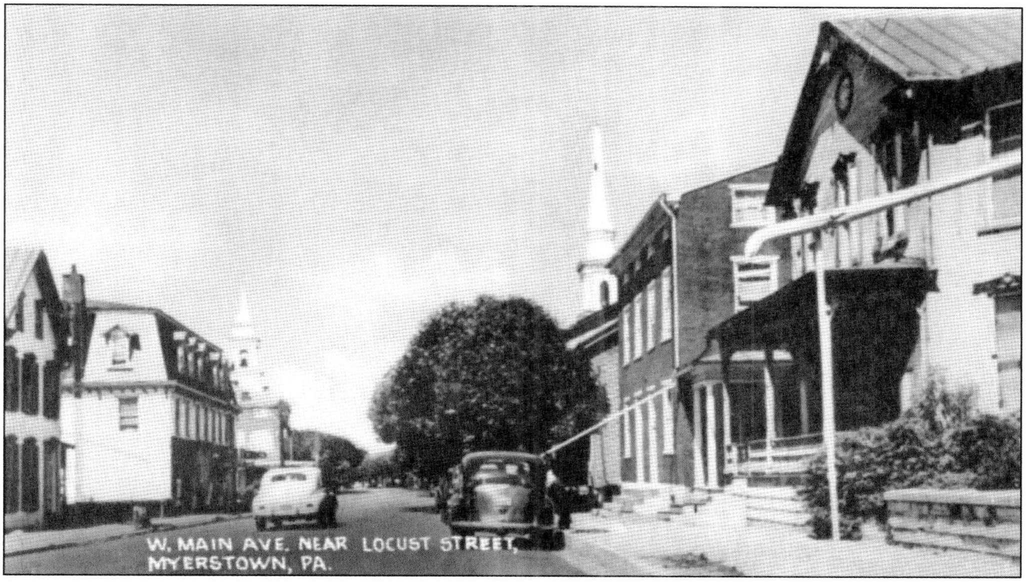

This 1940s view shows Main Avenue in Myerstown, one of a series of small towns along the course of the original William Penn Highway between Harrisburg and Reading. Originally settled in the 1750s, it has a modern population of more than 3,000. Just five years after being established in 1926, Route 22 was realigned to a highway far to the north, and Main Avenue became US Route 422, which continues to travel through the region today.

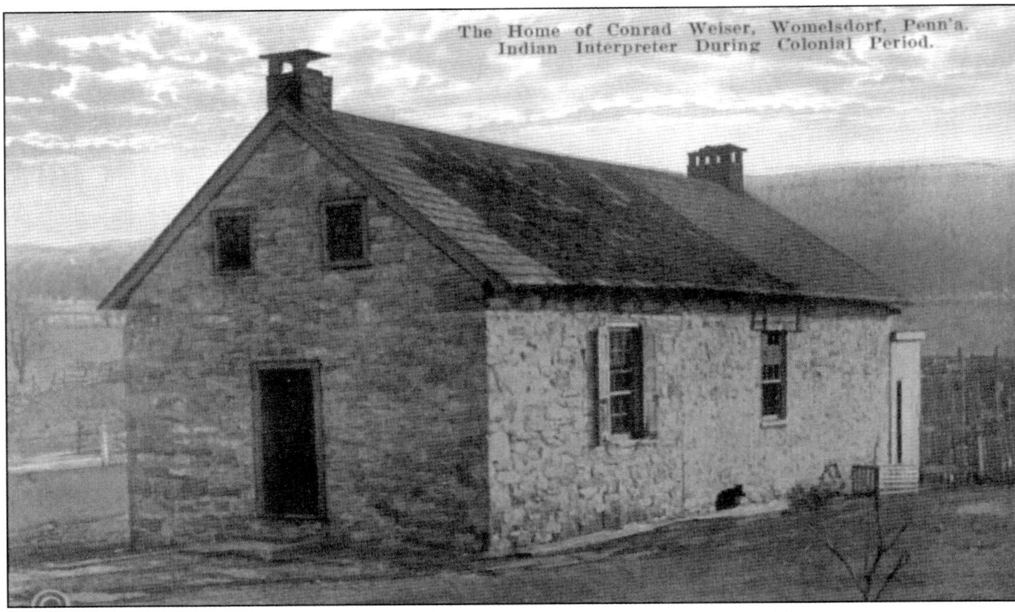

Conrad Weiser was a native German who came to America in 1710 and later spent a great deal of time living among the Native American tribes of east-central Pennsylvania. He helped to negotiate several treaties between settlers and the native Iroquois while helping to establish the city of Reading. His homestead has been preserved as a historic site and stands along the original course of Route 22 near Womelsdorf.

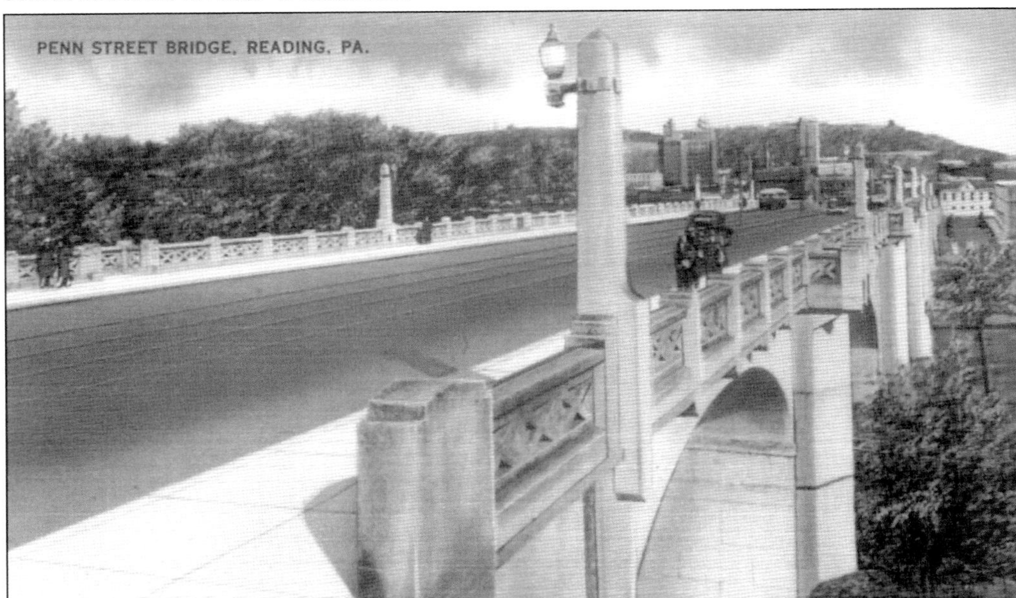

The original course of the William Penn Highway crossed the Penn Street Viaduct over the Schuylkill River on the west side of Reading. Shown here in the 1930s, the arched concrete bridge was built in 1913 and is more than 1,300 feet in length. Now more than a century old, it remains in use today carrying Business US Route 422.

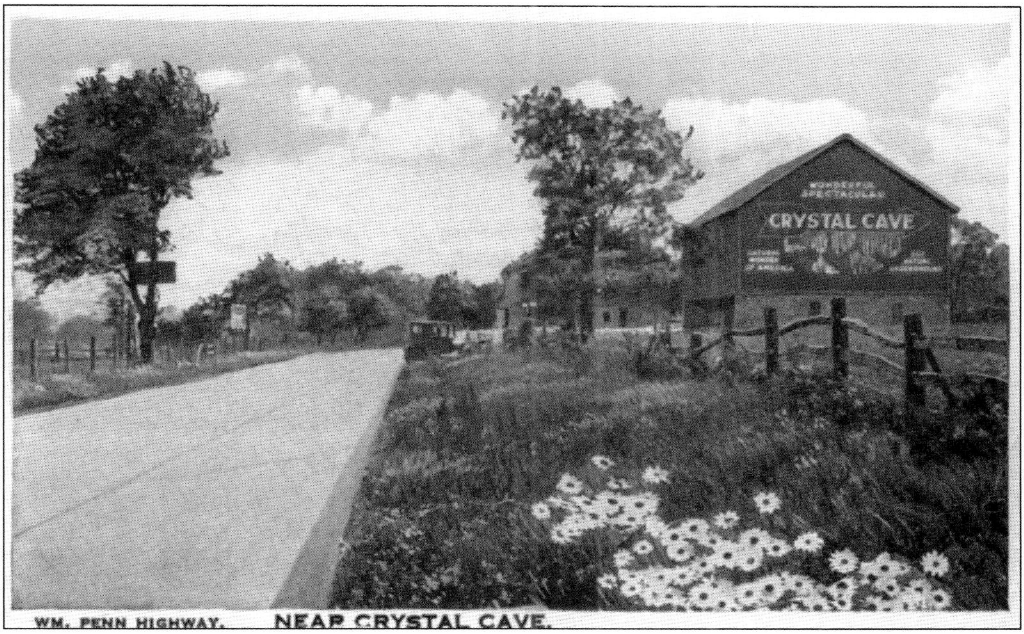

Pennsylvania's oldest operating cavern, Crystal Cave was discovered in 1871 on the farm of Gideon Merkel. Situated in the countryside between Lenhartsville and Kutztown, it has always been within a short distance of both the original and modern alignments of Route 22. Since its opening, it has hosted millions of visitors, who take the 45-minute tour of the underground caves and their crystal and rock formations, some thought to be as much as 500,000 years old. Above is an image of a sign for the cave on the side of a barn along the William Penn Highway in the 1920s. Below is the entrance to the cave in the 1940s.

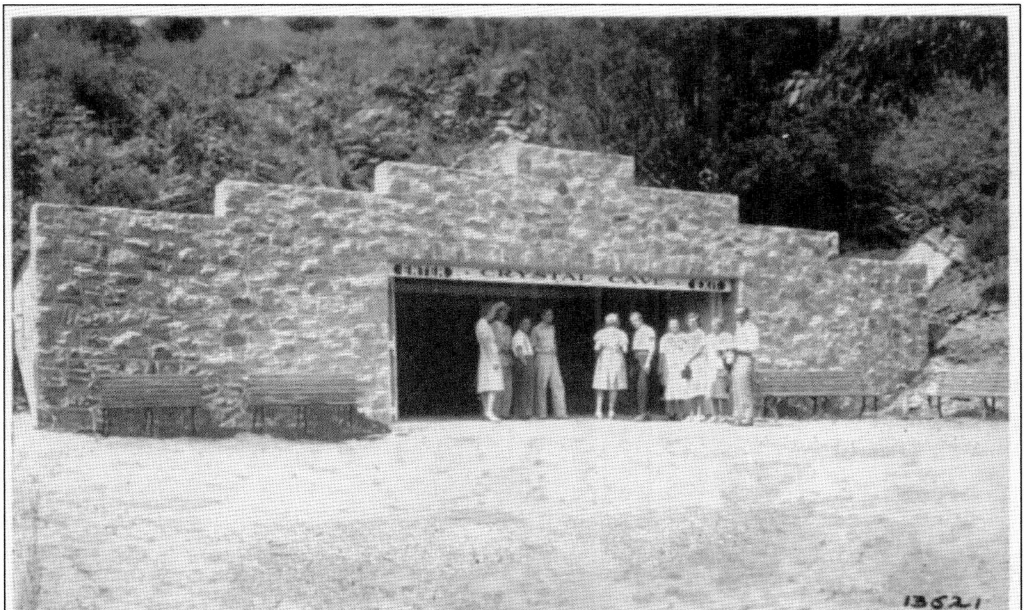

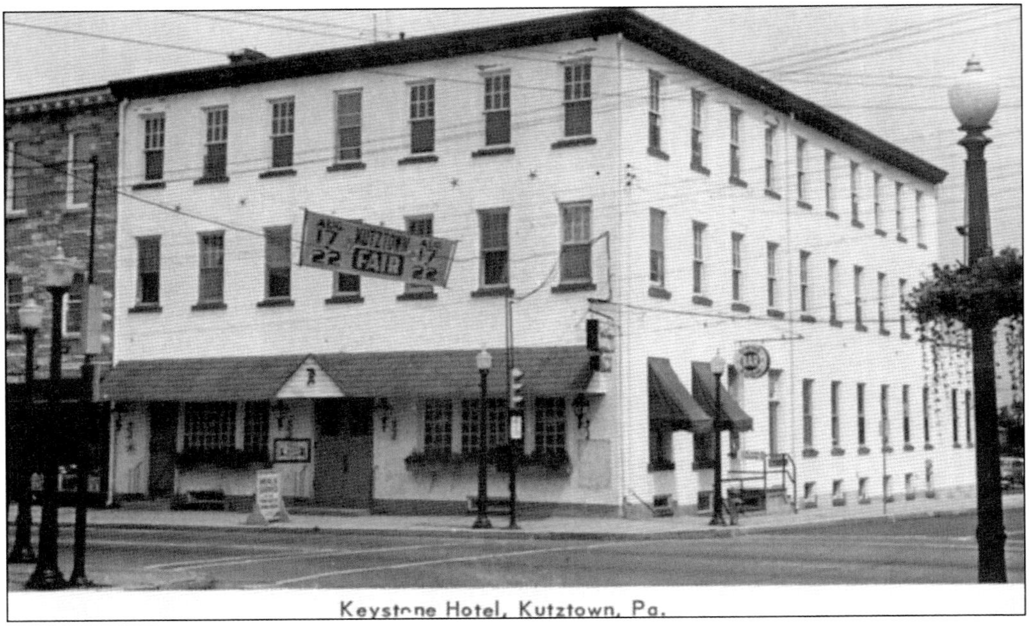

Founded in 1755, the borough of Kutztown is primarily known for Kutztown University and nearby Crystal Cave. Until 1931, the William Penn Highway traveled through the town as Main Street. Shown here in the 1930s is the 19th-century Keystone Hotel, at West Main and Whiteoak Streets. Although no longer in operation as a hotel, the building remains standing today.

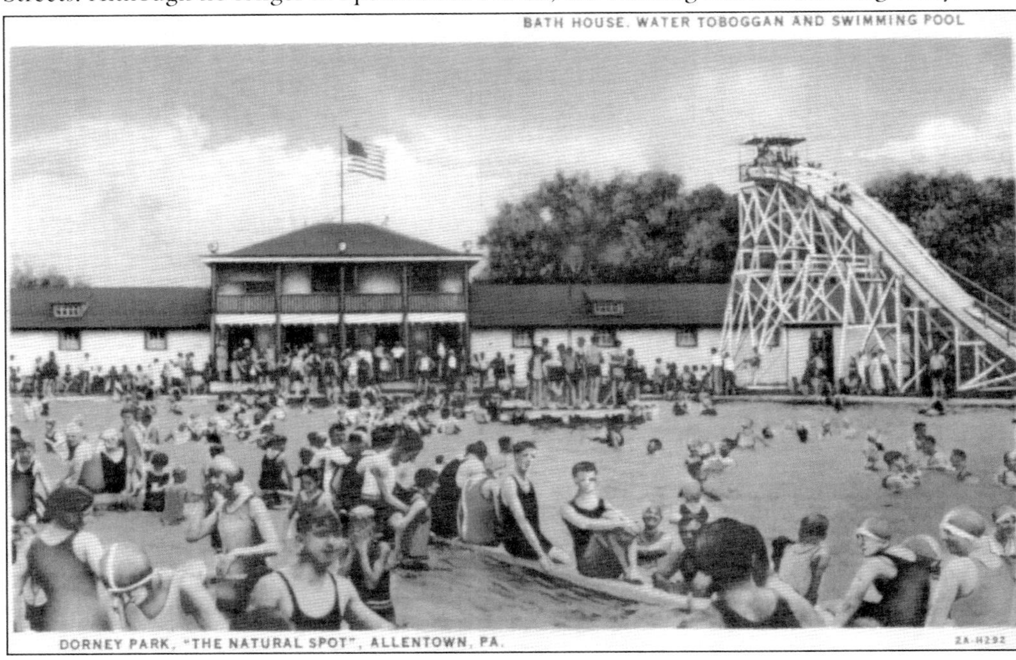

Dorney Park stood along the original course of Route 22 on the south side of Allentown. Established in 1860 as a resort and fish hatchery, it became an amusement park in 1884 with the addition of mechanical rides. Seen here in the 1920s, it also had a huge swimming pool, which was open during the summer. Still open today, it has eight roller coasters and 59 overall rides.

Seven

Harrisburg to Allentown after 1931

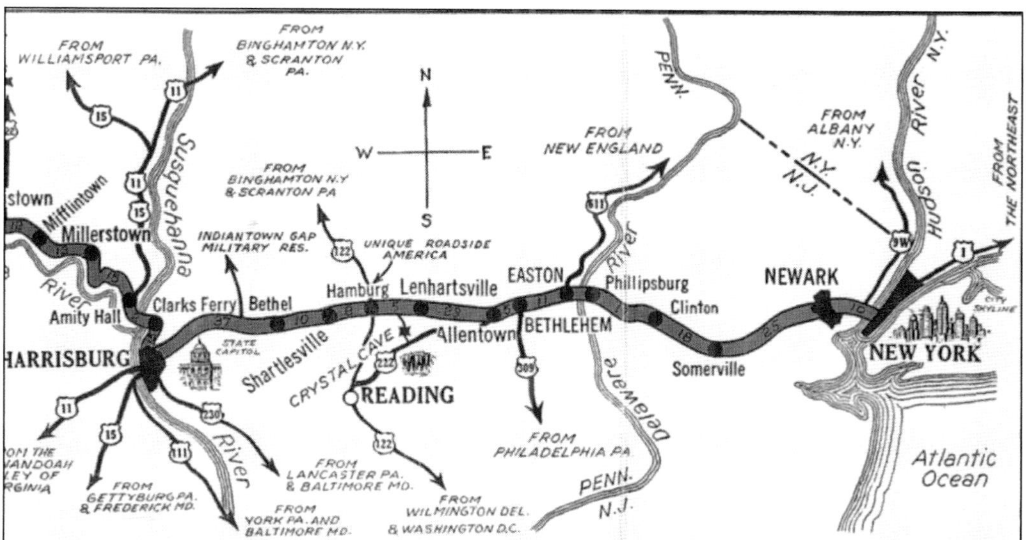

This map from 1951 shows the William Penn Highway from Harrisburg to Newark, New Jersey. Very little of the highway in this region had retained the same alignment from 1916; the route from Harrisburg to Allentown had originally gone through Reading, while the New Jersey portion originally continued directly east from Phillipsburg, through Morristown to Elizabeth.

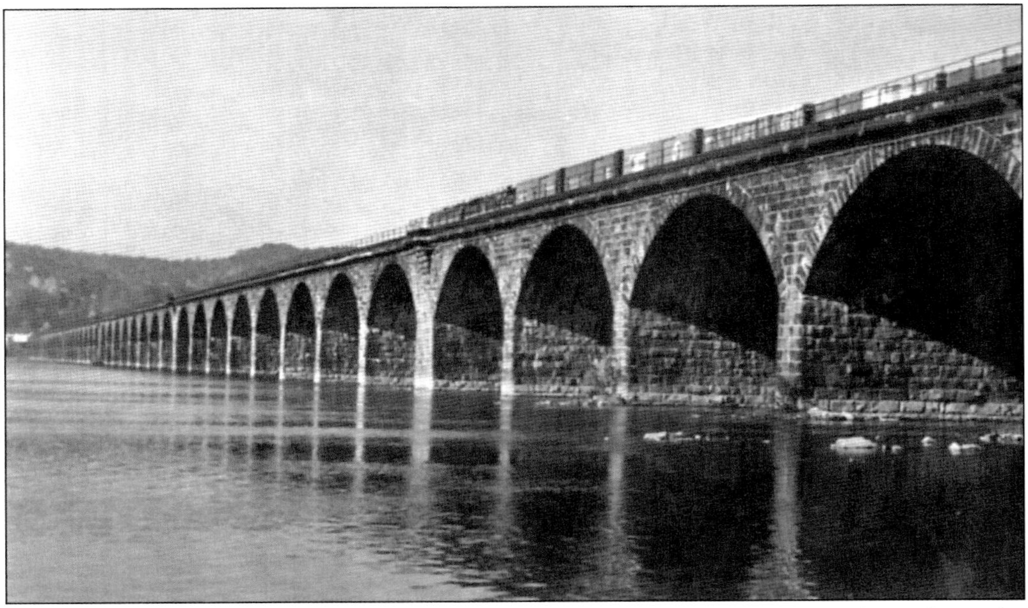

The Rockville Bridge crosses the Susquehanna River and the William Penn Highway five miles north of Harrisburg. Opened to rail traffic in 1902, it is more than 3,800 feet (three-fourths of a mile) in length, making it the world's longest arched stone railroad bridge. Originally carrying four rail lines across the river, it now carries only two.

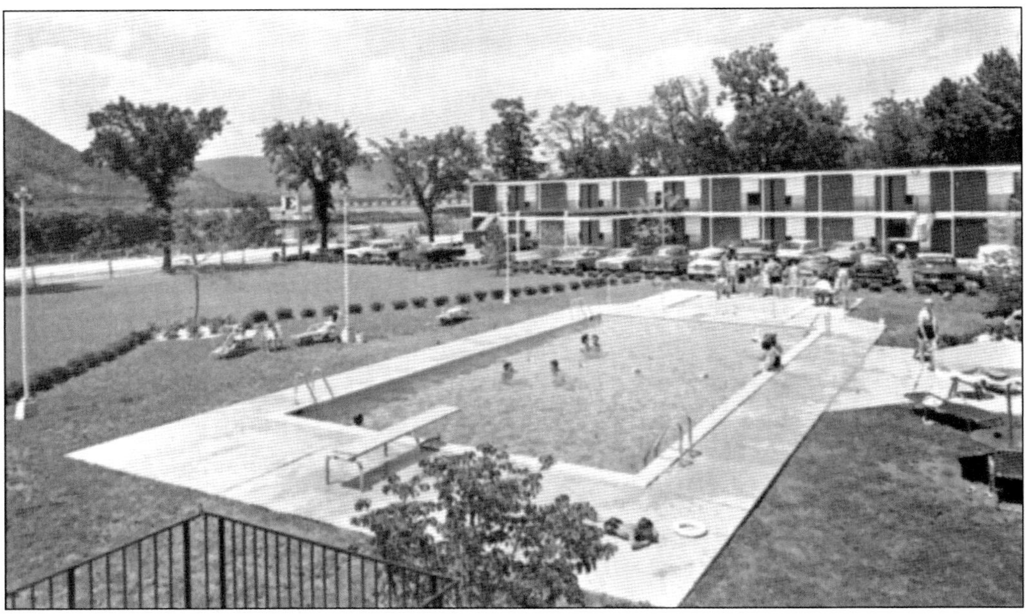

The Excellent Inn, shown in the mid-1970s, stood along North Front Street (the original course of Route 22) on the north side of Harrisburg. The site was across the street from the Susquehanna River and within view of the Rockville Bridge. Although the motel was not owned by a larger chain, it was built in a more modern style than most similar independent motels.

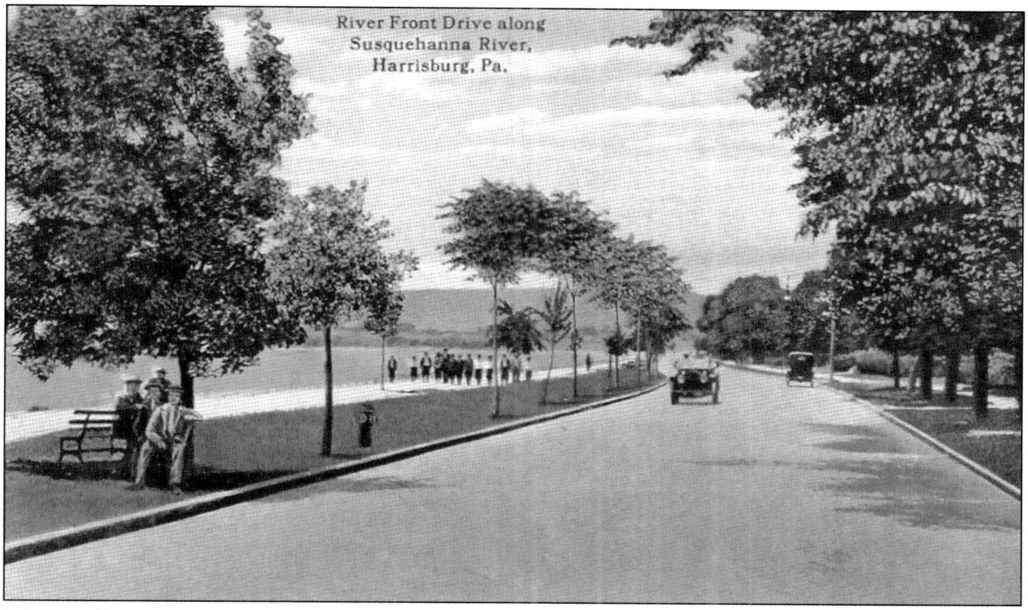

The William Penn Highway traveled for roughly seven miles along Front Street in Harrisburg (shown here in the 1920s as River Front Drive) until 1979, when it was routed onto the newly completed highway that bypassed downtown altogether. A lengthy portion of Front Street passes scenic Riverfront Park, which lines the Susquehanna River.

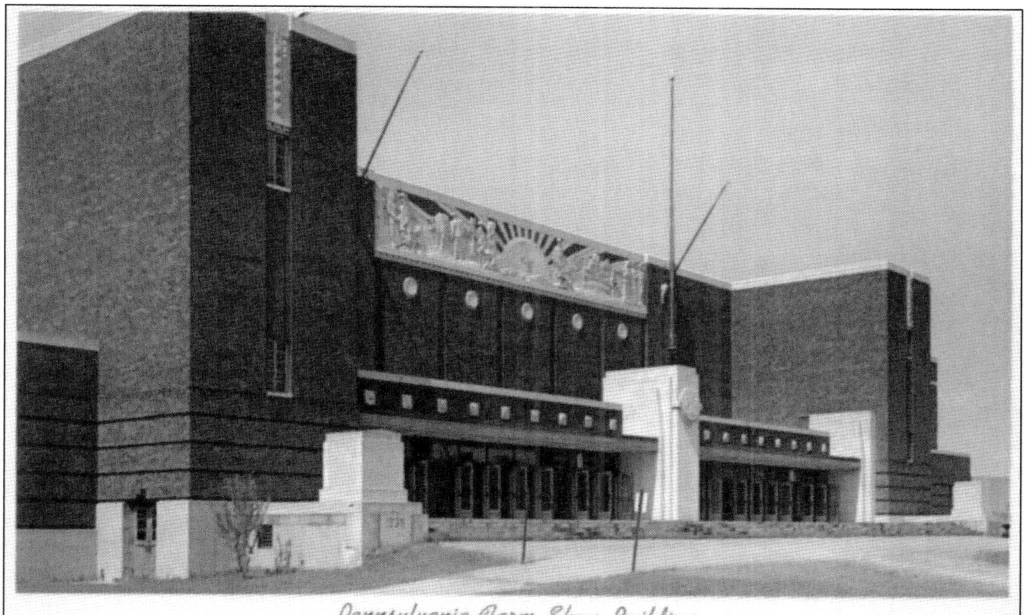

Directly along the modern alignment of Route 22 on the north side of Harrisburg is the huge complex that is home to the annual Pennsylvania Farm Show. The nation's largest indoor agricultural event, the show attracts half a million patrons each year. The complex consists of 11 buildings, the oldest of which was constructed in 1931. It also contains an arena that is home to sporting events.

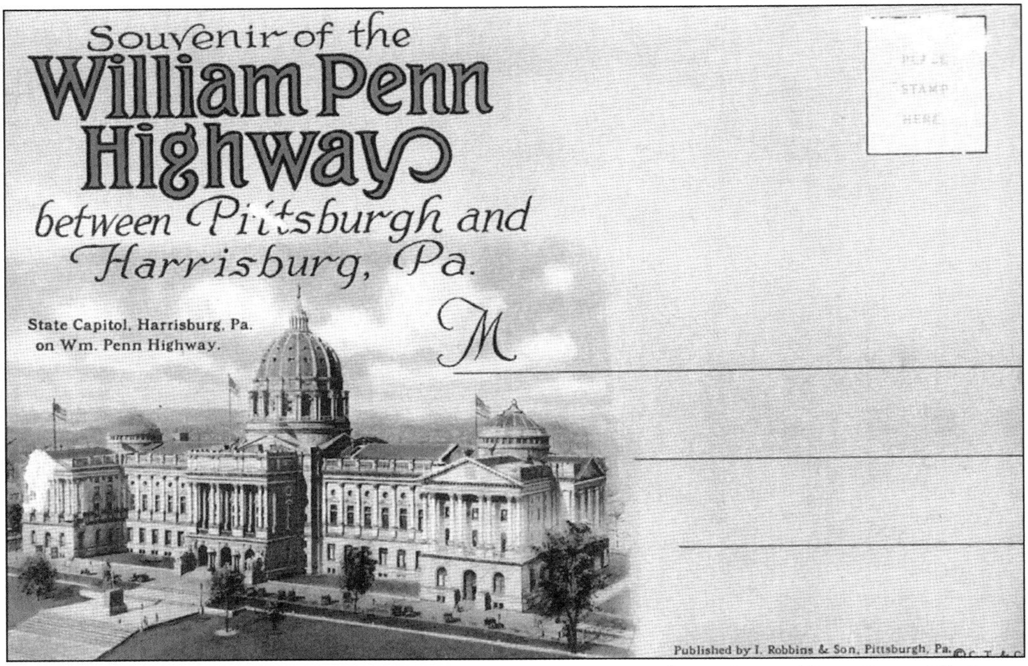

Above is the cover of a souvenir booklet of random images from the William Penn Highway to be used as a postcard and to help publicize the road. With the booklet having been made in the mid-1920s, there is no reference yet to Route 22. The cover image shows the state capitol in Harrisburg, which opened in 1906 at Third and State Streets (originally passed directly by the highway, and later Route 22). Shown below, the capitol building is covered by Vermont granite and is part of a large complex of government buildings. The dome rises to a peak of 272 feet in height and was inspired by St. Peter's Basilica in Rome. It is topped by a 14-foot gilded brass statue titled *Commonwealth*.

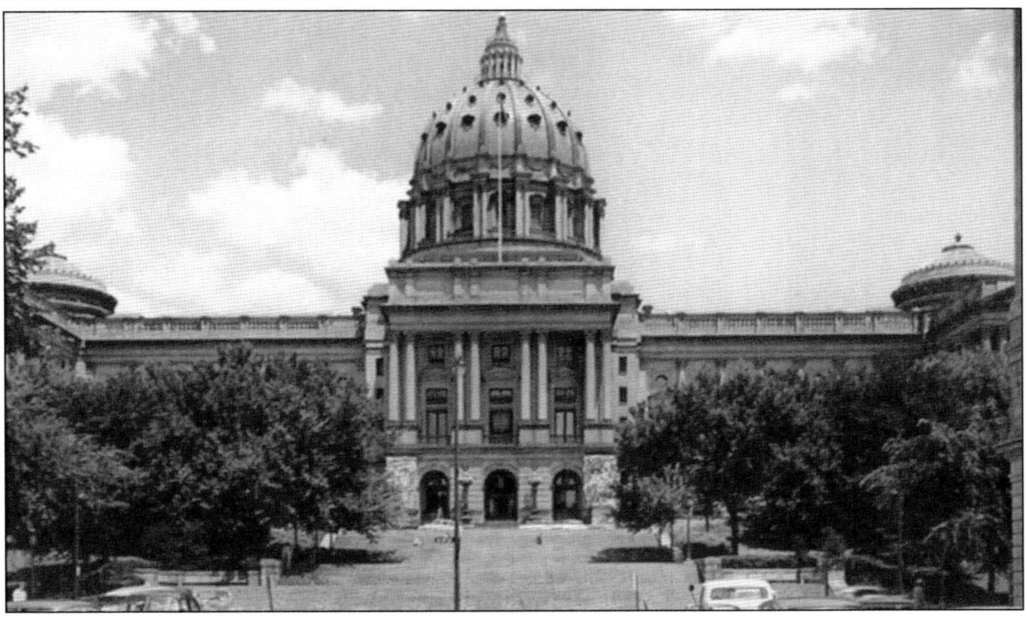

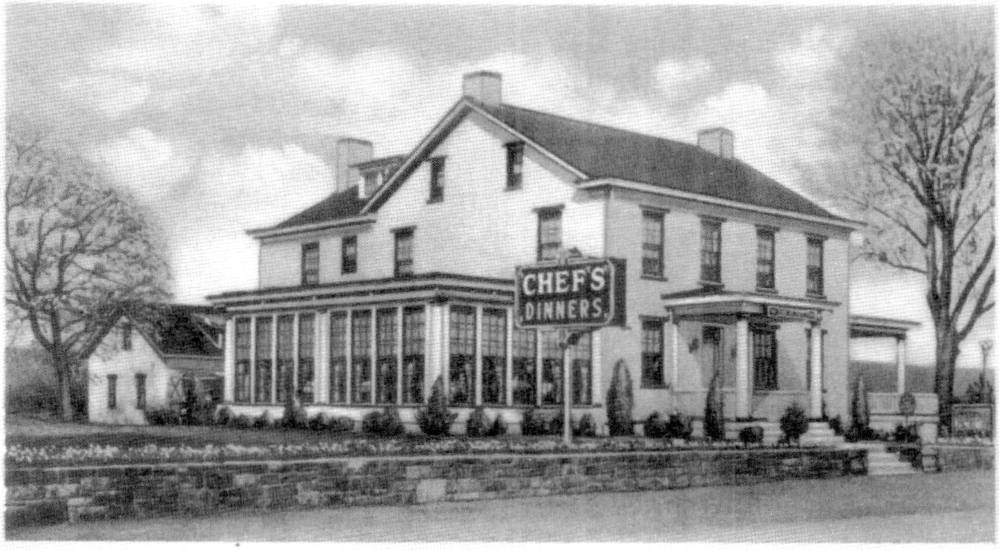

CHEF'S PAXTONIA INN
5½ Miles East of the State Capitol :: Route 22 (Formerly 43) :: The Short Route to Allentown and New York

The building shown here was originally a residence along Jonestown Road (State Highway 43) in Paxtonia, a suburb east of Harrisburg. In the mid-1930s, Route 22 was realigned onto Jonestown Road as a more direct path to Allentown, and many restaurants and motels began to appear along the road. By this point, the building was in use as Chef's Paxtonia Inn restaurant, shown above. By the end of World War II, it was being operated by Ruth and Ben Friedman and had been renamed Inn 22, as shown below on this card from the 1950s. This area continued to see commercial development over the years, and older structures like this were gradually eliminated in favor of modern businesses that line the road today.

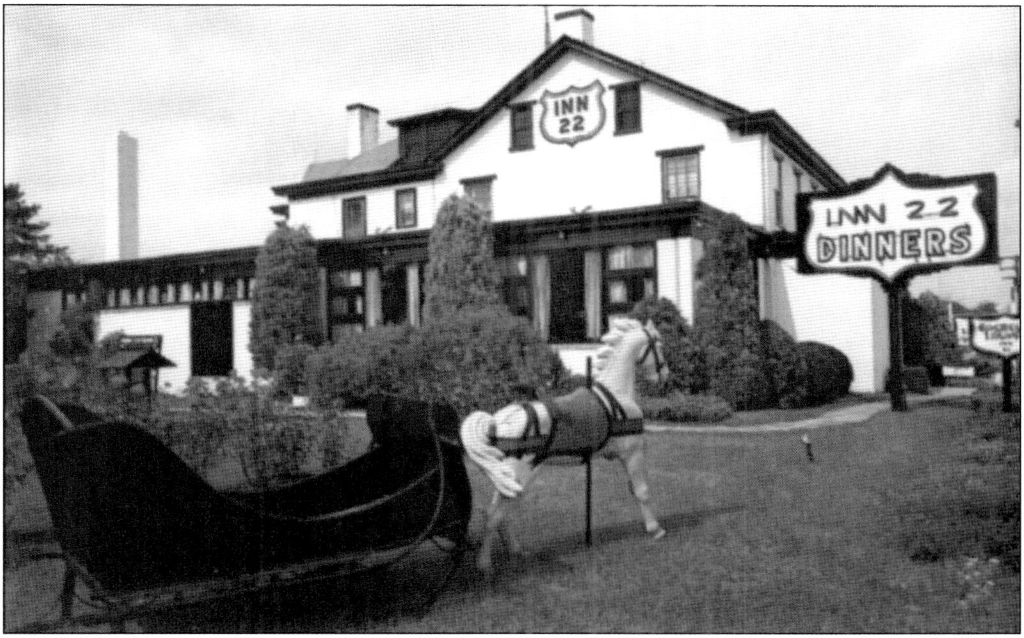

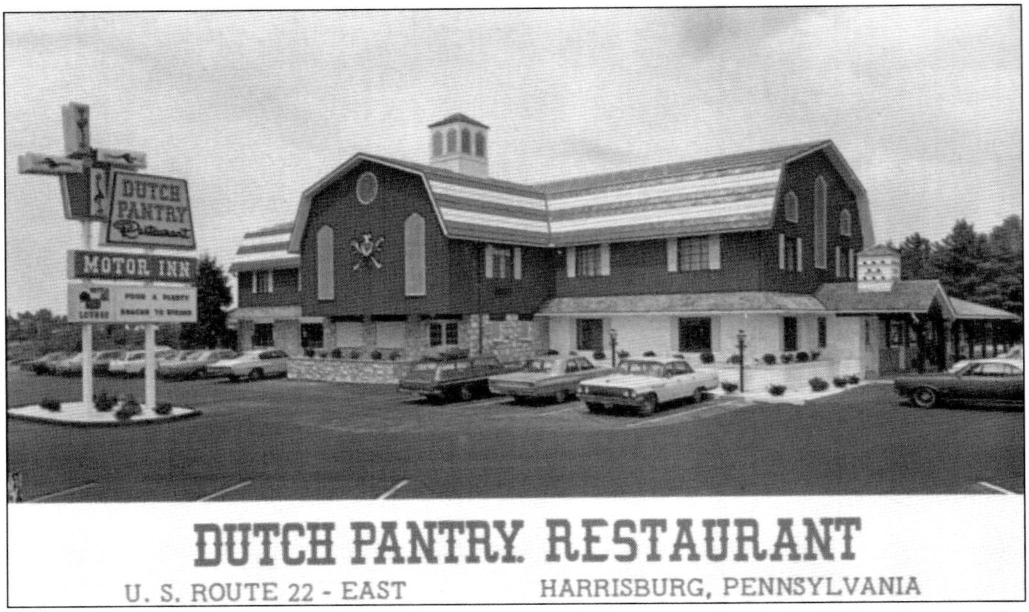

Dutch Pantry was a chain of restaurants that was founded in Pennsylvania in 1945 and eventually grew to more than 50 locations in 12 states. Featuring Pennsylvania Dutch–style food, the restaurants were painted red and white and featured hex signs and large cupolas. After peaking in popularity in the 1960s, the chain went into a gradual decline. This large restaurant, seen above in the early 1970s, was located adjacent to the Quality Motel, shown below, at 5680 Allentown Boulevard (Route 22), several miles east of Harrisburg. Established in 1939 as the Quality Courts chain of motels, the Quality Inns are today seen nationwide as part of the Choice Hotels International chain. This motel remains open today as a Comfort Inn, also part of Choice International. The Dutch Pantry is no longer standing.

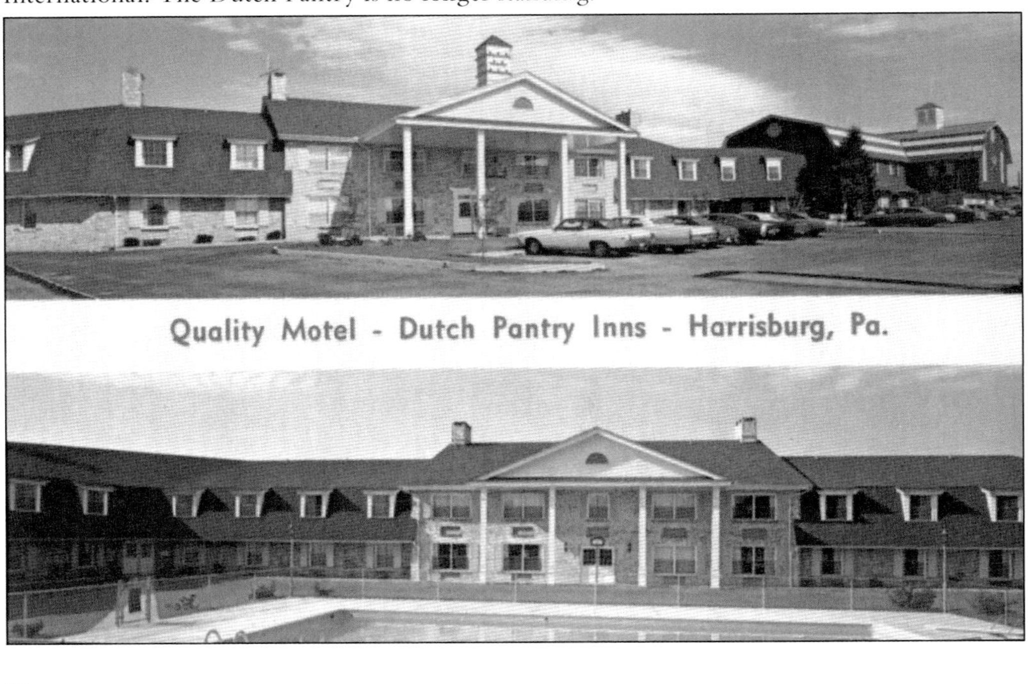

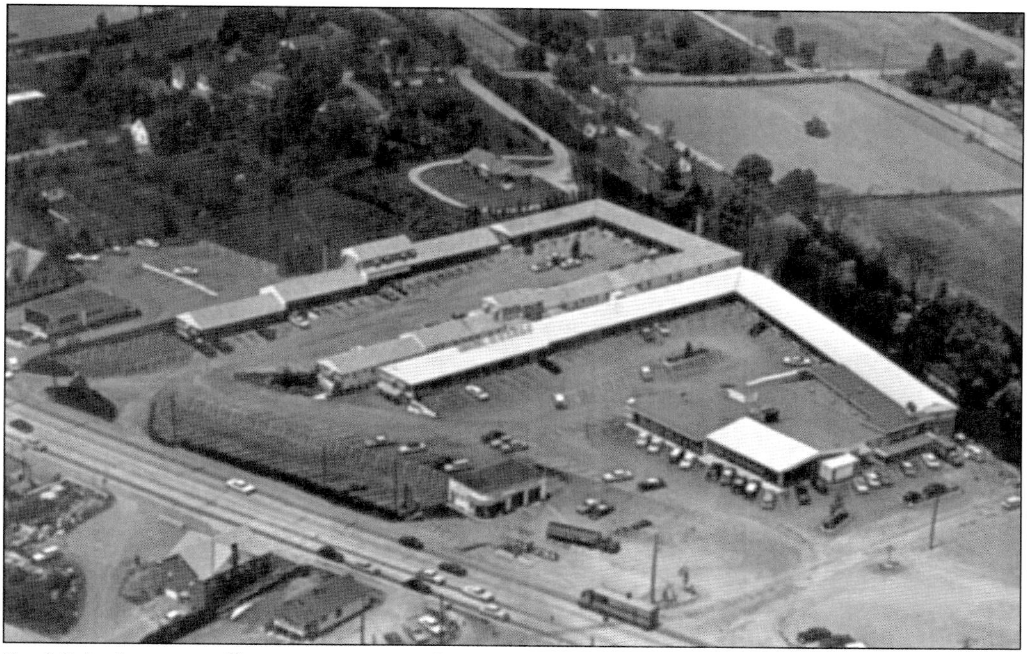

Established as a small motor court in the 1940s, the Capitol Motel stood four miles east of Harrisburg along Walnut Street (Route 22), near the present-day intersection of the Route 322 highway. Offering only 26 rooms when first open, the motel later expanded to 55 rooms by the early 1960s. In the aerial view above, from about 1970, the complex had expanded further, doubling in size with the addition of the rooms on the right side, with a white roof. Now with 115 rooms, the motel continued to operate for many years, with an adjacent coffee shop, dining room, cocktail lounge, banquet room, and conference rooms. The postcard below shows one of the motel's rooms around 1970. The complex is no longer standing.

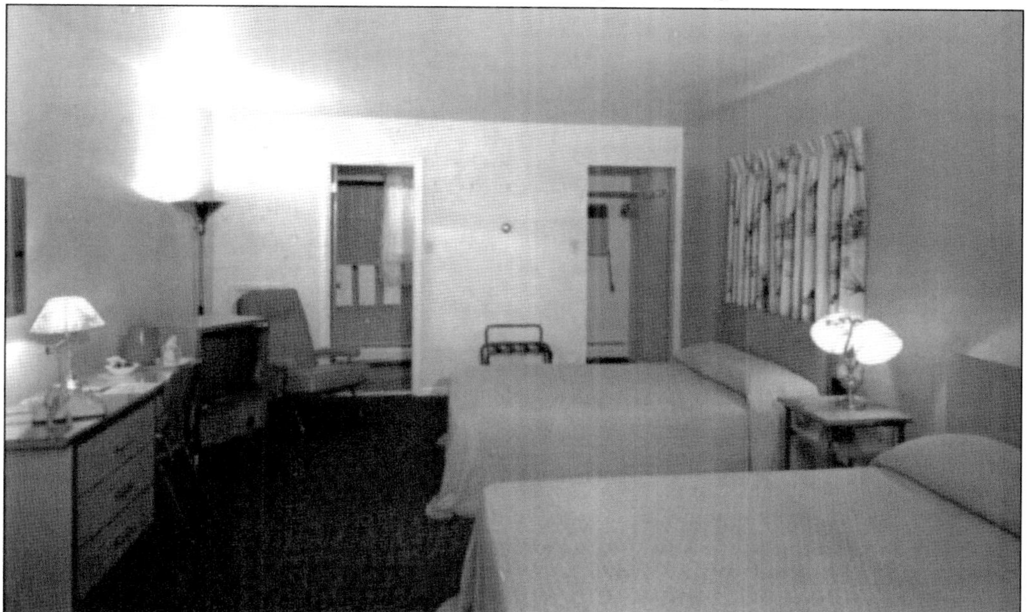

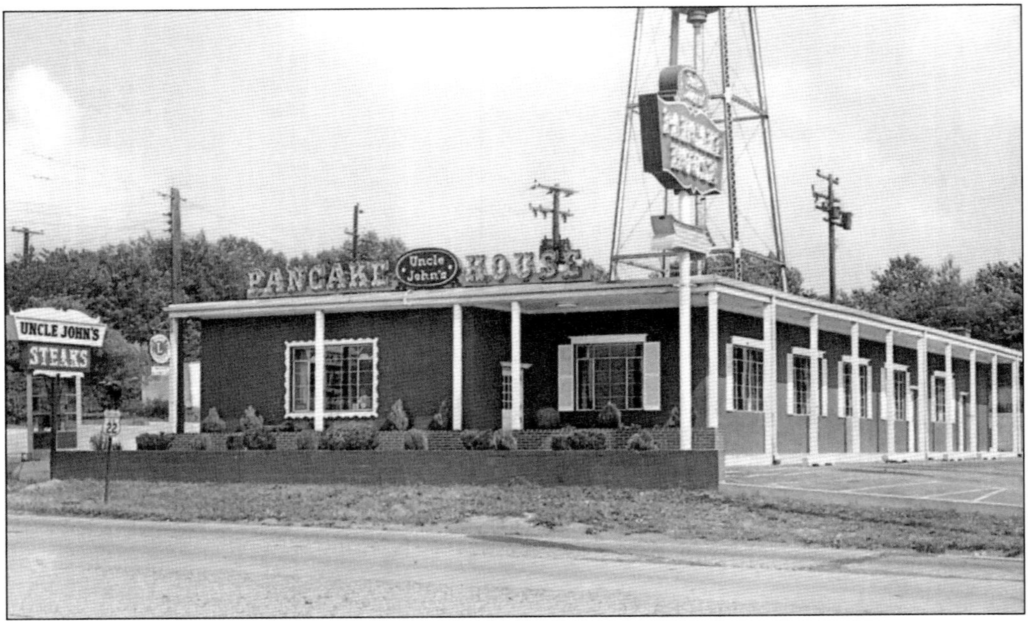

Uncle John's Pancake House, seen in 1964, stood along Route 22 on the eastern edge of Harrisburg. Similar family-owned establishments were a common sight along the federal highway system during the era, before chain restaurants began to dominate the industry. A Route 22 shield can be seen in front of the building.

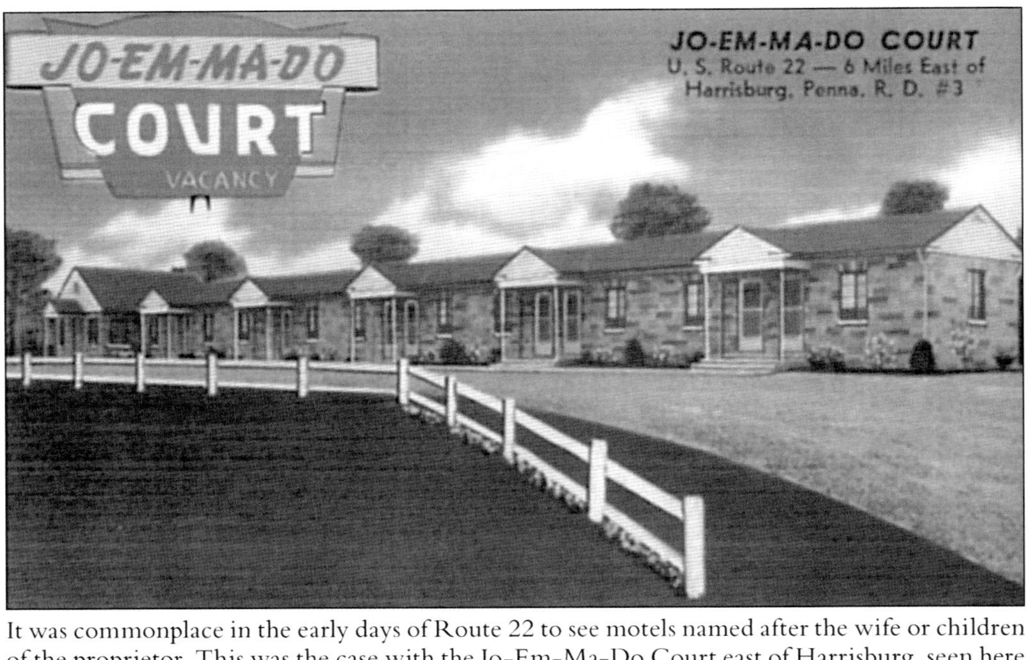

It was commonplace in the early days of Route 22 to see motels named after the wife or children of the proprietor. This was the case with the Jo-Em-Ma-Do Court east of Harrisburg, seen here around 1950. By this time, many roadside establishments were moving away from individual cabins in favor of more efficient single buildings with multiple units.

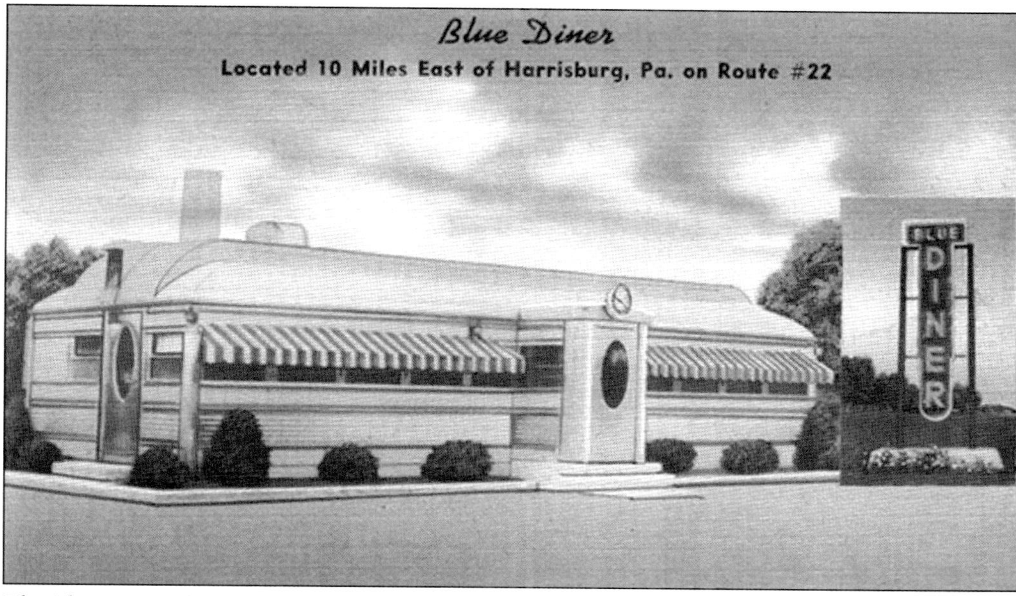

The Blue Diner, shown here in the late 1940s, was a small independent restaurant along Jonestown Road (which carried Route 22 at the time), approximately 10 miles east of Harrisburg. While most of these small, early establishments in the city's eastern suburbs are no longer standing, Route 22 continues to be lined with restaurants and motels through the area, due to its proximity to Hershey and Interstate 81.

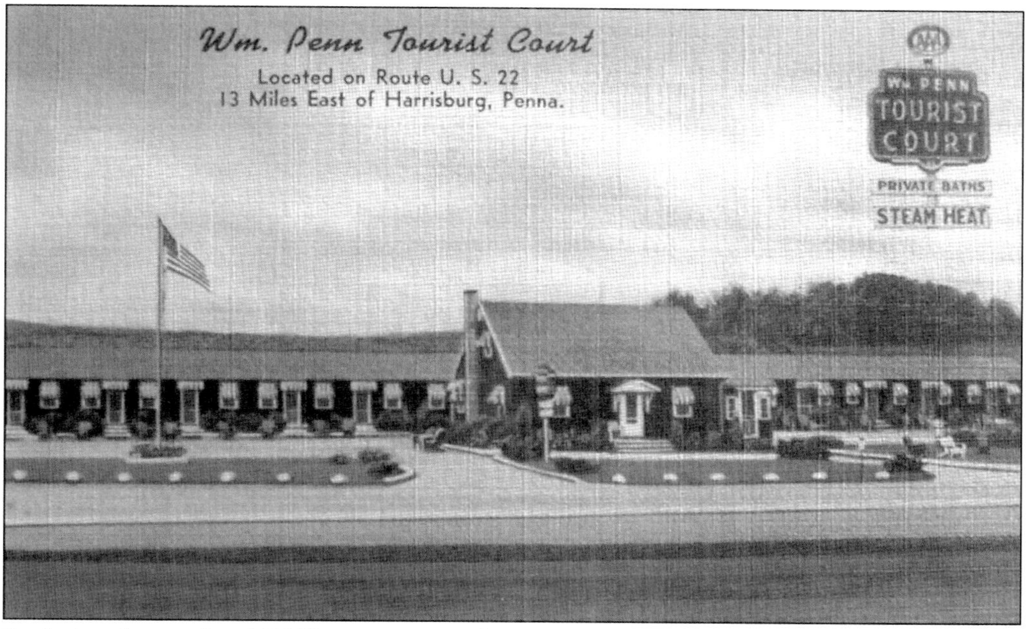

Predating the unrelated William Penn Motel in Monroeville, the William Penn Tourist Court stood 13 miles east of Harrisburg. It was typical of the many motels along the federal highway system in the years prior to the appearance of chain motels. The appearance of the AAA logo from the American Automobile Association gave travelers some assurance that the establishment was of acceptable quality.

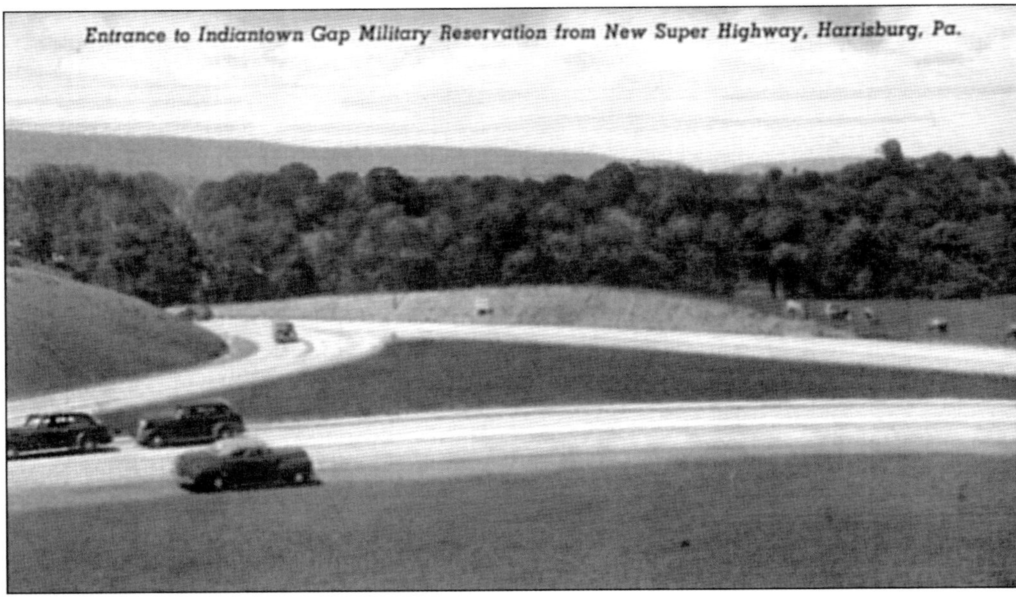

Fort Indiantown Gap is an 18,000-acre military post used jointly by the US Army and National Guard. Standing just north of Route 22 and Interstate 81, roughly 20 miles east of Harrisburg, the post was established in 1931, on the site of a fort that had originally been established by Colonial Pennsylvania in 1755. Employed heavily for training troops during World War II, it has been used during every American military conflict since then. Shown above is the entrance to the post from the new Route 22 superhighway in the 1940s, and below is a view of the mess hall and tents inside the camp from the same era. Both images show Blue Mountain in the background.

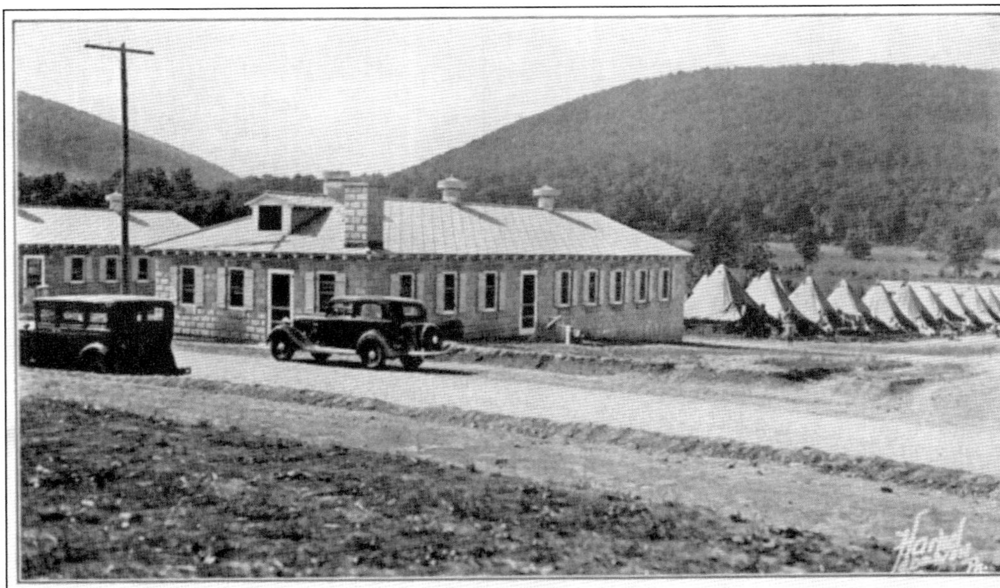

Mess Hall and Battery Street—Indiantown Gap, Pa.

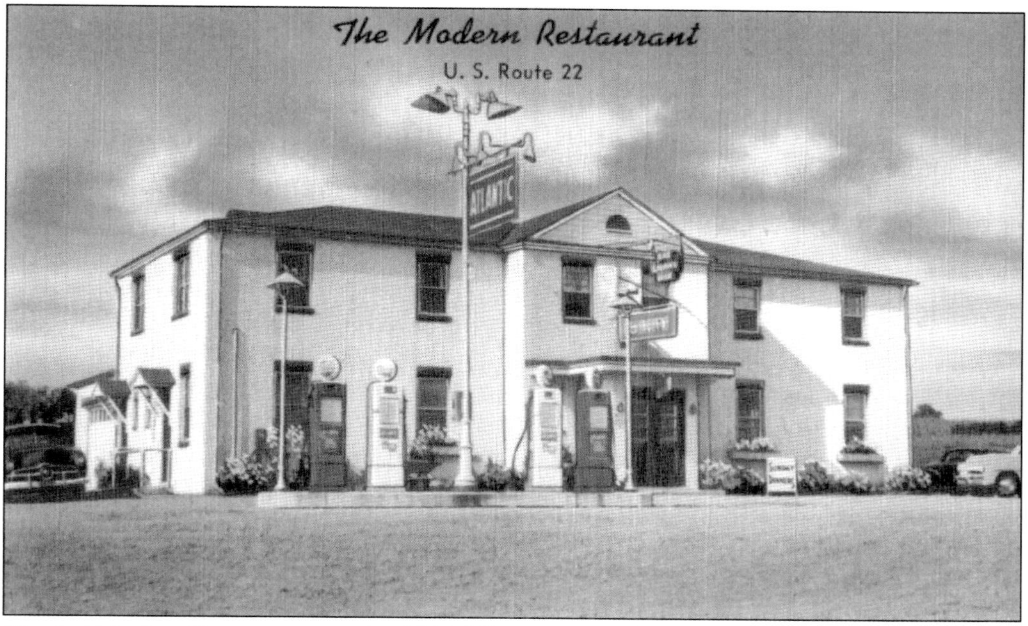

Charles' Modern Restaurant stood at 9916 Allentown Road (Route 22), at the northeast corner of its intersection with State Route 743 near Grantville. Shown around 1950, it also featured an Atlantic gasoline station and 10 rooms for overnight stays. The building remains standing today and is occupied by the Villa Rosa Italian restaurant.

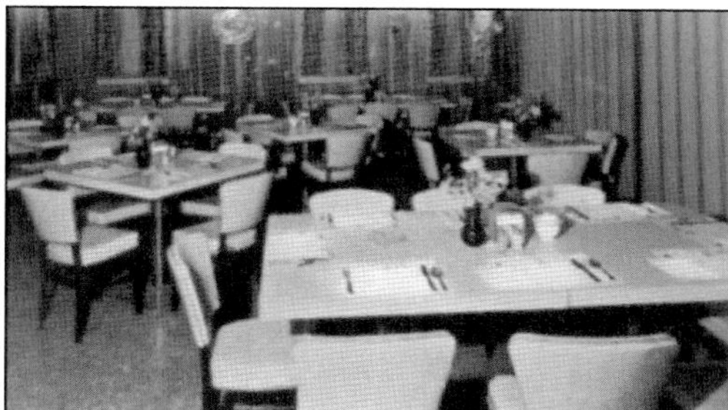

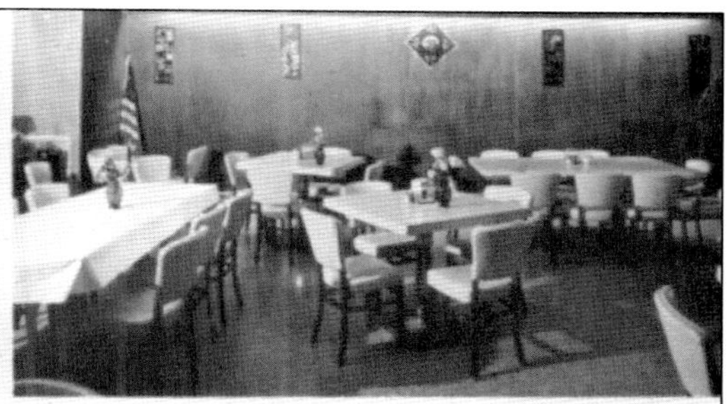

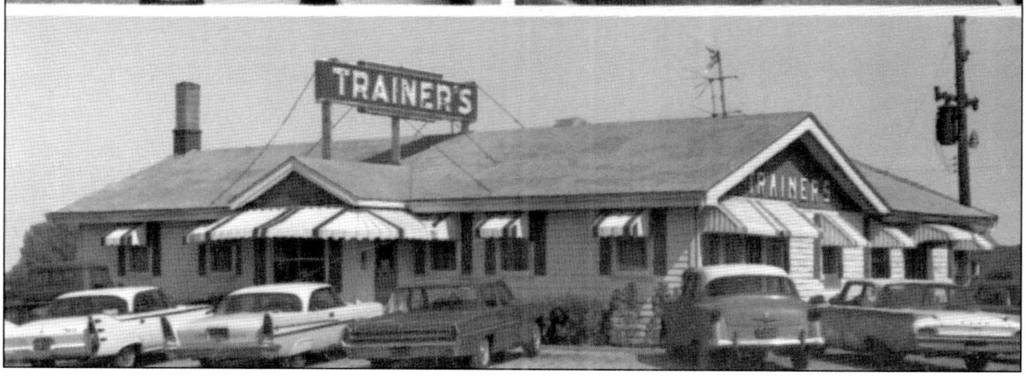

The segment of Route 22 between Harrisburg and Allentown is mostly rural but is dotted with small towns where travelers could rest and eat. Trainer's Restaurant, shown here around 1963, stood along Route 22 in Jonestown. Despite offering more upscale dining than the typical roadside diner, it is no longer in business.

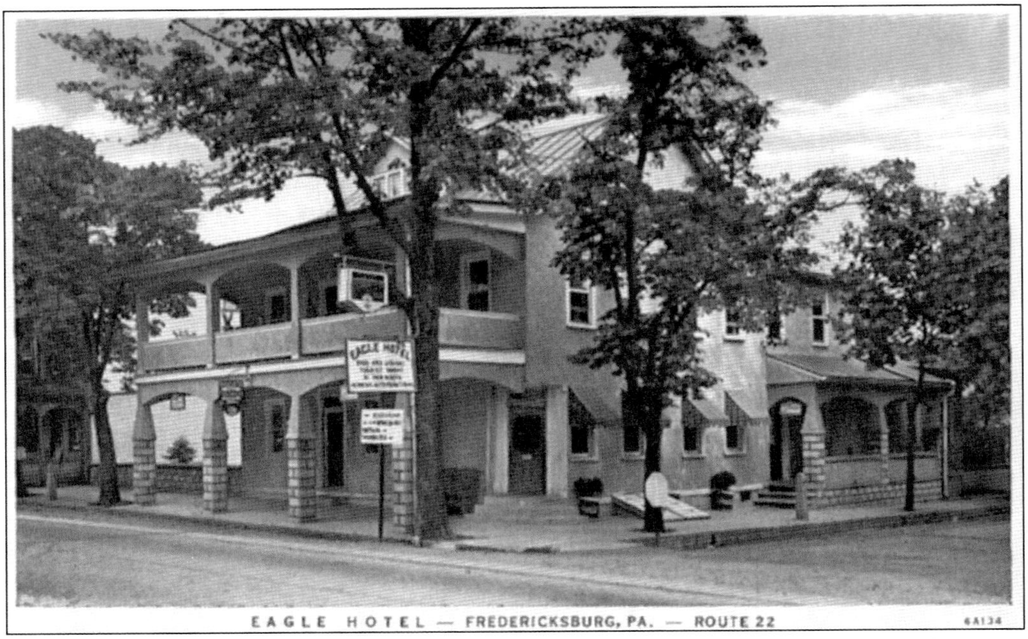

The Travelers Repose was established as a hotel in 1866 at 123 East Main Street (formerly Route 22) in Fredericksburg. Operating under a series of different names in its lifetime, it was the Eagle Hotel, with a restaurant and bar, in the 1930s, when this postcard was made. Since 1991, the structure has been home to Gubba's Pizza restaurant.

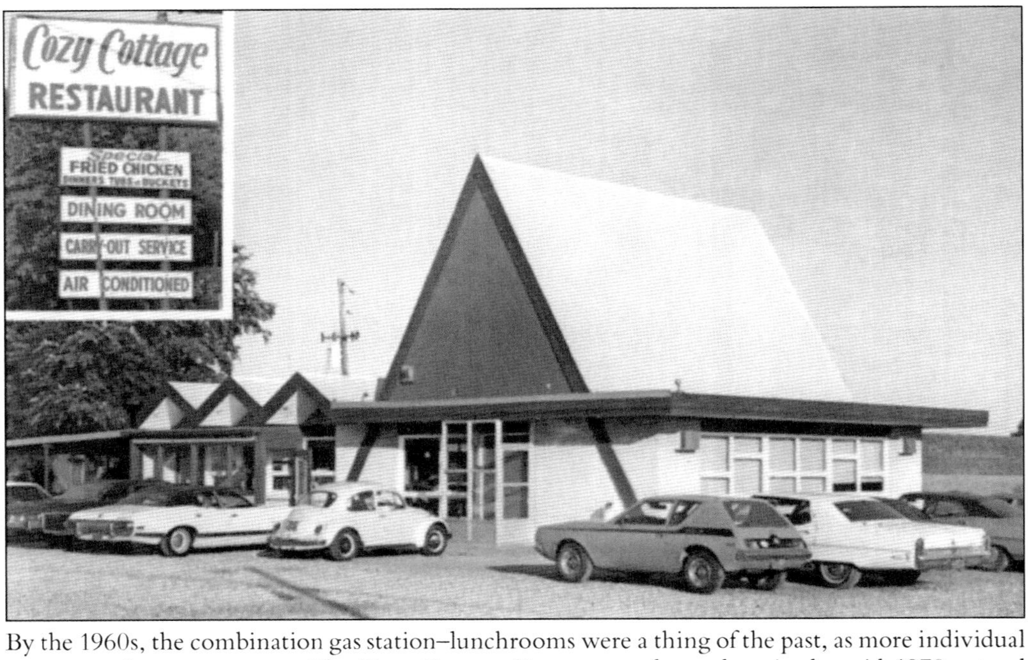

By the 1960s, the combination gas station–lunchrooms were a thing of the past, as more individual restaurants began to appear. The Cozy Cottage Restaurant, shown here in the mid-1970s, stood along Route 22 in Fredericksburg. The modern, eye-catching, A-frame architecture stood in stark contrast to the basic architecture of most comparable restaurants of the era.

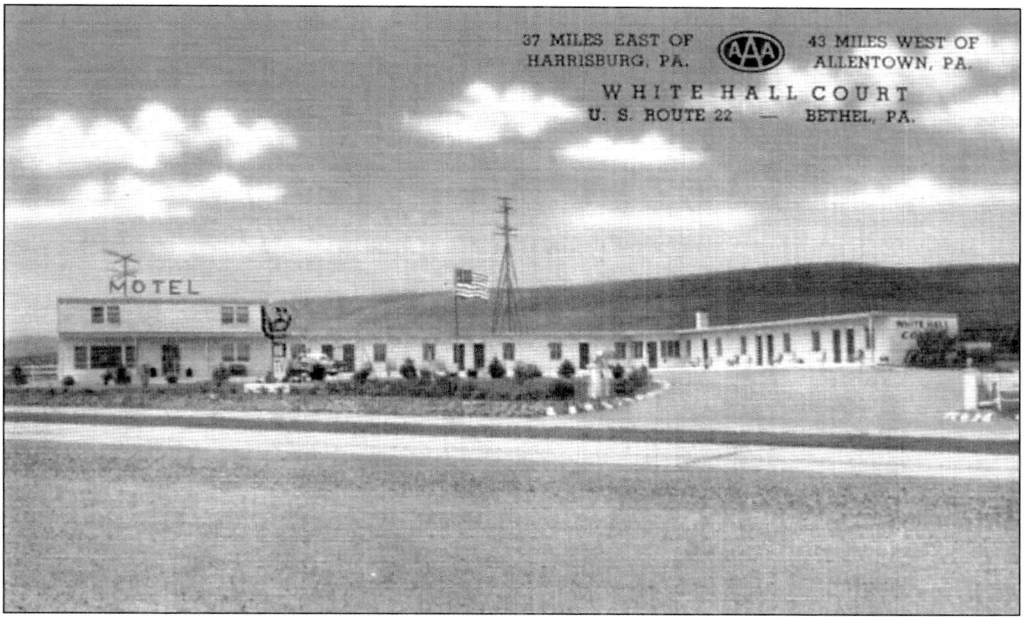

The village of Bethel is nearly halfway between Harrisburg and Allentown and has been the site of several motels over the years. Shown here in the early 1950s is the White Hall Court, directly along Route 22. By the postwar era, the days of individual tourist cabins were giving way to long motel buildings with individual rooms.

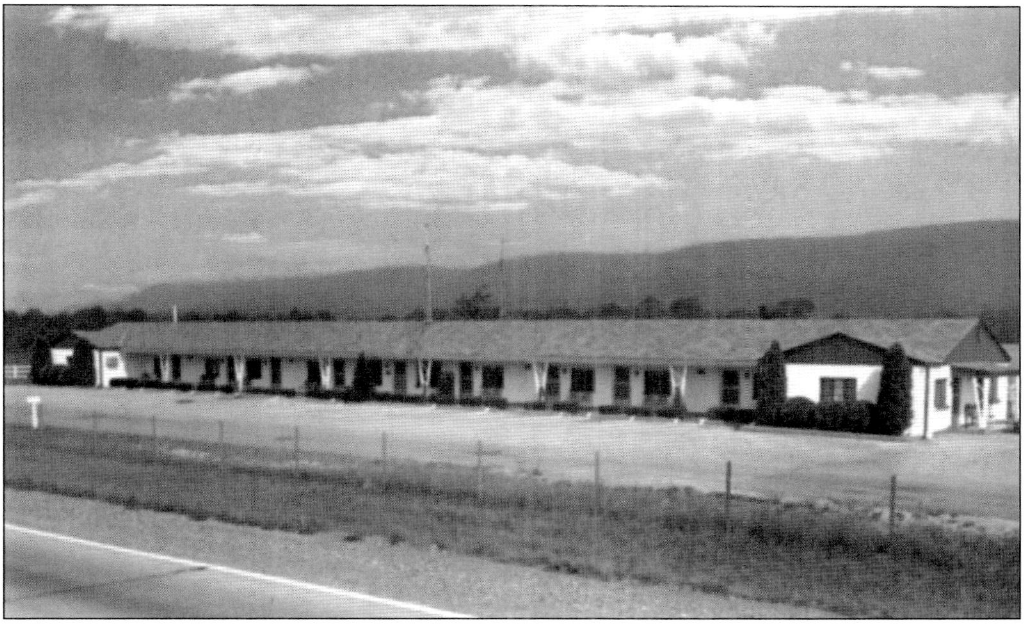

Some establishments offered travelers only the most basic amenities, such as the Lamp Lighter Motel in Bethel, shown here in 1973. In the background is the lengthy ridge known as Blue Mountain, which stretches 150 miles from the New Jersey state line to northern Maryland, ranging between 1,400 and 2,200 feet in height.

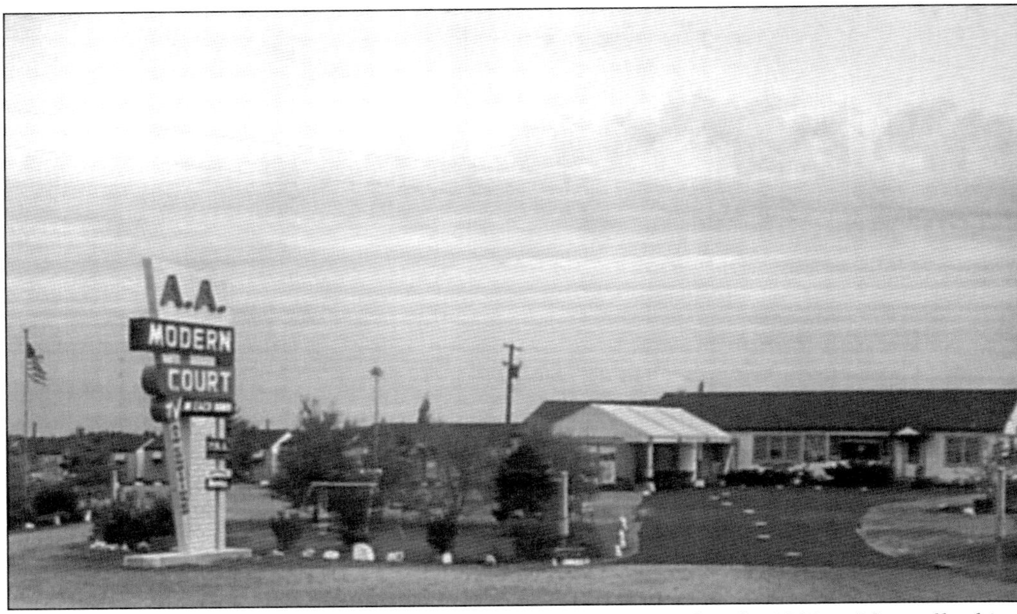

Many successful motels along the William Penn Highway opened in the 1930s with small cabins, often without running water, before modernizing them into tourist courts by the 1950s. The A.A. Modern Courts in the village of Bethel, seen here in the mid-1950s, was an example of this, having opened in the highway's early days with only the most basic lodging and gradually offering more amenities to travelers over time.

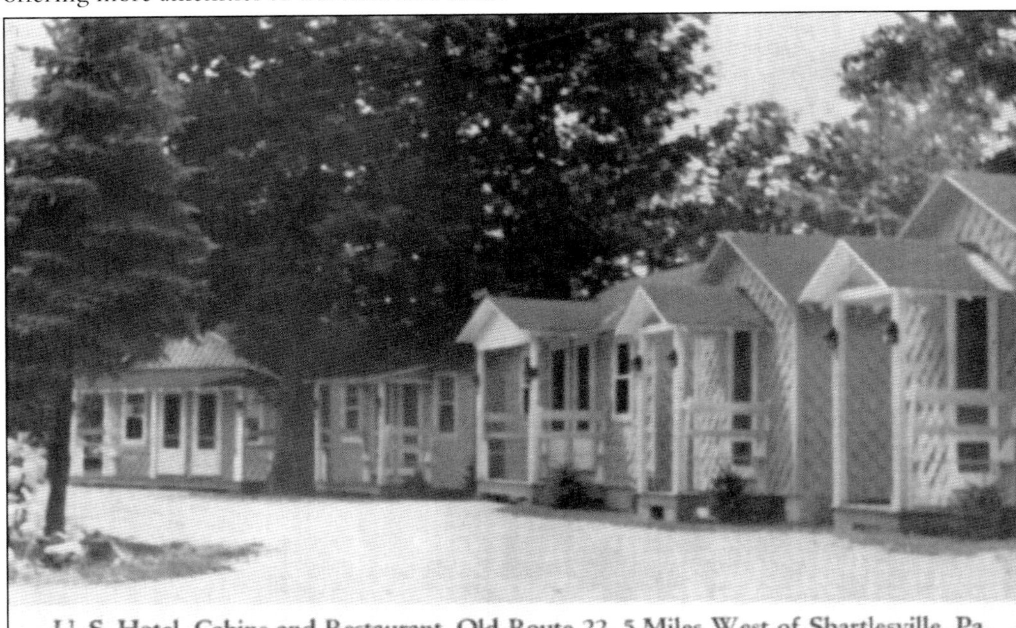

The US Hotel, Cabins, and Restaurant opened in the 1930s in the countryside five miles west of Shartlesville. Seen here in the late 1950s, it was well maintained despite its age and the fact that Route 22 had been realigned onto the new highway nearby (which would later carry Interstate 78 as well) by this time.

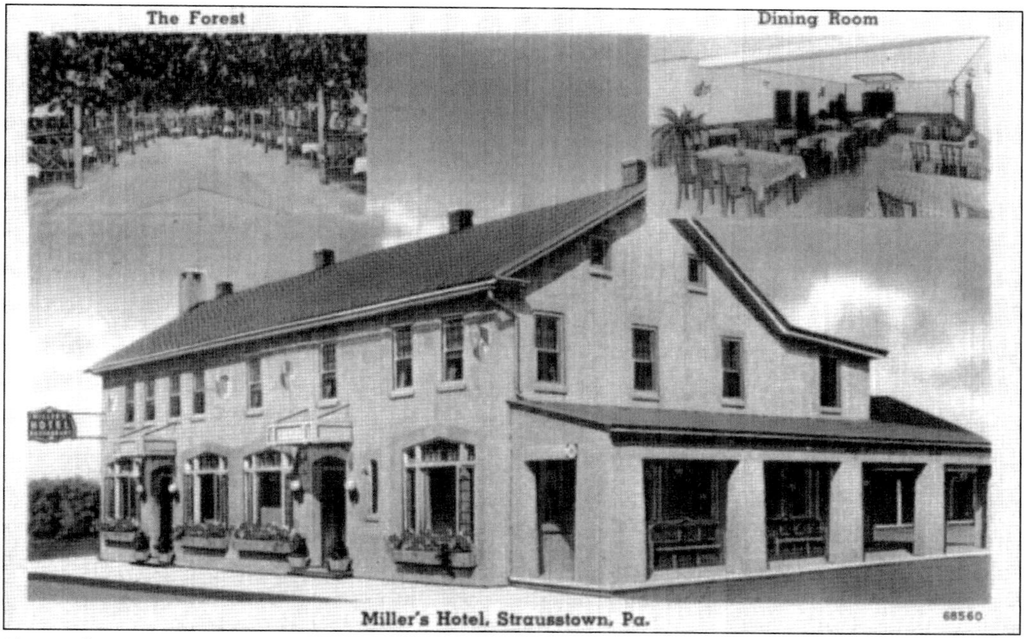

Shown here around 1940, Miller's Hotel operated in one of the oldest buildings in the village of Strausstown, and its use as a hotel predated by many years the realignment of Route 22 through the village. Although the hotel has long since closed, the stone building remains standing on Main Street (also known here as Olde 22) today.

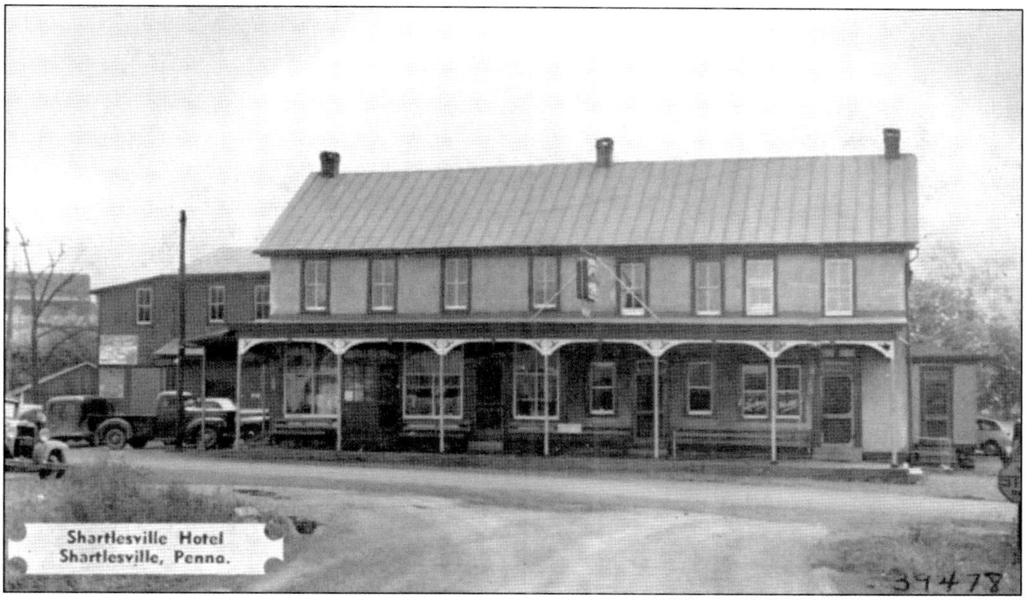

The century-old Shartlesville Hotel, shown here in the 1930s, was a local favorite for its seemingly endless menu of Pennsylvania Dutch food, available on a daily basis. Despite its popularity, however, the small hotel and restaurant closed in August 2012. Located at 5727 Old Route 22, the building is still standing today.

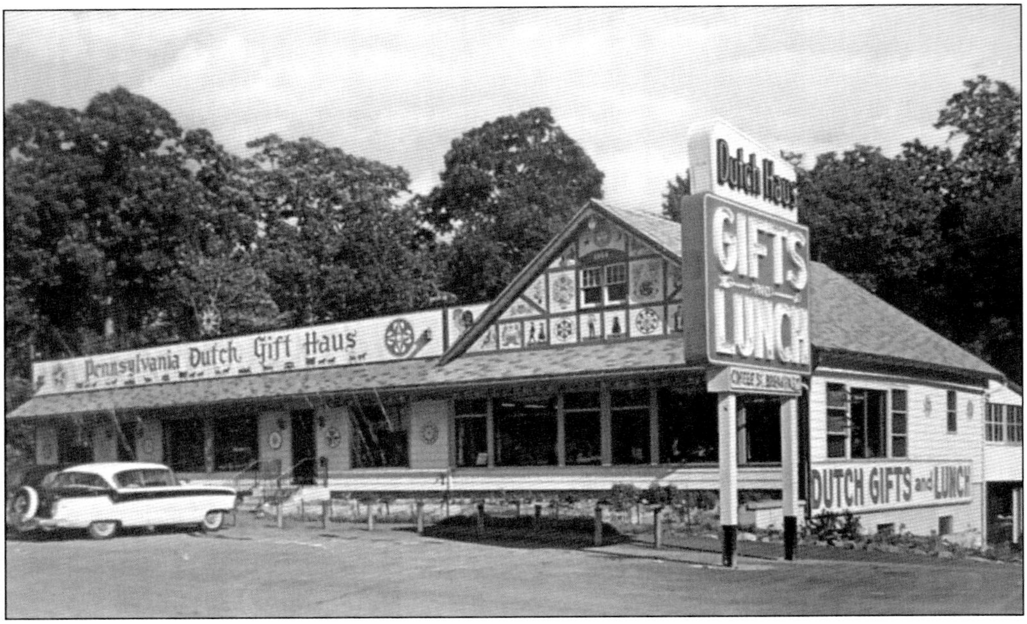

Located in the village of Shartlesville, facing Route 22 and Interstate 78, is the Pennsylvania Dutch Gift Haus (shown above), a souvenir shop filled with items typical of the Pennsylvania Dutch culture, such as hex signs, recipe books, dolls, candy, and so forth. Next door is Roadside America (shown below), billed as the "World's Greatest Indoor Miniature Village." Typical of the tourist attractions that were commonly seen in the early days of the federal highway system, it has stood at the site for more than 60 years. Both attractions are owned and operated by the family of Roadside America founder Laurence Gieringer.

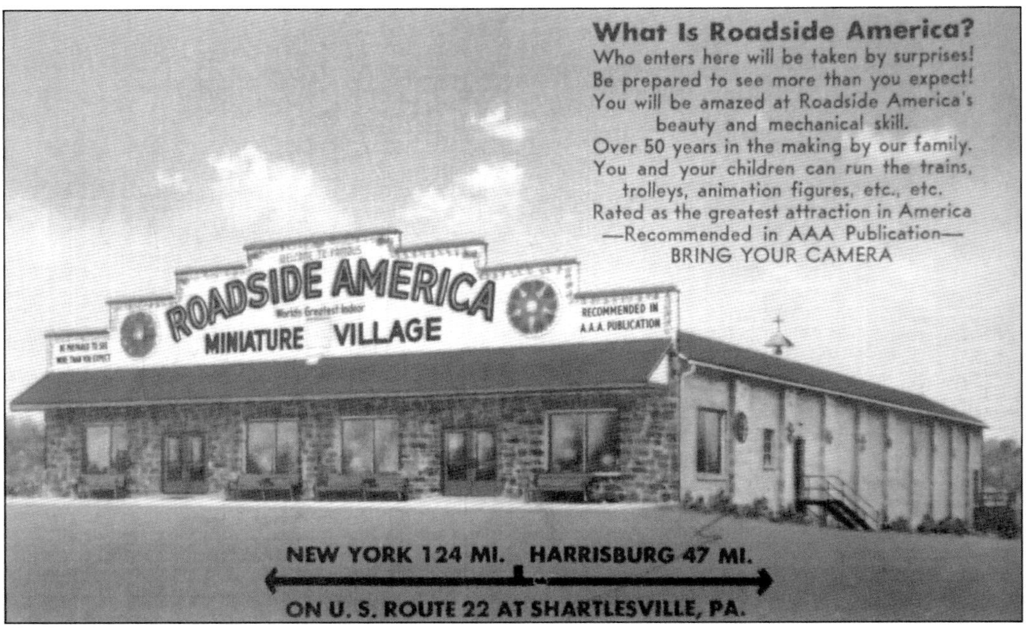

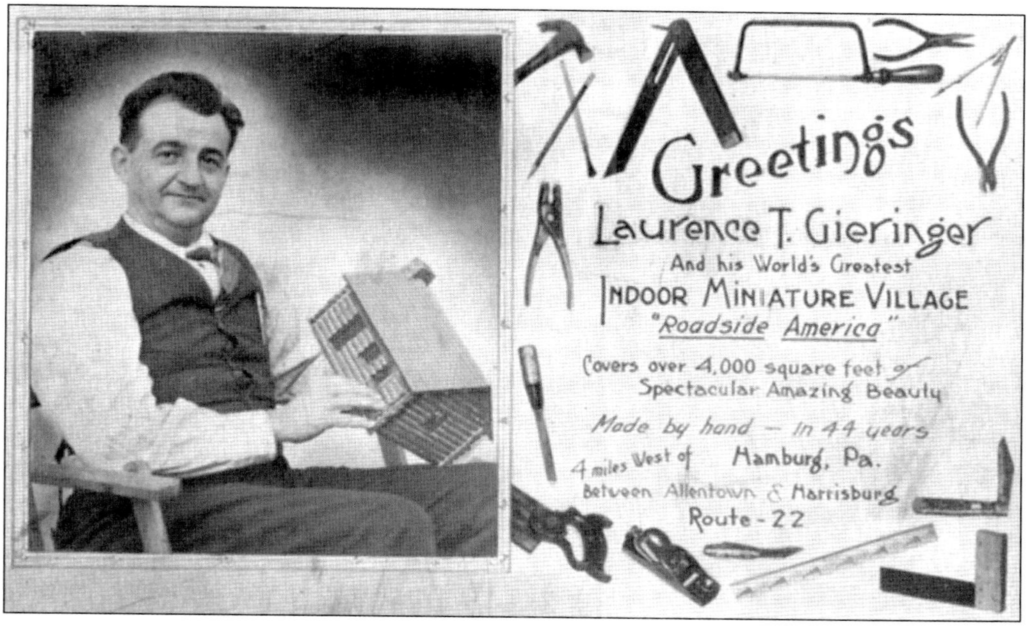

Roadside America was established by Laurence Gieringer (shown above), a master carpenter and painter, who began building miniature houses, towns, landscapes, and railroads in 1899, at the age of five. After opening his first version of Roadside America in Reading in 1939, he moved it to its current location in 1954. The display covers 8,000 square feet and contains over 300 miniature structures, 18 trains, trollies, and cable cars, 10,000 trees, more than 4,000 miniature people, and more than 21,000 feet of electrical wiring. One of its many city scenes is shown below. Gieringer died in 1963, but his family keeps the display in operation today.

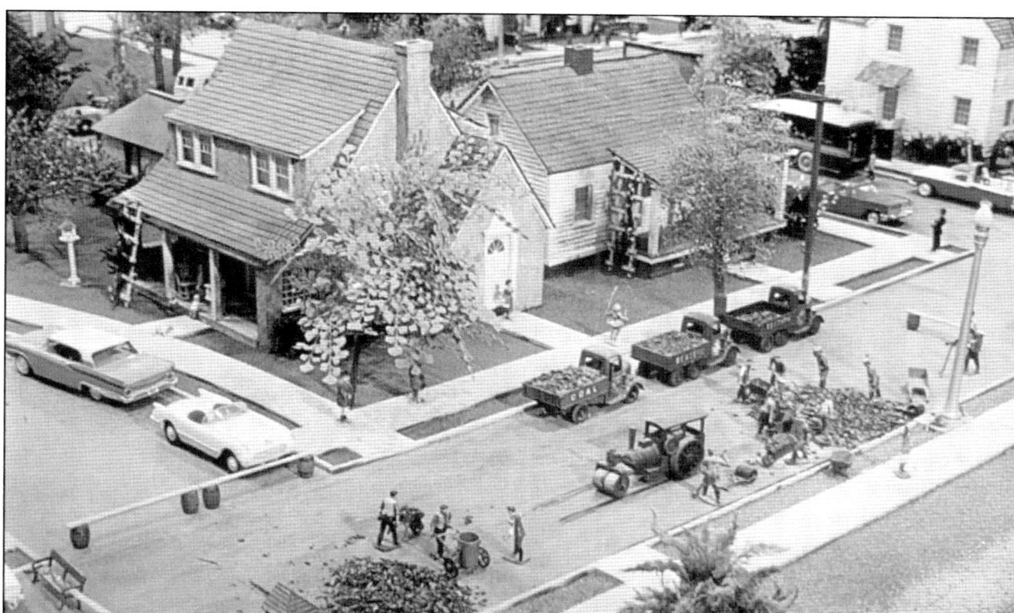

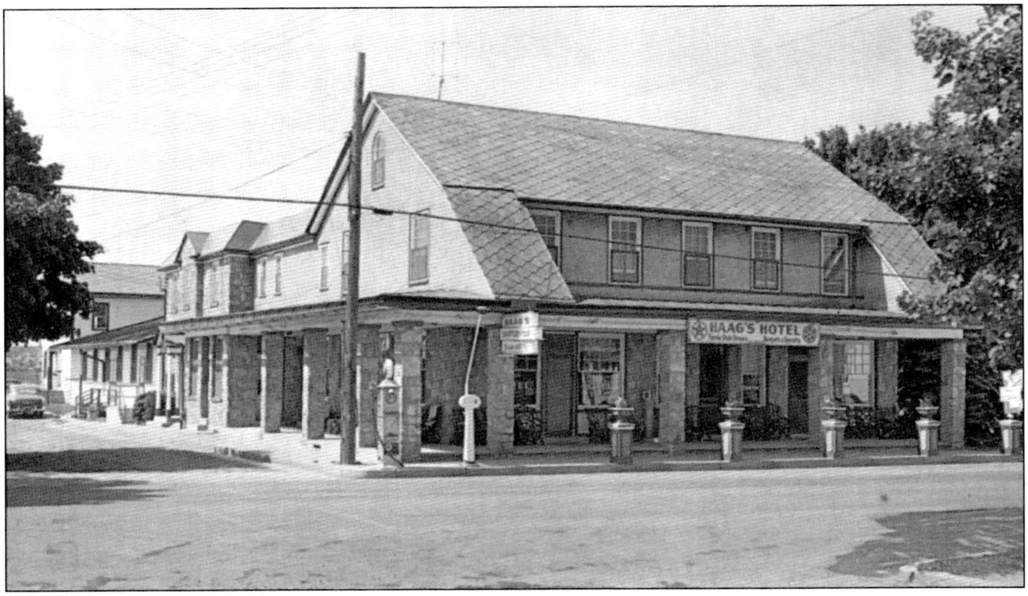

Haag's Hotel, shown above in the 1950s, opened in 1916 in the village of Shartlesville, midway between Harrisburg and Allentown. Located at Third and Main Streets (Old Route 22, also known in this area as Hex Highway), the small hotel has seven rooms available for overnight stays, and five of these have private baths. Known mainly for its extensive menu of Pennsylvania Dutch food (shown below), it recently celebrated its 100th year of business despite the fact that Route 22 was rerouted onto its modern alignment many years ago. The old Texaco gas pump seen at street side remains in place today, although it no longer pumps gas.

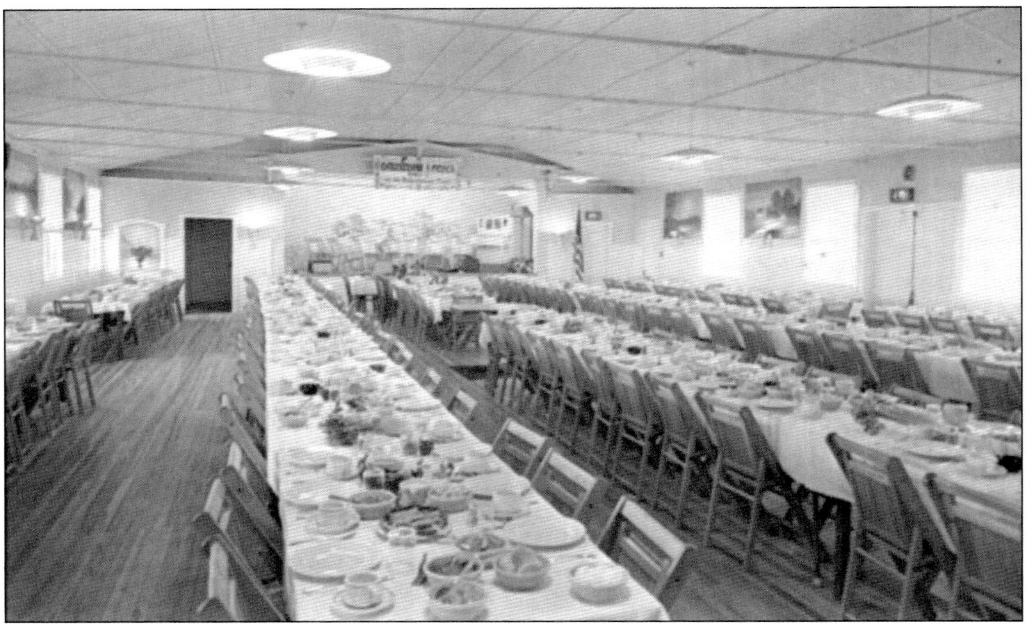

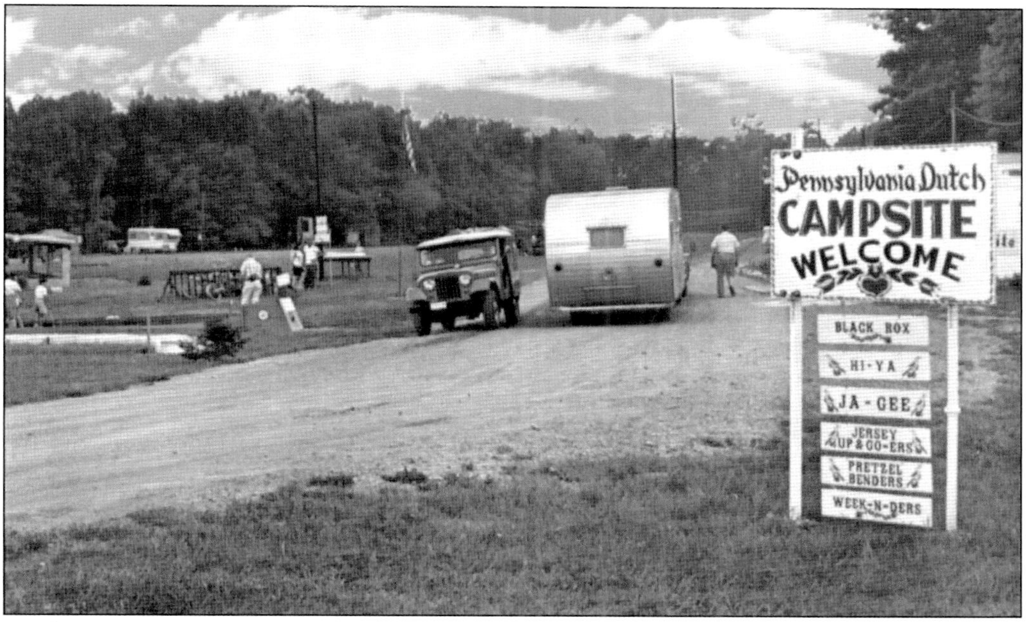

In addition to the many small motels that lined Route 22 in the early days, there were numerous campgrounds along its course as well. The Pennsylvania Dutch Campsite in Shartlesville, shown here in the early 1970s, provided amenities for campers in both tents and trailers for overnight as well as extended stays.

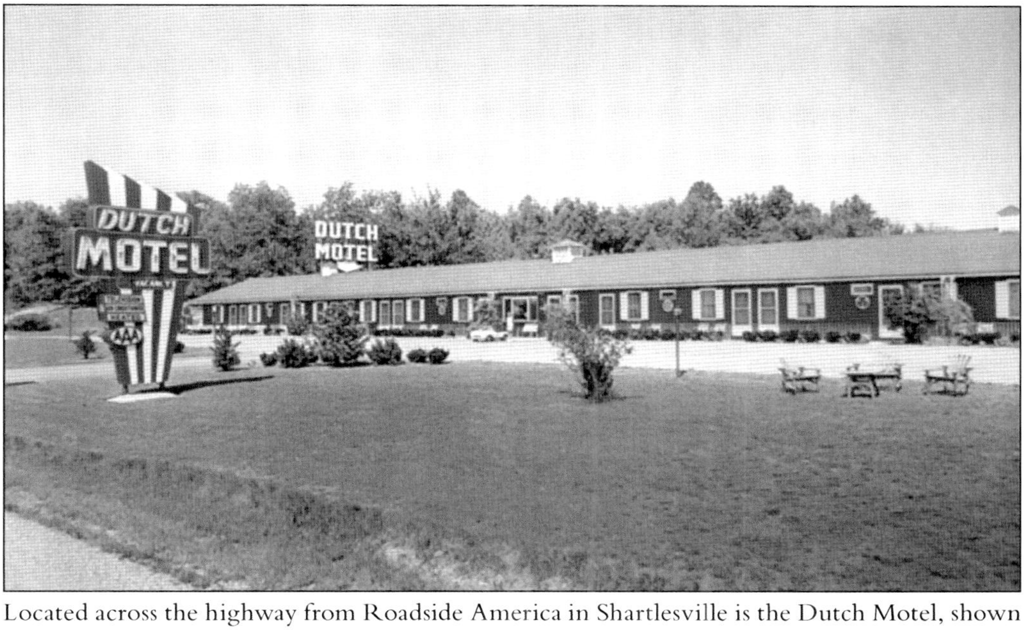

Located across the highway from Roadside America in Shartlesville is the Dutch Motel, shown in the 1970s. Still open today, the motel has a Pennsylvania Dutch influence like most other businesses in the village. The sign noting approval by AAA was a common sighting on motels for many years, assuring a specific level of quality in the accommodations.

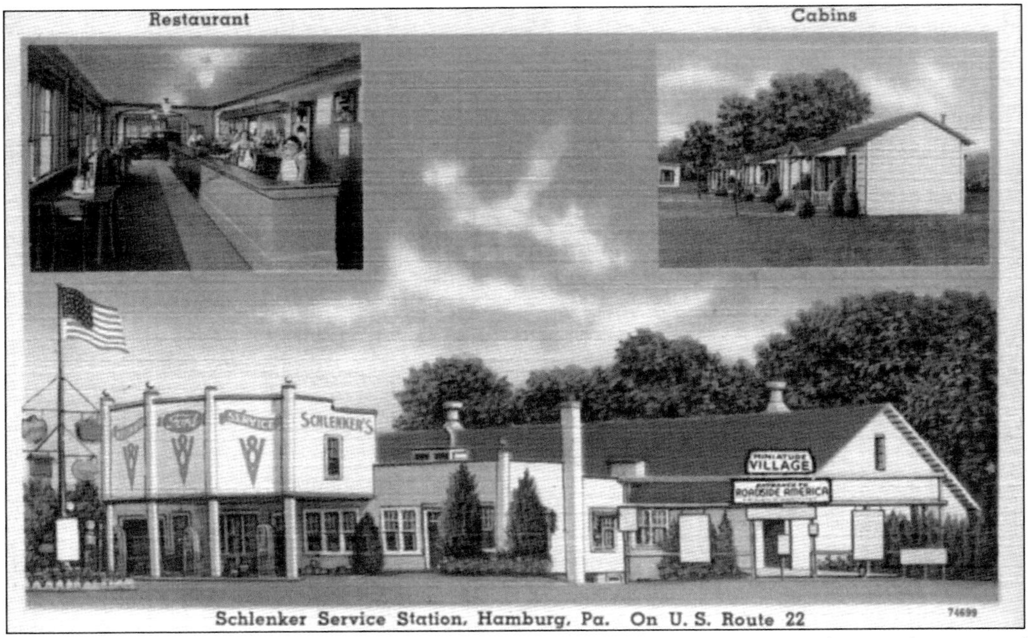

Pictured here in the 1930s, the Schlenker Motor Company was located four miles west of Hamburg. It was a dealership and service station for Ford, Mercury, and Lincoln Zephyr cars and sold Esso gasoline. It also had cabins for tourists, a restaurant, and a bar serving local Sunshine Beer. Its Art Deco canopy over the service area gave it the appearance of being somewhat larger than it actually was.

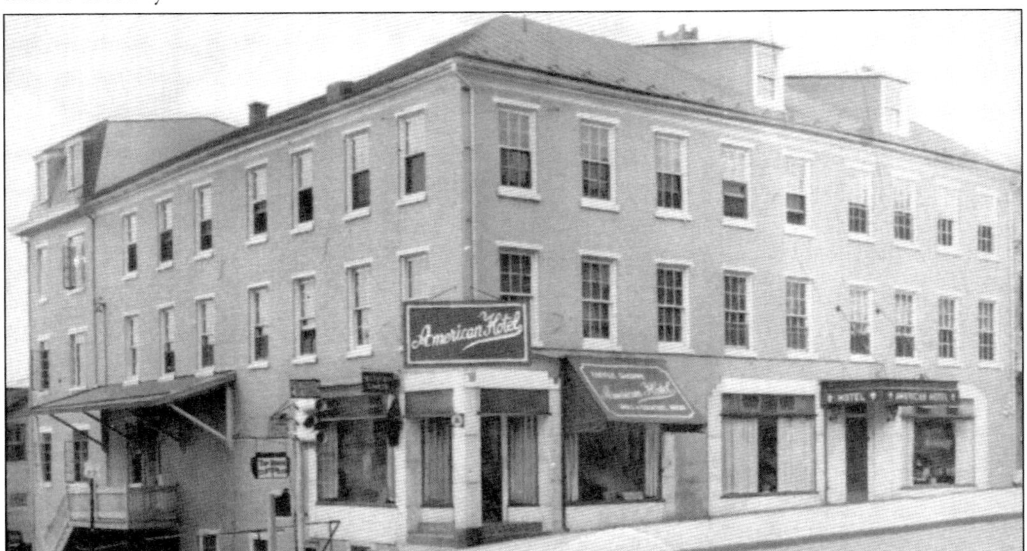

Pictured here in the 1930s, the American House Hotel stands at the corner of State and North Fourth Streets in the borough of Hamburg. Built between 1813 and 1853, the structure is a historic landmark in the town, having served travelers for more than a century. After being closed for many years, it was renovated and reopened in the 2000s for fine dining, before closing again in 2013.

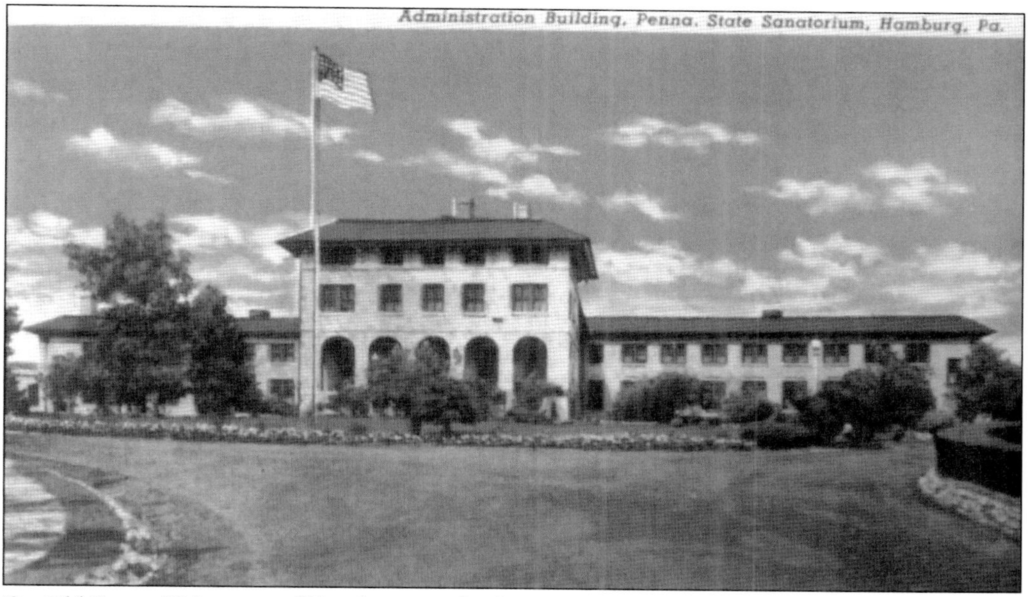

On Old Route 22 just east of Hamburg stands a large complex that originally housed the Hamburg tuberculosis sanatorium. Built in 1914, the complex consists of 43 buildings on 164 acres. After the facility had become obsolete in the late 1950s, it was converted into a home for people with mental and physical disabilities. Shown here is the administration building.

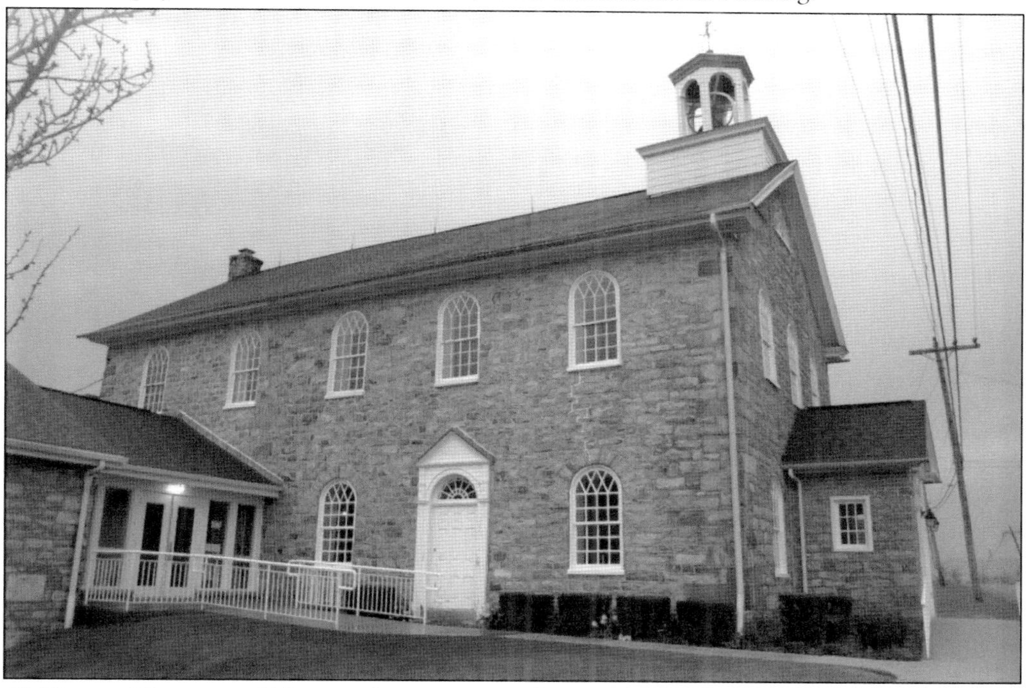

Old Route 22 runs parallel to modern Route 22 for much of the span between Harrisburg and Allentown. Along the road just east of Hamburg stands St. Paul's Lutheran Church. Shown as it appears today, the stone building was erected in 1832 to replace a log church that was first built on the site in 1756, making it one of the oldest congregations in the region.

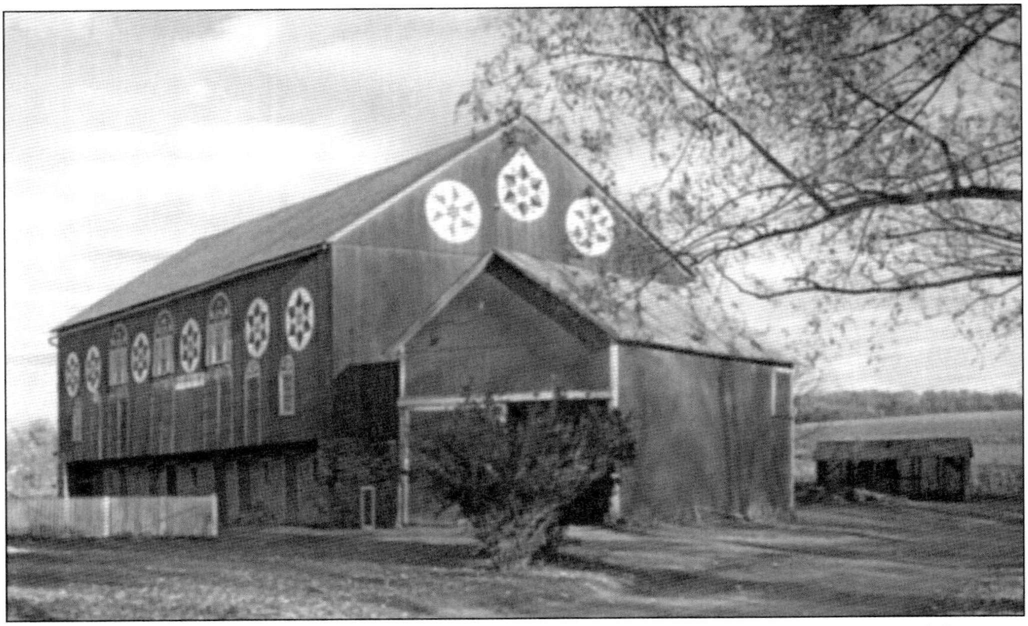

Much of eastern Pennsylvania is known for its Pennsylvania Dutch culture, and one of the most prominent aspects of that are the hex signs seen on barns and other buildings throughout the region to this day. This postcard shows a barn adorned with multiple hex signs along Route 22 in the countryside between Hamburg and Allentown.

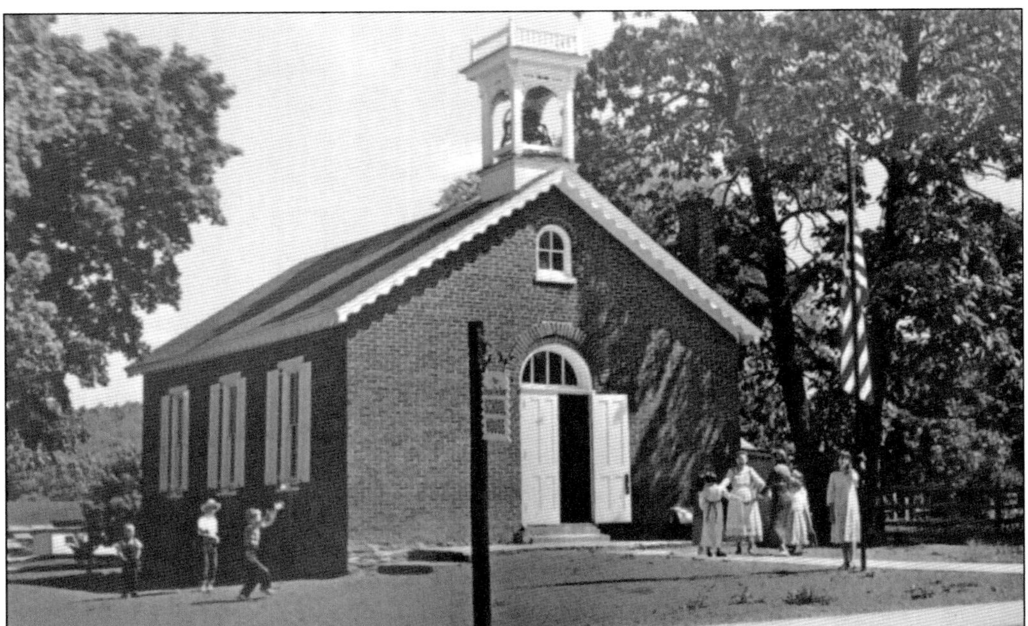

The Little Red Schoolhouse was a traditional one-room brick structure, built in the 19th century in Lenhartsville, half a mile south of Route 22. Shown here in the 1950s, it was being maintained by the Pennsylvania Dutch Folk Culture Society and visited by hundreds of local school children and tourists every year.

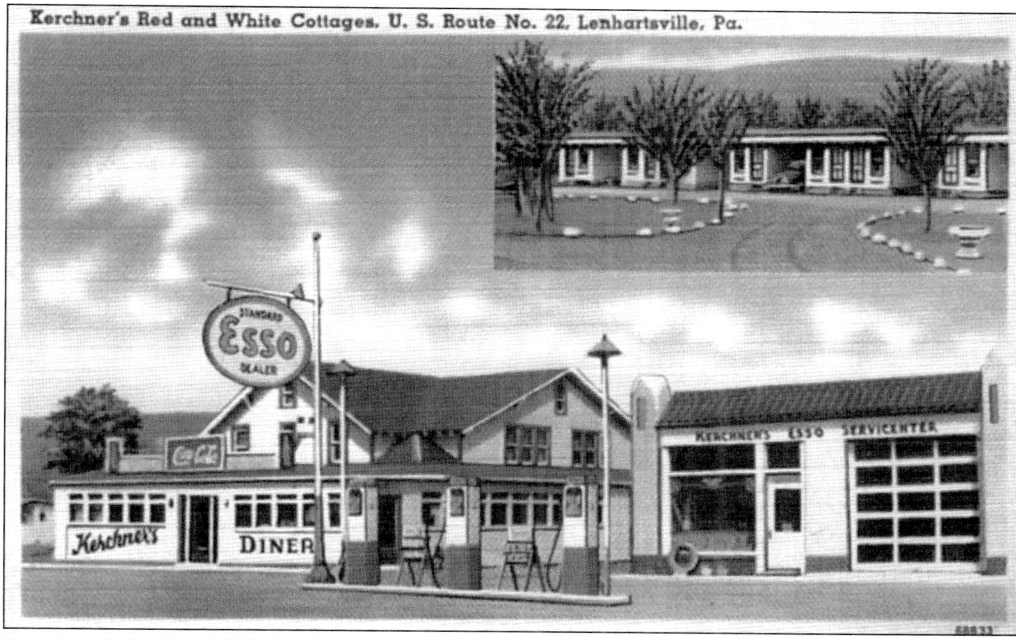

Kerchner's Red and White Cottages, seen here in the early 1950s, was one of several popular stopping points for tourists in the small village of Lenhartsville, roughly 20 miles west of Allentown. Like many similar establishments, it featured an Esso gasoline station, a diner, small cottages for overnight stays, and an automobile service station.

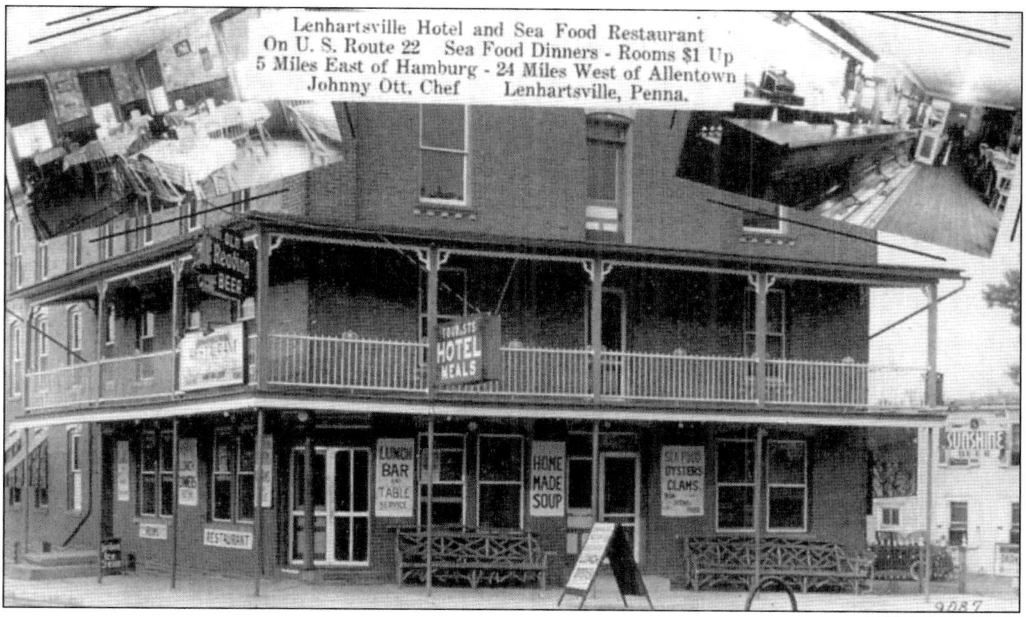

Situated along Route 22/William Penn Highway in rural territory between Hamburg and Allentown, the Lenhartsville Hotel and Sea Food Restaurant, featuring rooms beginning at $1, is seen here around 1940. The restaurant operated under the direction of chef Johnny Ott. The bar served Old Reading and Sunshine Beers, both local favorites that were made in Reading.

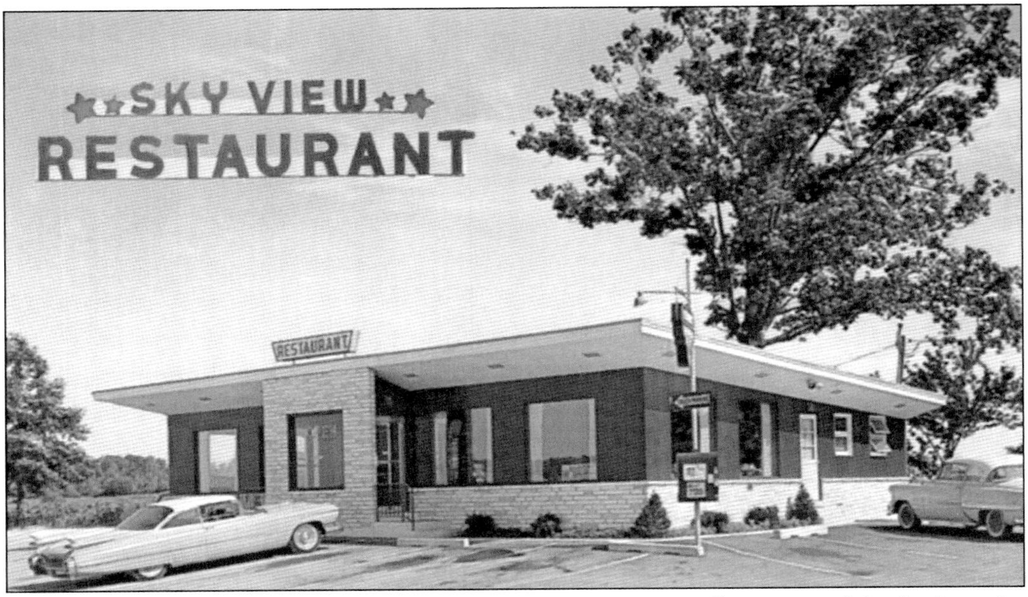

The Sky View Restaurant operated in conjunction with the small Top Motel, both along the Route 22 highway in the small community of Krumsville, between Hamburg and Allentown. Small family-owned restaurants such as this were common sights along the road from the 1940s to the 1970s, before national chain restaurants began to dominate the food industry. This view shows a 1959 Cadillac Coupe de Ville parked outside the restaurant.

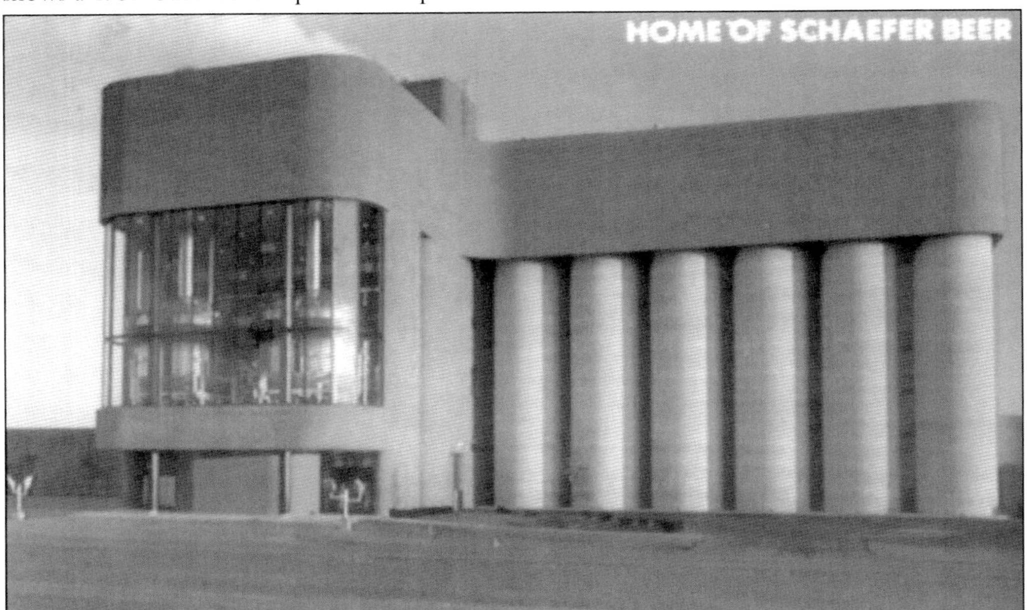

This huge brewery stands along modern Route 22 in Fogelsville, several miles west of Allentown. Built in 1972 by the F. & M. Schaefer Brewing Company, it produced Schaefer beer for many years. After a series of ownership changes, it is currently owned by the Boston Beer Company and produces Sam Adams beers. Its bright copper kettles can easily be seen by drivers passing on the highway.

Eight

Allentown to Easton

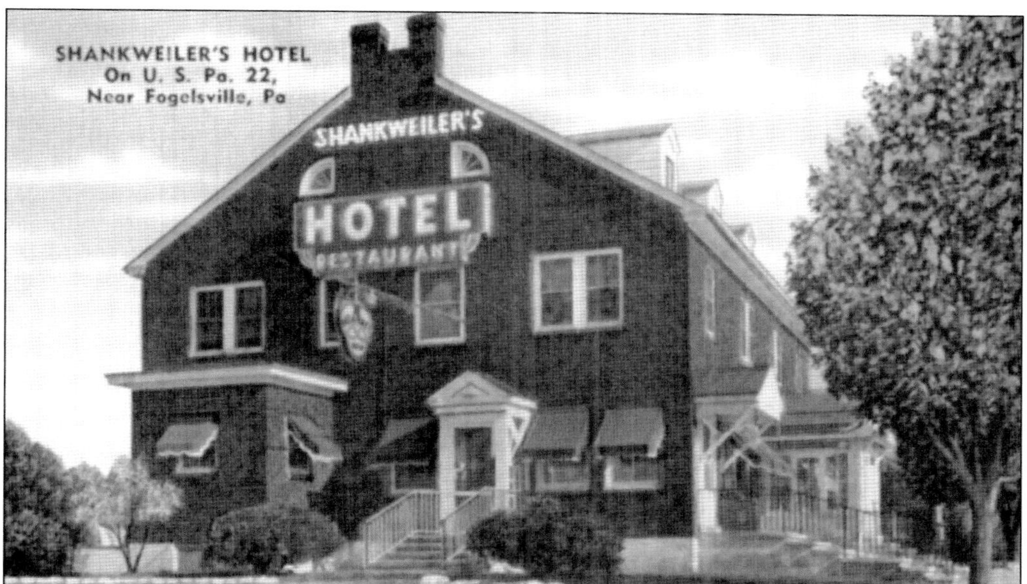

Shankweiler's Hotel and Restaurant, shown in the 1940s, operated between 1936 and 1993 in this large former residence near Fogelsville, just west of Allentown. The building, at the northeast corner of Old Route 22 and State Route 100, remains standing today and is used as a bank. Note the hanging sign for Ballantine Beer, a popular brand along the East Coast for many years.

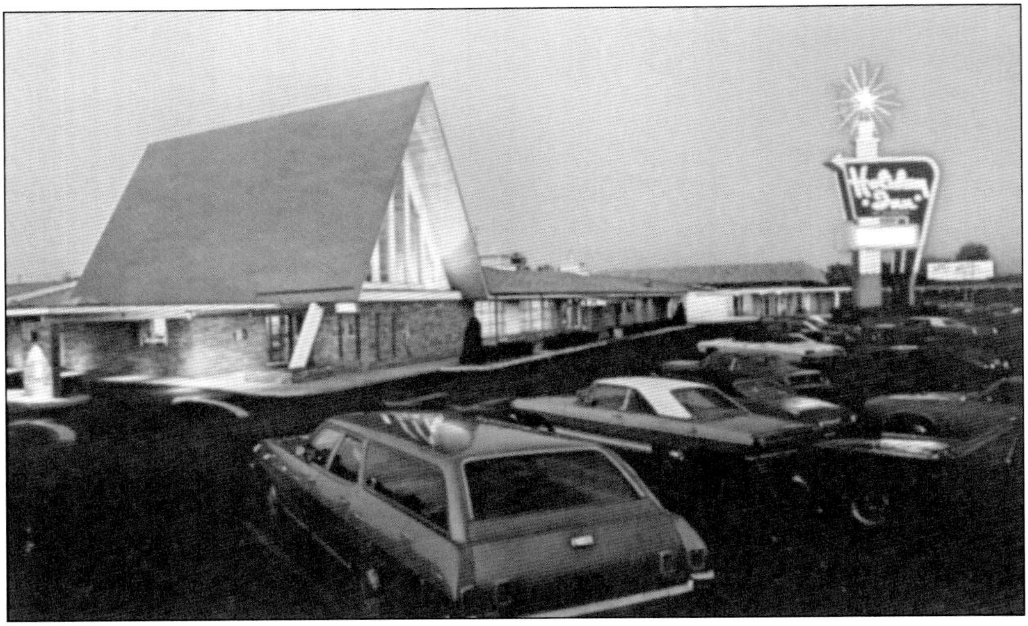

The huge iconic neon sign for Holiday Inn motels was a staple of American highways for many years. Established in 1952, the company gave travelers consistent lodging in an era when every motel experience was different. By 1968, it owned more than 1,000 sites in the United States and was known as the "Nation's Innkeeper." This particular motel was along Route 22 on the west side of Allentown in the mid-1970s.

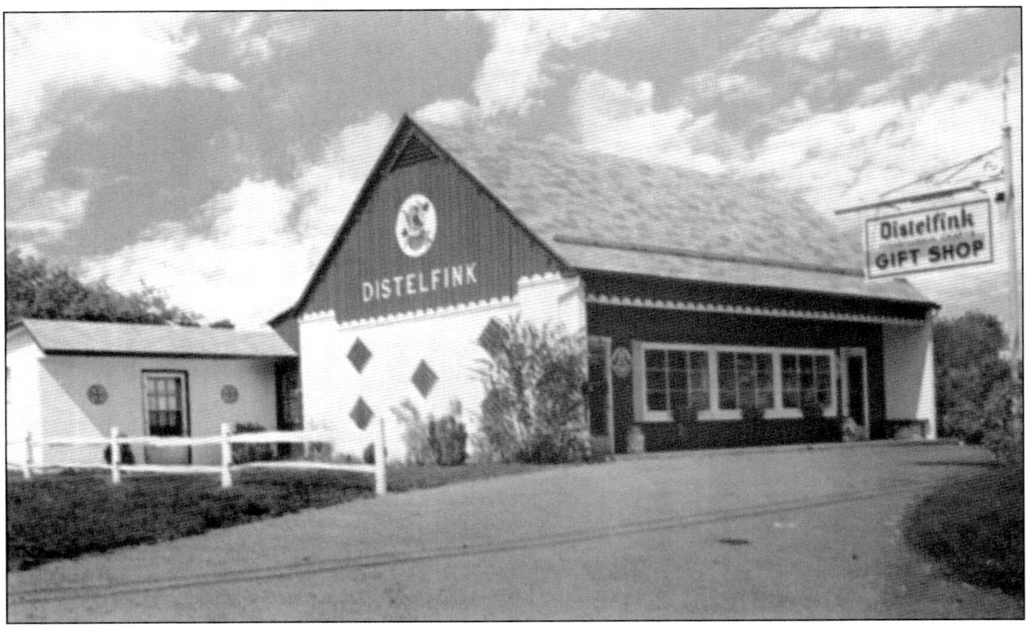

The Distelfink gift shop stood at Tilghman and Thirty-First Streets on the northwest side of Allentown for many years. Selling primarily Pennsylvania Dutch souvenirs, it was operated by local residents Marjorie Conover and Phyllis Greenall from 1948 to 1989. After closing, the barn-shaped building was razed in favor of a modern shopping center.

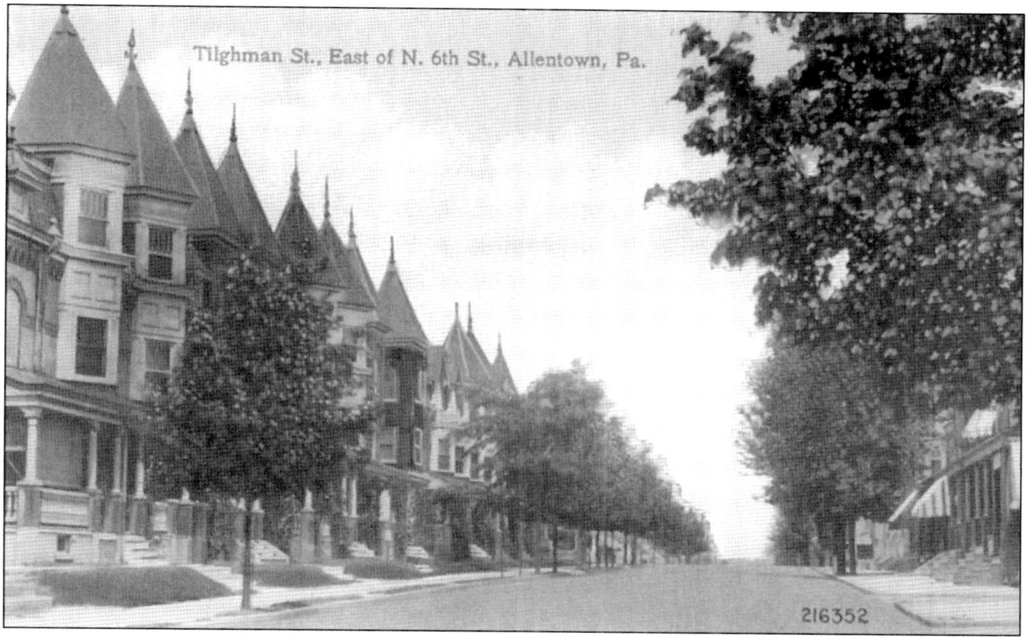

Until 1955, when the Lehigh Valley Thruway opened, Tilghman Street carried Route 22 through northern Allentown. A two-mile stretch of the road features a series of block-long townhouses, mostly built around the turn of the 20th century for some of the city's wealthier residents. Varying between two and three stories and featuring various styles of Victorian architecture, each block was somewhat unique. The image above, from about 1910, shows one block of the street in its prime. While the neighborhood remains almost entirely intact today, some architectural elements have been altered or removed, as can be seen in the image below, taken in 2015.

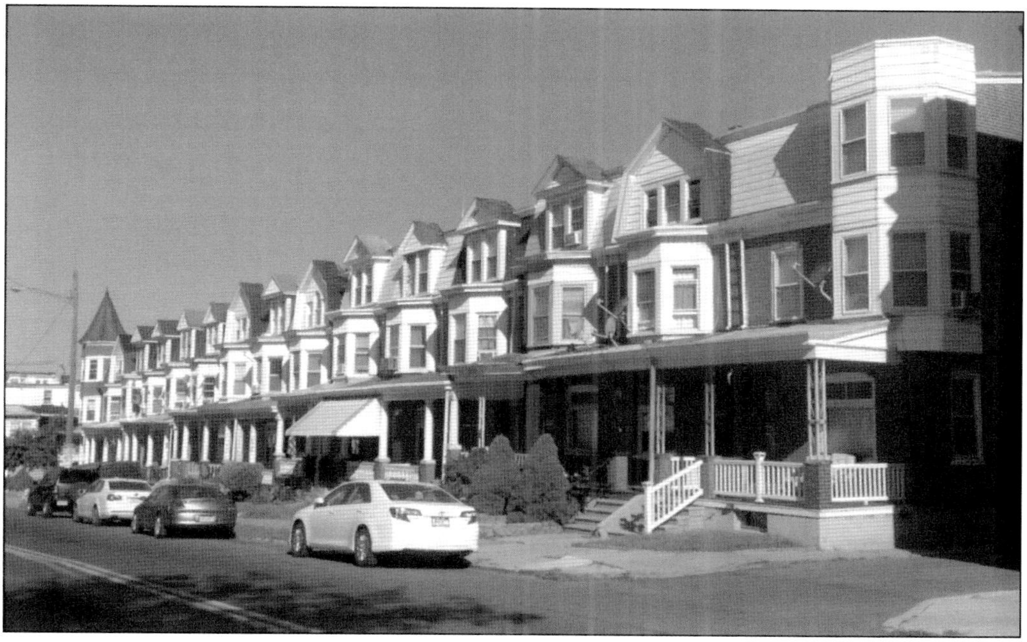

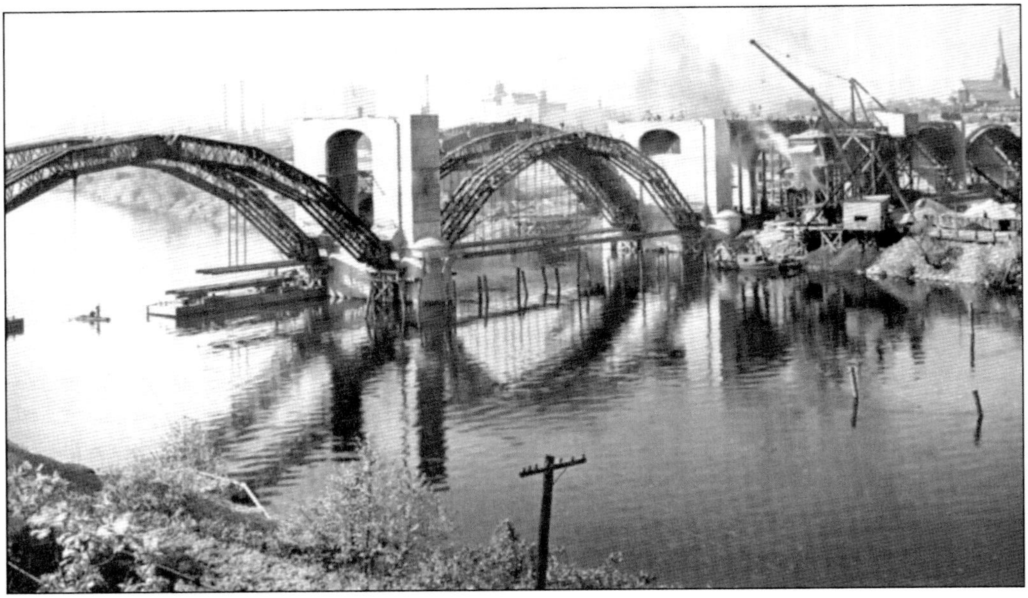

The establishment of the federal highway system in 1926 led to the improvement of many roads and structures along the course of various routes. The Tilghman Street Viaduct opened in 1929 to carry the William Penn Highway and Route 22 over the Lehigh River on the northeast side of Allentown. The arched concrete structure is nearly 1,400 feet in length and replaced an earlier smaller steel-truss bridge. The current bridge is shown above in a real-photo postcard under construction in 1928 (with the historic Neuweiler Brewery seen in the background) and below in the 1940s after its completion. It remains in service today.

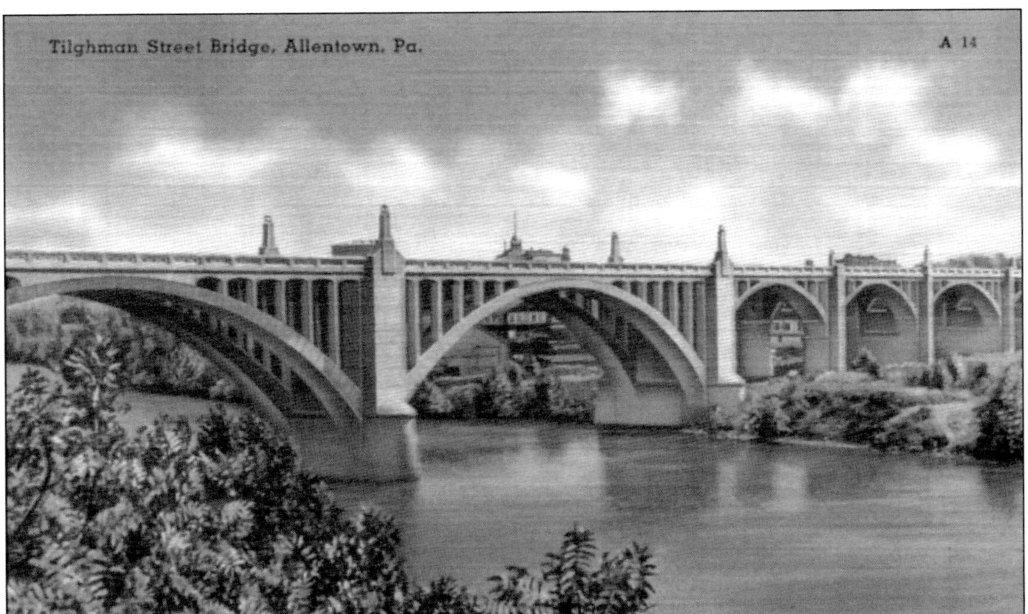

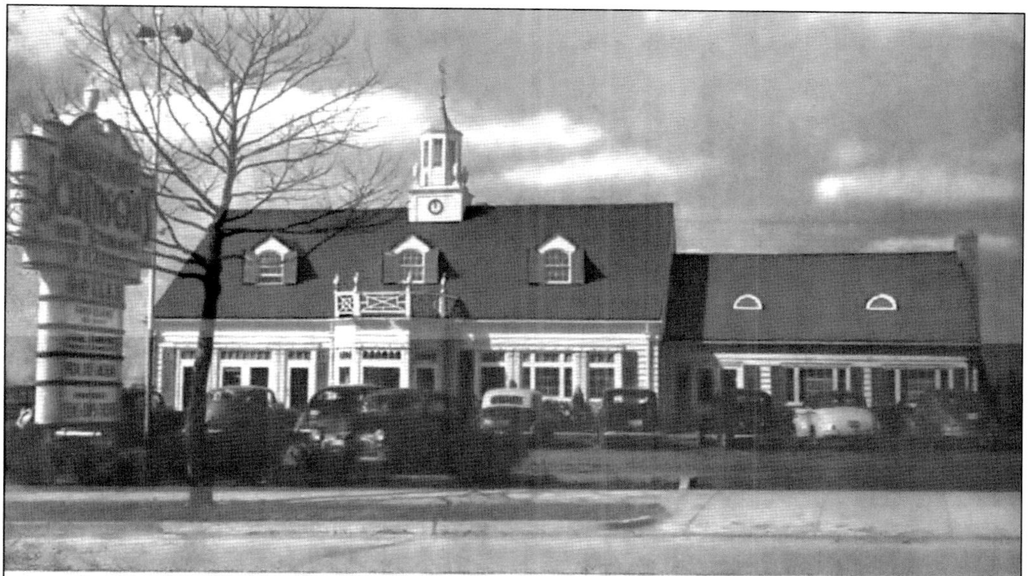

HOWARD JOHNSON'S RESTAURANT — ON U. S. ROUTE 22 BETWEEN ALLENTOWN AND BETHLEHEM

The Howard Johnson Restaurant chain was founded in 1925 in Massachusetts and quickly became well known for its 26 flavors of ice cream, as well as the bright orange roof and tall cupola on each restaurant. The chain achieved even higher visibility when it became the exclusive operator of restaurants at rest stops along turnpikes in Pennsylvania, Ohio, and New Jersey in the 1940s. After peaking in the 1970s, the chain has virtually disappeared from sight over the years. Above is a restaurant that was between Allentown and Bethlehem along Route 22 in the mid-1950s. Later, the company entered the motel business as well, and many of its properties dotted highways in Pennsylvania. At right is a card showing two views of a motel and restaurant in Bethlehem in the late 1960s.

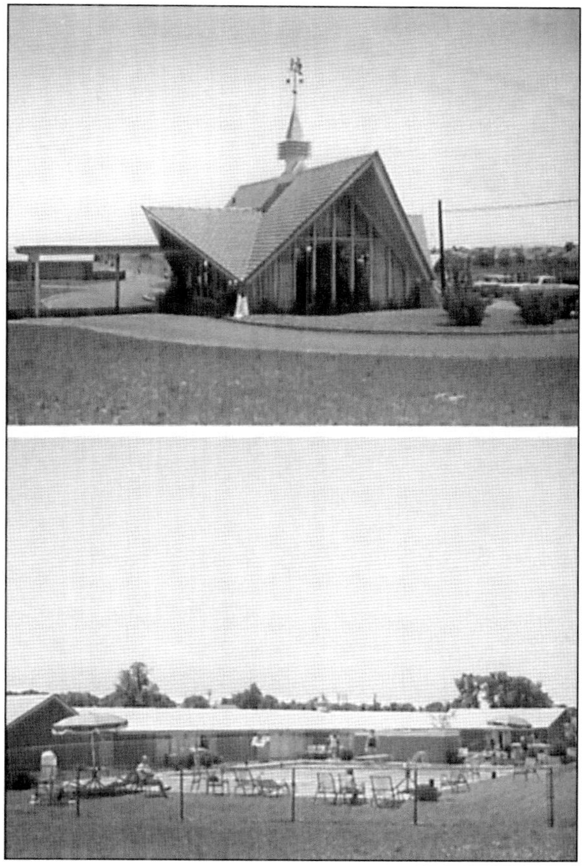

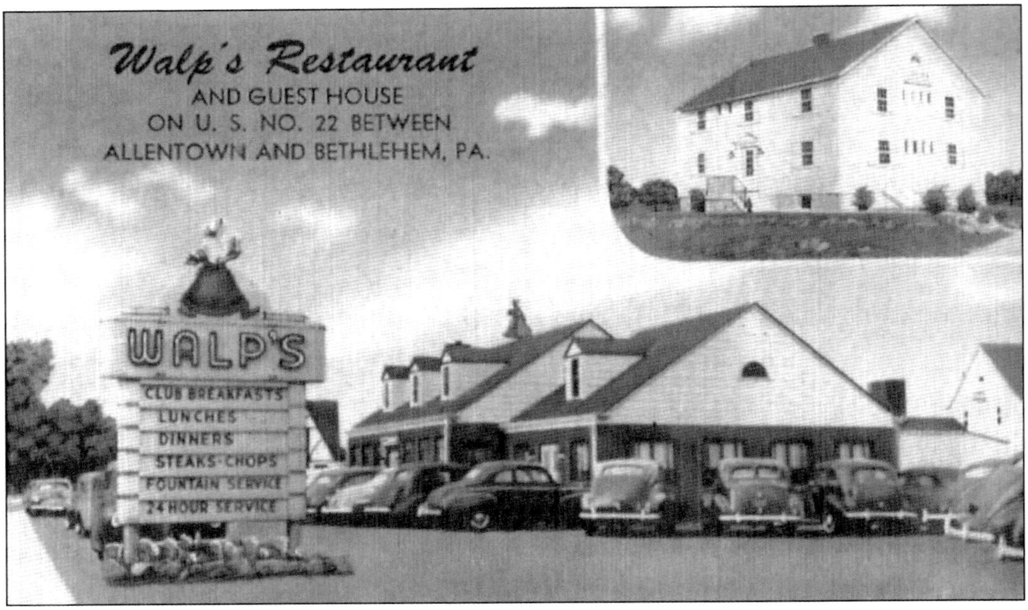

Walp's Restaurant stood for more than 60 years at the intersection of Union Boulevard (formerly Route 22) and Airport Road on the northeast side of Allentown. Established in 1936 by Robert and Blanche Walp, it was famous throughout the Lehigh Valley for its Pennsylvania Dutch cuisine. The restaurant grew from the small diner shown above around 1950 to the much larger modern restaurant shown below around 1960. It continued to be family owned until its closing in 1998. In recent years, a cookbook of favorite recipes used by the restaurant has been published and has been a popular item in the area.

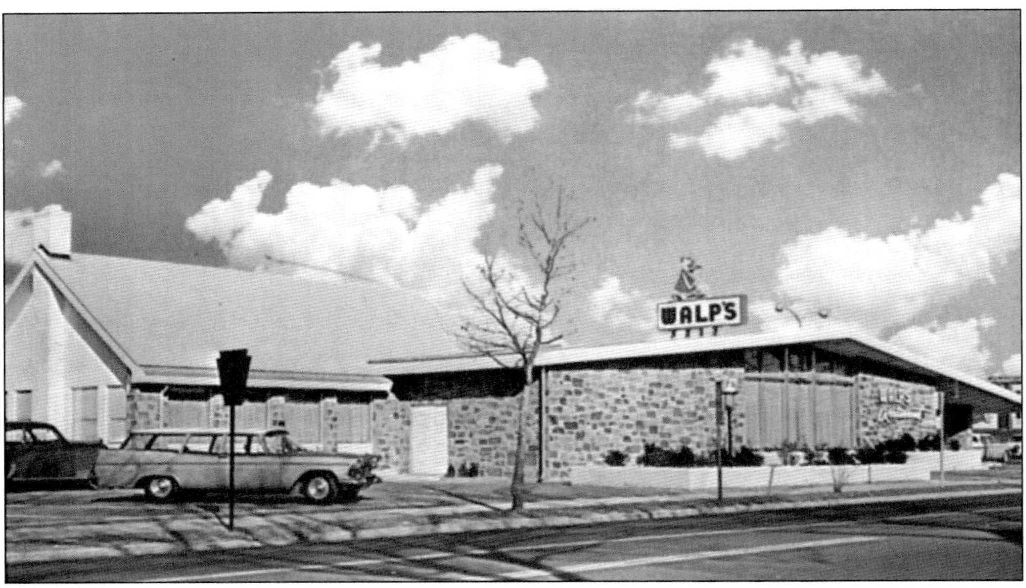

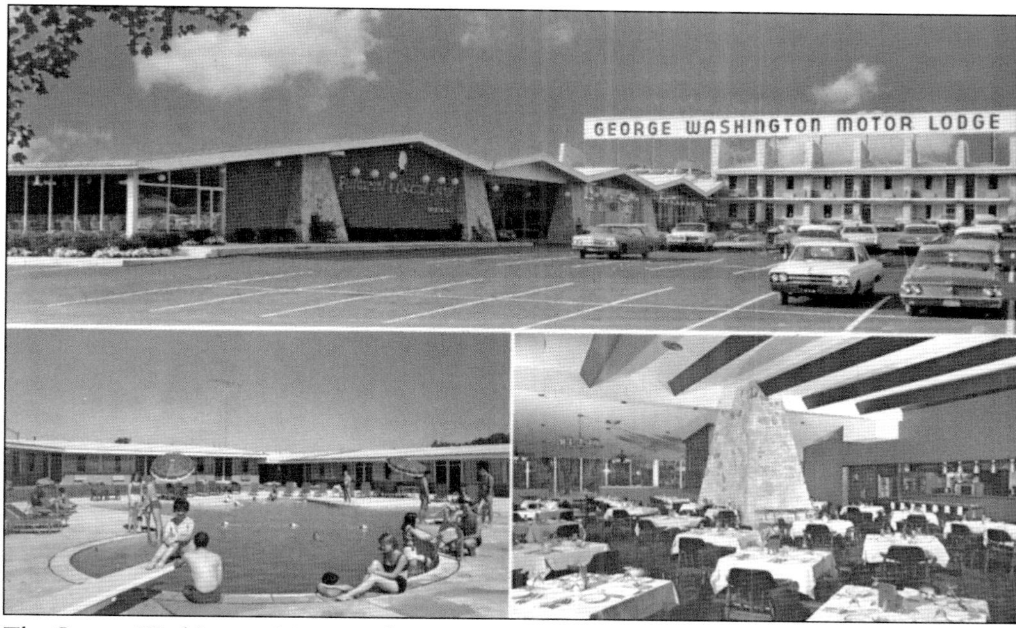

The George Washington Motor Lodge stood at the intersection of North Seventh Street and the modern Route 22 highway, just north of Allentown. Shown here in the late 1960s, it was one of the largest independent motels along the entire route. Although it boasted 250 rooms with air-conditioning and both indoor and outdoor pools, it eventually closed and was razed in 1994.

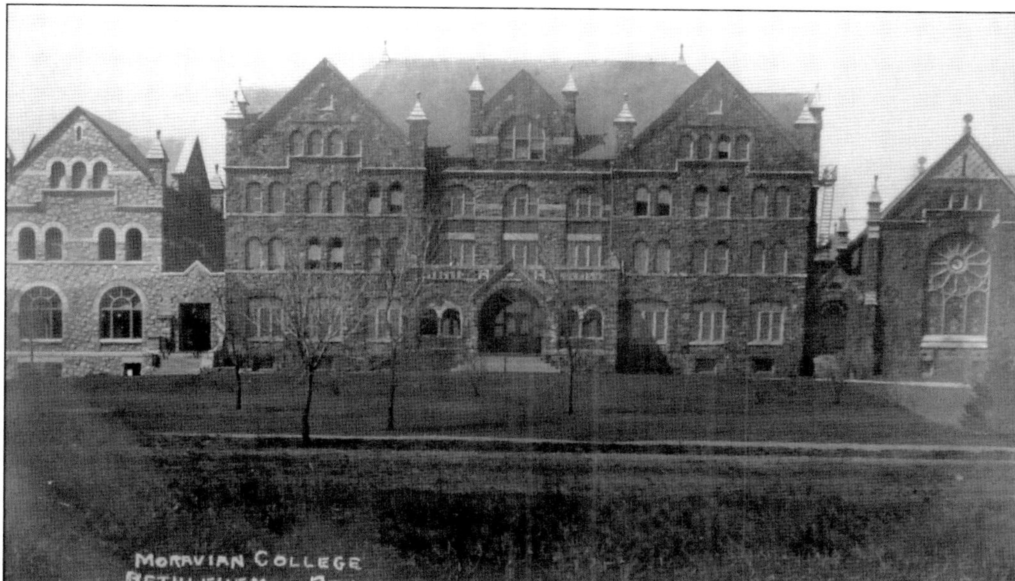

Moravian College was established in Bethlehem in 1742 by Countess Benigna von Zinzendorf of Moravia (today part of the Czech Republic). Still in operation today, it has two campuses in the city; the Main Street campus stands along the original alignment of Route 22. Shown here is the ornate Comenius Hall, built in 1891 and holding offices and classrooms. The college has more than 1,500 students today.

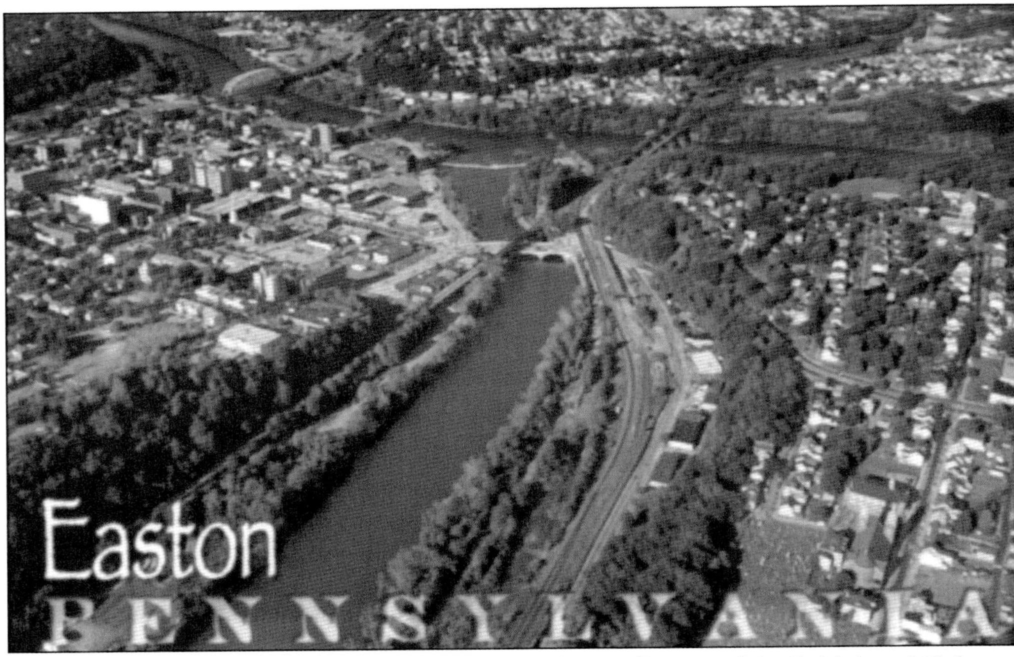

This aerial view of Easton from the 1980s shows the confluence of the Lehigh and Delaware Rivers. At the top left is the Easton-Phillipsburg toll bridge, which carries Route 22 over the Delaware today. To the right of that is the Northampton Street Bridge, nearly 120 years old, which carried Route 22 over the river until 1942.

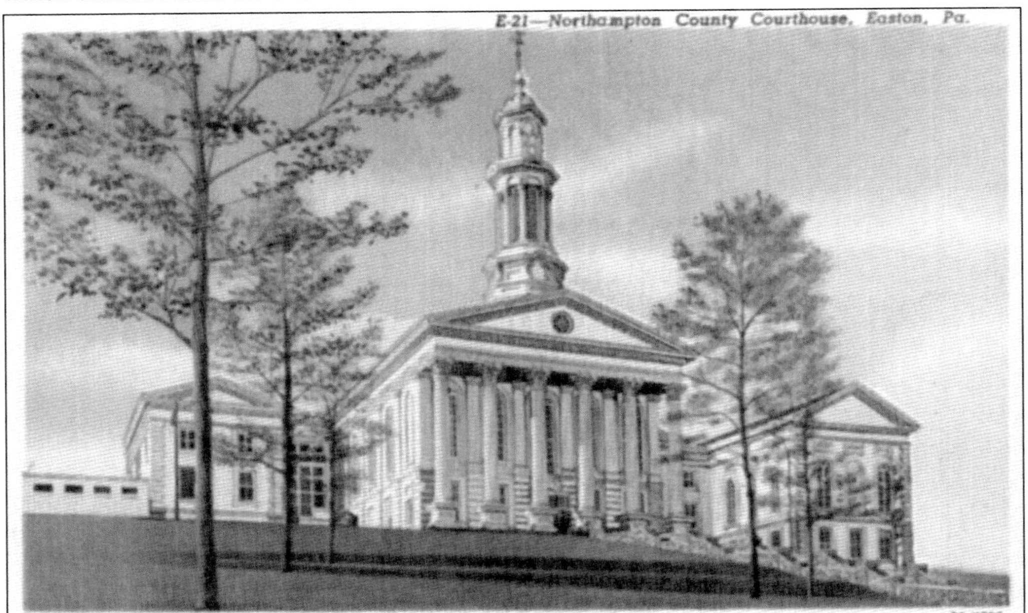

The Northampton County Courthouse stands atop a high hill overlooking the city of Easton. Built in 1860 to replace a nearly century-old courthouse at Centre Square, the current structure is located at the intersection of South Seventh Street and Walnut Street, the original course of the William Penn Highway and Route 22 until 1934.

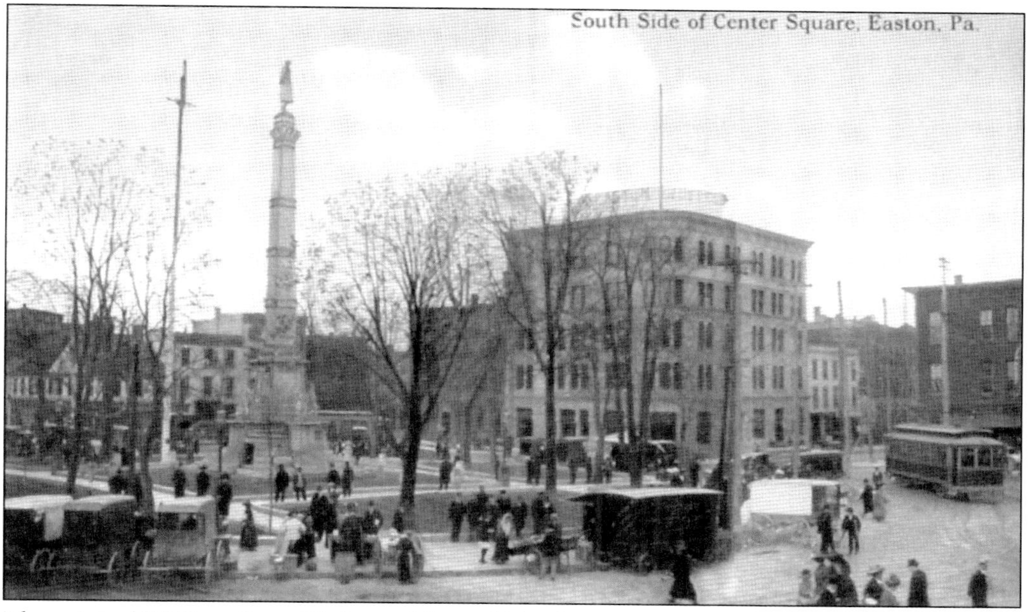

The original William Penn Highway followed Northampton Street past the Victorian buildings that line Easton's Centre Square. This postcard shows the square and the obelisk known as the Soldiers and Sailors Monument around 1915. Built in 1900 to commemorate Civil War veterans, the monument is converted into a peace candle every year during the Christmas season.

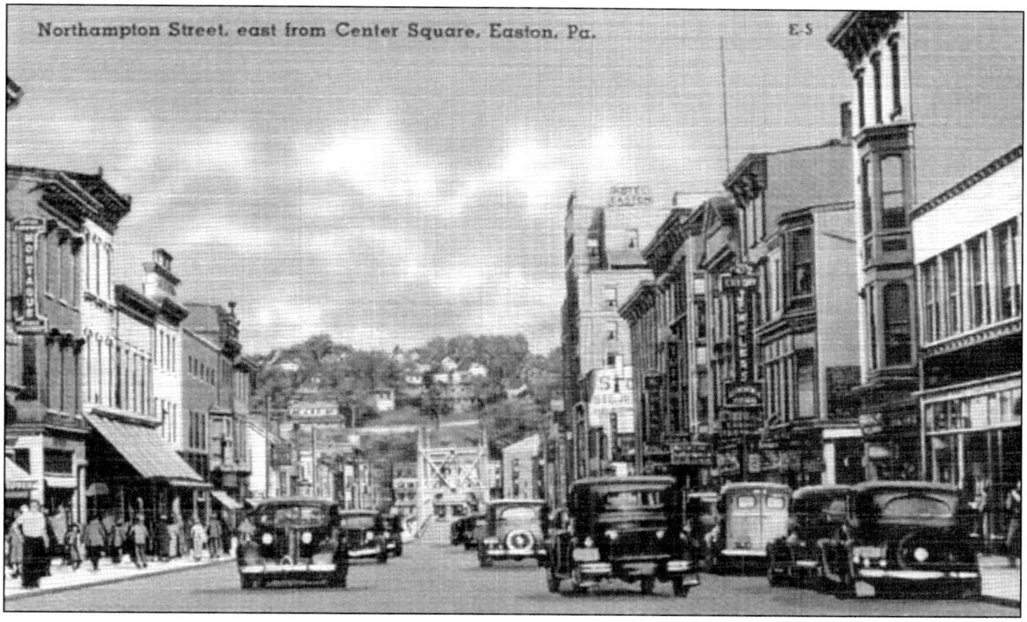

Northampton Street, seen here in the 1940s, originally carried the William Penn Highway through Easton. In this view looking eastward from the center of town, one can see the suspension bridge that crosses the Delaware River, just three blocks away. The tall building in the distance is the Hotel Easton, built in 1926; it remains open today as the Grand Eastonian Hotel. The hillside in the distance is in Phillipsburg, New Jersey.

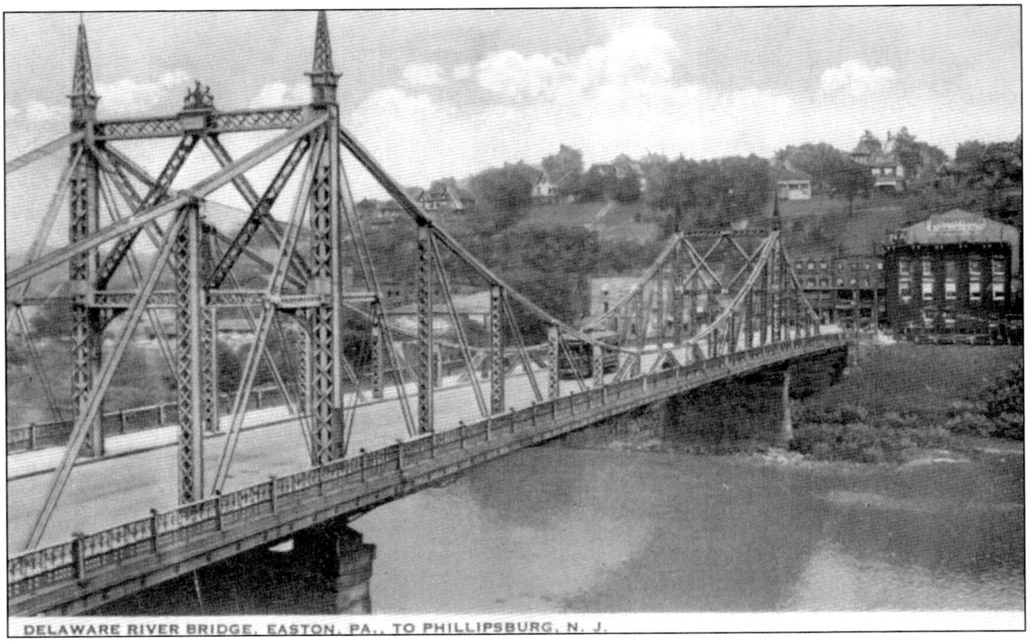

The ornate Northampton Street Bridge in Easton crosses the Delaware River and into New Jersey. Built in 1896, the bridge carried the William Penn Highway and Route 22 until 1942. The old bridge was damaged by flooding from Hurricane Diane in 1955, and although it was repaired and remains in use today, the damage left an irregularity in the bridge's structure that is still visible.

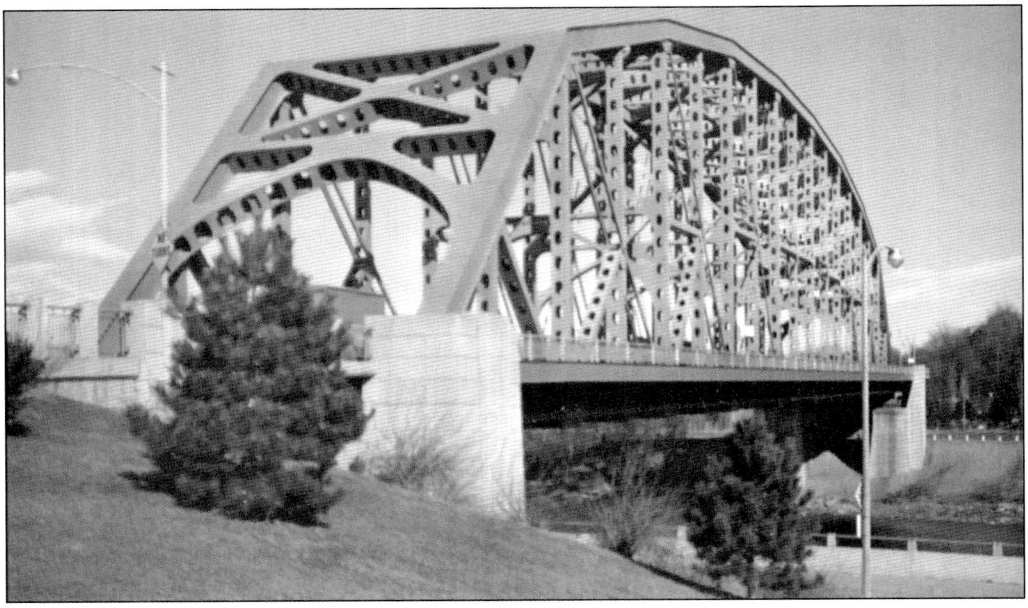

Built in 1938, this 1,000-foot-long steel-truss bridge was built across the Delaware River, less than half a mile north of the Northampton Street Bridge. Four years later, Route 22 was realigned onto this bridge, which later became part of the Lehigh Valley Thruway. Still in use today, the bridge requires a $1 toll from motorists traveling westward into Pennsylvania.

Nine

Continuing Eastward

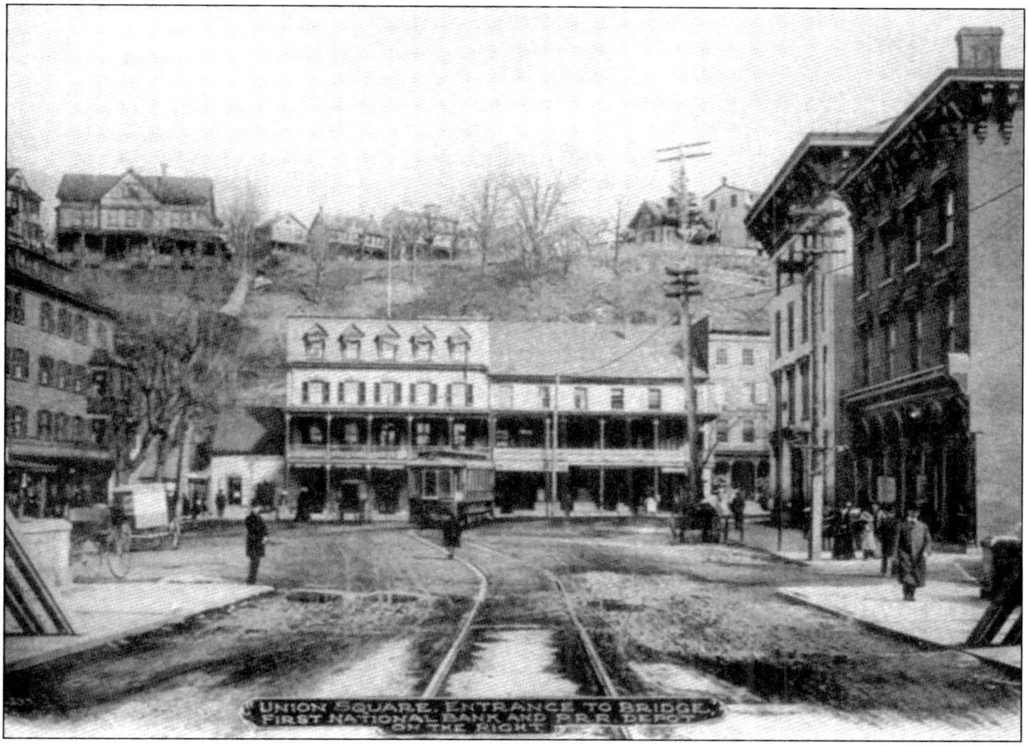

Immediately after leaving the Northampton Street Bridge and entering Phillipsburg, New Jersey, the William Penn Highway encountered Union Square, a block-long district of buildings from the early 19th century, including the city's railroad depot. Although the depot is no longer standing, many of the other buildings remain today, and attempts are being made to preserve them for future use.

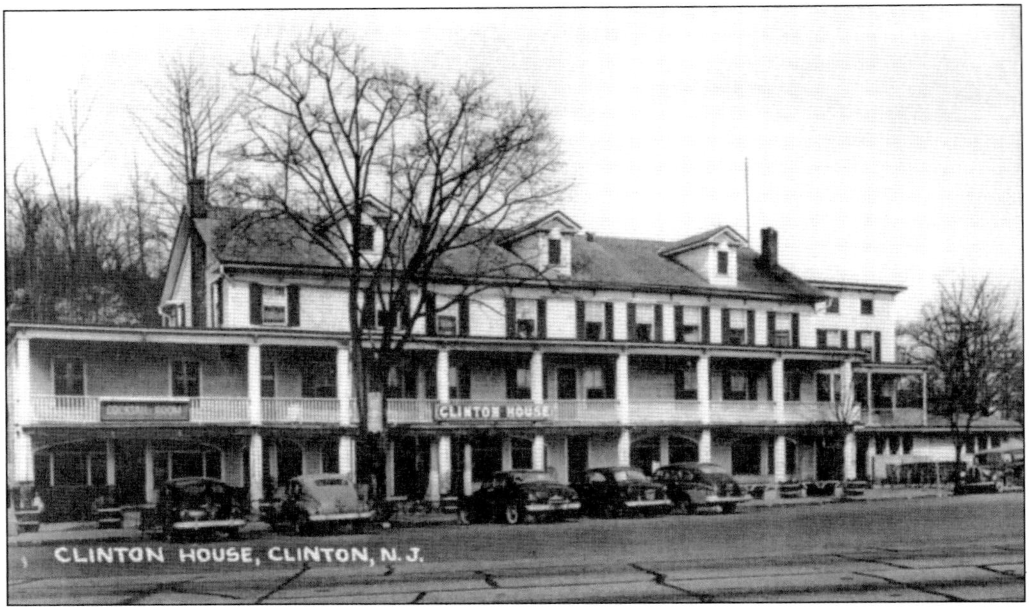

Although the modern Route 22 highway bypasses the small town of Clinton, the route originally traveled through the town on Main Street. As it crosses a branch of the Raritan River, it passes the Clinton House, shown here in the 1940s. Originally built in 1743 as a stagecoach stop along the old Easton-Brunswick Highway, it remains in operation today as one of the area's finer restaurants.

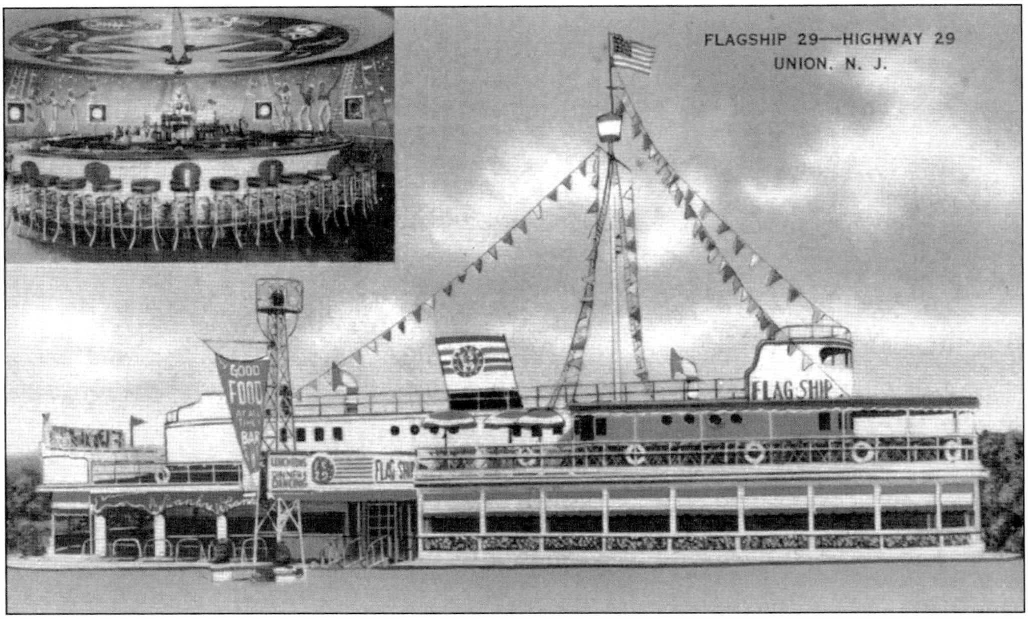

The Flagship nightclub in Union was one of the most notable attractions along Route 22 (formerly known as State Route 29). Sitting between the eastbound and westbound lanes of the highway, it was built in the shape of a ship in 1938. It was rebuilt and redesigned several times, and today it remains open as an electronics store, without a smokestack or any other nautical elements.